Dunkirk to the Rhineland

Dunkirk to the Rhineland

Diaries and Sketches of Sergeant C.S. Murrell, Welsh Guards

Edited by
NICK MURRELL

Pen & Sword
MILITARY

First published in Great Britain in 2011 by
Pen & Sword Military
An imprint of
Pen & Sword Books Ltd
47 Church Street
Barnsley
South Yorkshire
S70 2AS

Copyright © Nick Murrell 2011

ISBN 978 1 84884 389 9

Typeset by Acredula

Printed and bound in England
By CPI

Pen & Sword Books Ltd incorporates the imprints of Pen & Sword Aviation,
Pen & Sword Family History, Pen & Sword Maritime, Pen & Sword Military,
Wharncliffe Local History, Pen & Sword Select, Pen & Sword Military Classics,
Leo Cooper, Remember When, Seaforth Publishing and Frontline Publishing.

For a complete list of Pen & Sword titles please contact
PEN & SWORD BOOKS LIMITED
47 Church Street, Barnsley, South Yorkshire, S70 2AS, England
E-mail: enquiries@pen-and-sword.co.uk
Website: www.pen-and-sword.co.uk

CONTENTS

ACKNOWLEDGEMENTS

My thanks go to my sister Deborah for typing up all sixteen volumes of our father's Army and wartime, sometimes scarcely legible, diaries amounting to more than a million words. Without her Herculean efforts this book would never have been published.

The diary entries are as my father wrote them. I have checked them against the hand-written originals but cannot guarantee that everything he wrote is factually correct.

It has been difficult to identify everyone mentioned as, in some cases, only Christian or nicknames are used. In a Welsh regiment there is always a preponderance of names such as Jones, Williams, Evans, etc. In order to identify them further, the surname is preceded by the last two digits of their Army number, e.g. 08 Williams.

One of the more difficult tasks in editing these diaries was how best to deal with entries relating to those men who suffered from battle-strain, 'windiness' or those who 'cracked up'. My father's journals are honest, both when writing about himself and others around him and he well appreciated the fine line between 'cracking up' and not doing so. He also knew that other men in the front line had a worse time than he did. I know that he would not have wished to cause offence to their families and descendants. Because of this I have deleted some references and blanked out names in others. I hope I have not offended anyone.

Note: There are usually two different spellings of place names in Belgium, e.g. Maas/Meuse; Hoegaarden/Hougaerde. I have stuck to the names used in the original diaries.

GLOSSARY OF ABBREVIATIONS AND SLANG

1WG/2SG	1st Battalion Welsh Guards/2nd Battalion Scots Guards etc
AA	Anti-aircraft
ADS	Advanced Dressing Station
AFV	Armoured Fighting Vehicle
Arty	Artillery
A/Tk	Anti-tank
BD	Battledress
BEF	British Expeditionary Force
Bill Browns	Grenadier Guards
Blighty	1. England. 2. A wound involving a return to England
Bob/bobbing	To duck, get nervous or jittery
Canvas	Denim – when applied to clothing
C/L	Centre Line
CO	Commanding Officer
Coldies	Coldstream Guards
CP	Command Post
CQMS	Company Quartermaster Sergeant
CSM	Company Sergeant Major
DR	Despatch Rider
Fluff	To 'cotton on'; to understand
GAD	Guards Armoured Division
Gyppo	1. Army cook. 2. General term for dirt, grease etc
HCR	Household Cavalry Regiment
HE	High Explosive
'I' Section/truck/trench etc	Intelligence
I/C	In Charge of
IO	Intelligence Officer/Office
IWGC	Imperial War Graves Commission (changed its name in 1960 to the Commonwealth War Graves

	Commission)
Jocks	Scots Guards
M/C	Motor-cycle
MG	Machine gun
Micks	Irish Guards
MO	Medical Officer
'Moaning Minnie'	German *Nebelwerfer* – Multi-barrelled Rocket Mortar
MP	Military Police
NAAFI	Navy, Army and Air Force Institutes
NCO	Non-commissioned Officer
O/C	Officer Commanding
OP	Observation Post
PIAT	Projector, Infantry, Anti-tank
PoW Company	Prince of Wales Company – aka the 'Jam Boys'
RA	Royal Artillery
RAP	Regimental Aid Post
RASC	Royal Army Service Corps
RE	Royal Engineers
RSM	Regimental Sergeant Major
R/T	Radio Transmitter
Sig/Sigs	Signals or Signallers
'Sobbing Sisters'	see under 'Moaning Minnies'
SP	Self-propelled (i.e. guns/artillery)
Stunt	Army exercise – manoeuvres
Swan/swanning	'A new word "swanning" means either roaming about in a vehicle – or advancing as a column at speed and into the blue – not quite a battle – rather a mobile recce or thrust along roads.'
Tapes	NCO's stripes/chevrons
TCL	Troop Carrier, lorry
TFO	0Till further orders
WO	Warrant Officer

LIST OF PLATES, ILLUSTRATIONS AND MAPS

PLATES:

ILLUSTRATIONS:

MAPS:

INTRODUCTION

There were two achievements in my father's life of which he was immensely proud. One was the courtship of, and marriage to, my mother. The second was his service with the Brigade of Guards who he regarded as the finest fighting force in the world, the best regiment of which was the Welsh Guards. He rarely talked about the war, in common, I believe, with a lot of old soldiers and he preferred to relate his experiences of the Guards Depot and Wellington Barracks during his peacetime Army days. Reading his war diaries after his death was something of a revelation.

I hope these diaries will be of interest to Welsh and other guardsmen past and present, their families and descendants and, indeed, other members of the armed services, many of whom would have experienced similar or worse experiences than my father.

Many of the entries were written while he was being shelled, mortared or bombed in his trench, travelling in the Intelligence truck or in billets.

My father kept extensive diaries during the war years of over 700,000 words. Writing appeared to be almost an addiction or compulsion which probably explains the detail and length of some of the entries. He also mentions at one point that during his active service, while being shelled in the trenches, it was a way of coping with fear. Generally the diary entries were in the form of cryptic notes and jottings, 'a sort of home-made shorthand', kept secretly and written up later, while still fresh in the mind. In 1944–45 he mostly wrote his 'notes' in the Intelligence truck or in his trench.

My father transcribed these diaries in the 1960s and '70s. I was aware that he had kept some sort of record of his Army years but it was not until after his death in 1987 that I realized the extent of them. During the 1990s my sister typed them up.

This book concentrates on his active service; Dunkirk in 1940 and the war in NW Europe in 1944–45. The entries on Dunkirk have more or less been reproduced in full but of necessity the remainder has been cut by over a half – the eleven weeks he spent in Normandy amount to over 100,000 words alone – possibly the most detailed military diaries ever written.

I have edited the diaries in order to iron out typing and spelling errors etc, divided them into parts, chapters, added summaries, footnotes, an introduction, contents, glossary etc. The entries remain my father's own work.

Throughout the war he served with the 1st Battalion Welsh Guards, initially as a signaller and then with the Intelligence Section. He served as a ranker for the major part of his Army years but ended the war as a sergeant, though he never really considered himself to be NCO material.

He produced many sketches and watercolours during this period, four of which were reproduced in *Welsh Guards at War* by Major L.F. Ellis (1946) for which he also did the illustrations of British and German Arms and Equipment.

Charles Stuart Murrell was born in Cardiff in 1912 of English parents and he never considered himself Welsh. During his first twenty-one years he led a nomadic and unsettled existence which included periods spent in Newport, Porthcawl, Chatham, Gillingham and Bromley with assorted aunts and uncles and a spell in France where his father was a major with the Imperial War Graves Commission. He spent four years at King's School Rochester, leaving early due to his father's financial problems.

He had a talent for art and in 1931 found work with a firm of commercial artists. He became increasingly restless, however, and in 1933 he handed in his notice. With the country in the throes of a depression this was a somewhat quixotic (some may say foolish) gesture. He returned to Art School for a while and was unable to find another job:

> I was scrounging from mother, and worse – I realized that I was hopelessly adrift, and a dead loss to my mother…I was slipping badly…I knew that I needed a really hard kick in the pants. I knew just where I could get it. On 2 September 1933 I presented myself at the Central London Recruiting Depot in New Scotland Yard, Whitehall and signed on for four years in the Welsh Guards. 'The die,' as the novelist might say, 'was cast.'

He survived the harsh and brutal discipline of the Guards Depot at Caterham Barracks and his first difficult few months at Wellington Barracks – but only just – ending up near to death in Millbank Hospital with pleurisy. He was close to being discharged but completed his four years in 1937 after which he found work with the Ordnance Survey until his call-up as a reservist in June 1939.

PART 1

DUNKIRK

1

Blitzkrieg and Retreat to Dunkirk

Charles (Charlie to his comrades) Murrell was working with the Ordnance Survey when he was called back to the Welsh Guards as a reservist in June 1939 for two months' training. He was in the Signals Section with the 1st Battalion Welsh Guards (1WG) with whom he served for the duration of the war.

War was declared on 3 September and the Battalion left for Gibraltar on the 5th where it remained on a war footing for nearly two months.

The 1st Battalion then sailed for France on 7 November 1939, landing in Marseilles and thence to Arras where their role was to provide protection for General Headquarters, then in and around Habarcq, 8 miles west of Arras and they became part of the BEF under the command of Lord Gort. The Battalion was based at Izel-les-Hameaux about 3 miles away, with companies dispersed in villages and the northern outskirts of Arras.

The billets were basic and the winter was a hard one. It was wet and stormy with long periods of frost and snow interspersed with periods of thaw and mud.

A sizeable chunk of his diary entries during this period revolve around bars, and on the whole it seems to have been a fairly bibulous time: 'Fairly tight again' is not an untypical entry.

> The trouble is that drink – wine, French beer, and spirits – are so cheap out here. Generally guardsmen drink only beer at home, and then only when they have some money – out here we drink everything – all mixed up and if we are not becoming hardened campaigners and veterans of battle, we are certainly becoming hard and heavy boozers. (March 1940.)

The tremendously favourable rate of exchange meant that they enjoyed a higher standard of living than people back in England. The army food was meagre and pretty awful and they usually ate their suppers at the *estaminets*. 'Without café meals we'd almost starve on army fare.'

As the weeks and months dragged on, boredom became the biggest enemy and generally there seemed to be an increasing desire for some sort of action. There was little relaxation in the Guards' discipline and 'bull'. In addition to a few exercises, many fatigues and training, there were guards of honour, visits and inspections by the King, HRH the Duke of Windsor and the Presidents of France and Poland.

***

In early March 1940 Lance Corporal Murrell was attached to General Headquarters, Royal Corps of Signals as a temporary relief, together with two other Welsh Guardsmen, 77 Johnson and Barlow. Between them they manned a 'passive air defence (PAD) telephone' twenty-four hours a day: 'Why three infantrymen, even if battalion signallers, are required to do this simple task, I don't know.' They were billeted in Dainville, a few miles outside Arras.

He was later to regret this attachment as he was separated from his battalion when the *Blitzkrieg* came and he was not with his comrades in the fighting in and around Arras and the subsequent evacuation from Dunkirk.

Charles Murrell was very fortunate to get leave on 3 April and married his beloved Stella on the 6th. All leave was cancelled on his return.

8 March 1940 – Dainville, near Arras

I thought about Arras. This town, blacked out at night, yet full of troops and airmen seeking relaxation or excitement as an antidote to the boredom of a war that is no war – a war of frustration and not of fear. It is almost like a game of charades. As though France and England, out of sheer nostalgia, have recreated this echo of the 1914–18 Arras, a town behind the front; like a gigantic stage-set for a play about the last war and we, the extras, hired and uniformed, are play-acting the reconstruction. There is something unreal, what the Yanks call 'phoney' about it all, as there is in the sympathy the BEF gets from civvies back home, and the food parcels, and Red Cross, and the knitted woollens. Yet out here we are far better off as regards pay and cigarettes and drink than ever we were in a barracks in the heart of London in peacetime when, as sometimes happened, men, with rumbling bellies, half-seriously discussed breaking into the NAAFI for cigarettes or for a bite to eat. Here our money is worth about three times what it was worth in England. We get very cheap, often even free cigarettes and drink and food here are absurdly cheap.

Blitzkrieg hit Arras on 10 May 1940. While Murrell was attached to the Royal Corps of Signals, 1WG held Arras from 17 to 24 May when they were ordered to withdraw. The enemy had nearly surrounded Arras before the garrison left. Their story is summarized briefly in Lord Gort's despatches:

> This concluded the defence of Arras, which had been carried out by a small garrison, hastily assembled, but well commanded and determined to fight. It had imposed a valuable delay on a greatly superior enemy force against which it had blocked a vital road centre.

10 May 1940 – GHQ Arras, France

The long-anticipated *Blitzkrieg* – the invasion of Holland and Belgium by German troops – has begun. Like tales of dragons, I had begun to believe there was no such thing, but here it comes in dead earnest.

I was awakened at 4.30 am by the guns of the local AA batteries. A mild inferno. We were ordered out of our bunks and got outside in tin hats and carrying gas masks, to see, and hear, about a dozen bombs dropped on the aerodrome on the crest of a hill about half a mile from the billet. A series of dull, angry, orange glows, followed (seconds later) by the heavy reports. It seems two men were killed there.

As we drove into the town the streets were full of scared civvies discussing the latest news and rumours – one could feel the excitement and alarm. All morning the PAD 'phone was going full blast. Battle HQ here in the cellars of the Palais St Vaast was occupied by Army and RAF bigwigs. An air-raid alarm sounded in the town this morning.

15 May 1940 – Dainville – Noon

I wrote a bit too soon last night. Only five minutes after I put my pen away a plane droned low overhead and circled this area. No bombs were dropped – it seemed the plane's mission could well be the dropping of parachutists. We were ordered to stand to and we got outside, armed and equipped, and saw a mile off, the town of Arras silhouetted against the white magnesium-like glare of incendiary bombs. Parachutists were to be reckoned with on the outskirts of the town, and Johnson, and Maurice Sims the Grenadier, and Pat and I went along to the drying sheds of the brickworks, and we three guardsmen covered the ground as far as the bank, but did not continue beyond it because, in the brilliant moonlight, we would have been conspicuous targets, not only for any lurking Jerries who might be around, but also for any trigger-happy AA sentries just over the way. I kept looking up at the sky for square-headed Huns – or even nuns – dangling at the ends of parachutes, and felt that the whole business was slightly absurd, particularly when I found myself prodding sacks in the gloom with my bayonet – there seemed to be no parachutists about, and we returned to the billet. We all patrolled the area until midnight, and then most of them turned in, and Jock and I remained to patrol the area until 5.00 am and dawn broke. I often stopped and stared at the burning town – my first vista of the work of the 'Red God of War', and he seemed aptly named. Up till 3.00 am the fires seemed to increase, but after that they diminished in intensity. It was a grand, but awesome sight. Huge clouds of smoke drifted across Arras, lit from below by the fierce glare of the flames I could see licking up to well above the rooftops of the burning buildings.

These parachutists can easily get on the nerves at night. Every rustle, or the slightest sound, brought my rifle into my shoulder, but none came, and common sense told me that little military advantage was to be gained by Jerry dropping valuable soldiers to play hide-and-seek all night in a brickworks in the hope of popping off a couple of non-combatants of an HQ signalling unit – but it is not so easy to reason that way at night. Only in the light of day does the absurdity of it come to mind.

17 May 1940 – Arras

Here, in GHQ itself, the Headquarters and Signals office are packing up, and we are under two hours' notice to stand to. In fact things do look rather black and rumours are flying around thick and fast – that Jerry is breaking through and racing on Arras – has dropped parachutists behind the town – is planning a devastating air-raid on the place – that the British and French Armies are in headlong retreat. Nothing of much cheer, and I must confess that things are pretty gloomy. But a defeatist attitude is no help, though I find my ticker right now not as steady as I would wish, and even the British staff officers here (though outwardly calm and speaking in their usual modulation) are fidgeting with the cigarettes they hold behind their backs, as I can see from here.

7.30 pm

It appears that GHQ has moved out of Arras, and I believe one of the Army HQs has moved in. And now people are rushing out of Arras wholesale. Almost every café is closed. We did, however, find one open near the baths – there a plucky *Madame* and her charming daughter are carrying on. Previously we had gone to the YMCA canteen to buy some cigarettes – we were surprised to see a great pile of packing cases full of cigarettes stacked just inside the entrance. A young man, a civilian, was rather agitatedly rushing to and fro between the shop and a room behind. During one of his appearances we politely asked if we might buy some cigarettes. He waved his hand at the pile, 'Help yourselves' and disappeared again into the room behind. We looked at one another, and someone suggested opening a case and taking what we wanted and leaving the money as the young man seemed rather busy. But it seemed a sacrilege, and no one dared. He reappeared and we asked again. He looked exasperated and harassed, 'I told you – help yourselves. There'll be no transport coming for this lot now. Go on, take what you want before the Germans get them.' This was defeatist talk with a vengeance – somehow a canteen actually giving away fags brought home to me more fully than anything so far the seriousness of the situation. Hesitantly we seized a carton each – then more as no protest was made, and delighted, we bore off our loot in triumph. We gave a pile of fags to *Madame* and her daughter and they kissed us and gave us some wine. Planes droned overhead and I did my best to allay their anxiety by assuring them they must be British or French, or the AA guns would be firing. They were a plucky couple – the husband away somewhere with the French Army.

<u>18 May 1940 – Arras – 10.30 pm</u>

Am somewhat tight now, and am also somewhat ashamed of myself. Johnson turned up to relieve me. Barlow is OK, and still with the signallers at Dainville. We asked a sergeant if we might go out to get some food, and leave the useless telephone, and it was OK. Johnson and I went to a café near the cathedral – the place seemed full of women, and I wondered why they had all gathered there. They were not prostitutes I think – I noticed one dainty little brunette, quite the prettiest girl I have seen in France, and she, and the other women, seemed unnaturally gay, though they did not seem to be drinking much. There was no food to be had there. Johnson suddenly decided he wanted to pay a visit to No. 4 and we went there. Perhaps it was the sight of the women in the café that decided him – I couldn't imagine how he could feel that way in the present situation, but I can more so now. The drink has eased my anxiety, though it has not stimulated in me carnal desire for prostitutes.

Johnson has his 'regular' girl at No. 4, and he took her upstairs while I sat and drank a wishy-washy beer costing six francs a glass. Very few men there tonight – only 04 Dusty Smith, Rees, and Benjamin, who were out of bounds to the Battalion, and in risk of severe penalties if caught. Trade was not too good and *Madame* looked worried. The girls seemed optimistic, but said they had no intention of staying in Arras when the Germans came. It was not patriotism, still less virtue, that decided them. They seemed to think the Germans would take them upstairs and not pay or, if they did pay, that they would do so in some worthless currency they had printed prior to invasion. We moved on to other cafés, and drank a lot of wine and spirits.

<u>10.00 pm</u>

We left Hazebrouck after five hours and we are now in a farm somewhere in Flanders – we have no maps to tell us. Crowds of planes flew over last night. The searchlights made a fascinating pattern as they searched for planes in the moonlit sky.

This countryside is very peaceful (when the planes are absent). It is rather like England. We are still in the land of vast plains (at least vast by English standards) but locally it is quite enclosed with dusty roads and hedgerows, and thatched cottages, and lilac bushes surrounding wayside shrines, and pleasant, fresh, greeny, sun-dappled woods – less cultivation, and more meadows, here. Strange how destruction and danger whets the appetite for the peace and beauty of a smiling countryside. But I seem to see things more intensely in the presence of danger. It is as though the senses are sharpened by fear – the longing for peace and security is, I suppose, natural enough in war. I like the long avenues of poplars along the roads.

21 May 1940 – Location unknown – 10.30 pm

A glorious muck-up. We were ordered to stand to (ready equipped to move off) at 9.30 pm and have been hanging around in the street ever since. The Quartermaster of the Signals has just ordered us back into our billets and to wait here TFO. More and more does this QM seem to be taking over this unit. We rarely see any of the other Supplementary Reserve officers at all. They certainly haven't been killed or wounded – malicious gossip says they have 'done a nip', but where to I couldn't guess. It is possible. They seemed a poor lot – merely senior civil servants made into officers on account of their technical knowledge. But this QM is a good soldier – an old-time regular from a line mob – he fought in the last war and he is the only man holding this ramshackle outfit together.

Despatch riders are passing through, spreading alarm and despondency in their wake – tales of retreat and rout and of whole units decimated. And lorry-loads of odds and ends of men – Durham Light Infantry (DLI), Territorials or Militia and others, possibly stragglers, have passed through too, and I saw a Grenadier in the back of one truck. He shouted to me, and I ran up as the truck slowed at a corner. He had been caught coming off leave in all this turmoil and he told me that he had heard that my battalion was wiped out, defending Arras. This was ghastly news. About two hours later a lorry slowed near us and another man, seeing my cap badge, gave me the ominous thumbs down sign and, as I had a brief word with him, told me the same story. The news stunned and depressed me, and as I watched the crowd of ambulances full of wounded men pass by, I wondered what had become of all the men I have known for so long.

God knows what is happening. Surely this can't be the end? Unless this retreat is all part of some gigantic strategic plot – a trap perhaps? But it seems to have gone too far for that, and it looks indeed as though we are beaten. Yet I cannot, and will not, believe that. Neither can I really believe that my battalion and my friends, Joe, Sammy Cureton and dozens of others are dead, or are wounded, or are prisoners-of-war. If one only knew what to believe. One moment there is wild optimism here, the next deep depression. Never again will I permit myself to be attached to another unit, especially to a corps or army unit, if I can help it. We should have taken French leave and rejoined the Battalion when we were in Arras with them. Ironical I should write this (out of exasperation because I am not with the Taffs to know what is really going on) when, if these rumours are true, I myself would be dead or a prisoner with them. I am beyond caring about anything now. If the Welsh Guards can be snuffed out just like that, then nothing else we've got can do any better, and there's no holding Jerry.

It does seem that England and France, through gross negligence and stupidity, have given Jerry his victory. Yet I cannot get myself to believe that the Meuse bridges were left intact through treachery, or even negligence. These signallers here, now they have had some food, seem cheerful. They, like me, seem unable to grasp the awful truth. This is surely some ghastly nightmare? I can hear the German guns and see their planes but cannot yet accept them as the triumphant symbols of a conquering army. It is impossible that armies of millions can be defeated in a period of eleven days! Perhaps I am losing my sense of proportion. The loss of a whole battalion in a day went almost unnoticed on the Somme – a tiny cog in a mighty machine, as our battalion was to the massive armies out here. But it is different when it is one's own battalion that has perished.

Pray God I can read these words a year hence and know they were wrong. But God, and Stella, seem the world away from all this.

<u>22 May 1940 – 11.00 am</u>

Jock and I walked into a small IWGC Cemetery near here – beautifully kept – the grass fresh and trim, and the soil weedless inside the well-cut beech hedges. The calm and dignity that surrounded the 300 dead soldiers was suddenly shattered by the blasting of AA guns, and of bombs dropping near, and some shrapnel fell and twanged against the simple stones. Then it was quiet again except for the growling and rumbling in the distance – a sound that was not unharmonious to the setting of the cemetery. I glanced up at the inscription, 'Their name liveth for evermore.' And I glanced at the other inscription, 'He died that ye may live' and I thought how brutally Germany is giving the lie to that promise. I wondered how many more of the white stones will be needed when this war too ends. Somehow those graves, and the well-kept flowers, emphasized the folly of this war even more than the ever-spreading plague of destruction of French towns and villages can do. Wrote to Stella in answer to her nice letter. I wonder if (and when) she will get it.

We, Johnson and I, are now virtually stragglers – the most undignified and inglorious thing an infantryman can become. We have no job here. The whole of this part of GHQ is, or seems to be, thoroughly disorganized. These men are not field signallers – they are specialists in the working of office exchanges and teleprinters – they now have no equipment, and so no jobs and I don't see how, where or when they can come to roost now – certainly not until the front is stabilized – if ever.

Certainly we are not, by the wildest stretches of the imagination, a fighting unit. Nothing could be more ludicrous than such a claim, which (in all fairness) they do not make. Yet these men are dressed, and equipped, no differently to Johnson and me. Each man wears battledress – has pack, pouches, steel helmet, water bottle, everything, including bayonet, Lee Enfield rifle, and even ammunition.

But, except for a handful of beribboned old-timers from the last war, not a man of them knows how to fire a rifle, and very few even how to load one. When we left Arras someone gave the order to load with five rounds. A signaller asked Johnson what to do, and he came out with the old gag about shoving the rounds into the butt-trap, and Johnson then stared in amazement as the questioner asked where the butt-trap was and, on being shown, prised it open – pulled a round off his clip of five and solemnly dropped it in. But he was not joking. I showed them what to do as best I could in the crowded truck, and some enthusiasts must have followed my movements as I demonstrated the first time. I pushed the five rounds into my magazine, closed the cut-off automatically easing springs and squeezing the trigger with the rifle at the port, the barrel pointing to the roof of the truck. Then I remembered that a number of the men had no cut-offs in their rifles, and was just about to tell them to release their magazine springs, or to show them how to do it – take the magazines out and load them – close their bolts, and replace the magazines so that a round did not go 'up the spout' and would not do so until the bolt was worked. But suddenly a couple of shots whistled by, one out of the side of the truck and the other, I judged, close by my left ear. I imagine that nothing can make a man more temperamental than to be shot at by his own side.

I lost my temper and told them they were a right shower, and someone petulantly argued that they had only followed my instructions. I told him that I had only said watch (and not follow) the first time and that, whoever had fired the shot had not eased springs as I had shown – had they done so the round in the breech (and the rest of those in the magazine) would have been automatically ejected. I don't believe that all of them were so ignorant about their rifles – I doubt if many actually kept their oil bottles and pull-throughs in their butt-traps, but they have undergone rifle inspections and so pulled them through – but very few know how to load, and fewer still had ever fired a rifle. It seems insane to give men guns and not teach them how to use them. Some of these supplementary reservists must have been in uniform for nearly nine months. It is true, as someone said when I moaned about it, that never in their wildest dreams do members of a GHQ staff expect to find themselves using firearms in battle. Yet something very like that is happening now, even if it is only futile potting at enemy aeroplanes, and any day it could become more personal at any time.

Indeed, as this unit drifts around, seemingly aimlessly, I am beginning anxiously to wonder how I stand officially. I suppose, if any paper records survive from the Battalion (or from this unit) I am in the clear; but that is more than I can say for my conscience in that matter. If the Battalion is in fact destroyed and we, Johnson and perhaps Barlow and I, the only survivors, we are going to be marked men when the Regiment takes stock and I (as the only NCO) a very marked man indeed. It is too late now – there is no Battalion left.

The refugees continue to trek onwards, or backwards (one doesn't know which). Jerry is rumoured to be coming from all directions. Farm carts crowded mostly with women and children – many on foot. These are all poor people now, or seem to be. The exodus of the rich in their motor cars was in the early days. It must puzzle these people to see so many soldiers in khaki battledress just hanging about so far away from the battle. Indeed the ratio of non-combatant to combatant troops seems absurdly high, and makes nonsense of the claims of statisticians when they proudly claim to have landed a million British soldiers in France. Of these probably only 100,000 are true fighting men. But, if the refugees wonder, they still mostly greet us with wan smiles, until a plane is heard and then they rush into the barns and houses. I saw a woman who looked to be 70, and a younger woman, perhaps her daughter, trudge by on foot, and the older woman carried a pack every bit as large and as heavy as a soldier's. I still cannot really believe the Battalion is wiped out.

<u>25 May 1940 – Belgium – 8.00 am</u>

Still on the run. I was sent out yesterday morning with an anti-tank rifle to create, and man, a roadblock at a railway level-crossing near Caestre and the roadblock faced west, not east. The Germans must have practically surrounded us in this area. I had one rather reluctant signaller with me – Johnson was sent to man another roadblock also covering the village of Caestre. We were dumped by truck near the level-crossing, and the truck went off and I found myself at last face to face with the enemy (though there was no visible sign of him) and with a tactical problem to solve. I tried to remember the logical procedure of the many operation orders I used to write down when I was in the orderly room in peacetime, and all I could think of was 'OWN TROOPS' and 'ENEMY'. The former was simple enough – the answer, 'Two'; and so I suppose, was the latter – the answer, 'The German Army'. The orders given me were brief, if a bit vague and optimistic: 'Shoot up German tanks that are expected to come in from the west.'

I had no binoculars and I strained my eyes for any movement on the long stretch of road where the 'attack' was expected. There were the usual background noises of distant gunfire, nearer AA guns and bombs at times, and the drone of German planes as they passed overhead, but I, and the signaller, listened intently and heard, to the west, the clanking and roaring and squealing noises that armoured fighting vehicles would make at a distance, but at what distance these were, and if they were German, French or British, I had no idea. As far as my eye could see there was no sign of movement at the far end of the road. Not that I really expected to see tanks at all – from what I have heard of German *Blitzkrieg* tactics their armoured columns are preceded by motor-cycle troops who are, in turn, supported by armoured cars, and behind these come the tanks themselves. I rather doubted if I should see off enough motor-cyclists and armoured cars with one anti-tank rifle (and fifteen rounds of anti-tank ammo) to concern myself too much about the tanks.

We plonked the great cumbersome weapon behind some cover at the edge of the level-crossing and from here we 'commanded' the road for as far as we could see it. Common sense told me that this was a suicidal position to adopt for firing the A/Tk rifle at armoured cars which would, no doubt, plaster so easy and obvious a target with their gun and MG fire and obviously the safest position to adopt would be a flanking one, out in the fields from which, though it is harder to hit a moving target at right angles, it would be easier to escape since, if their fire did not see us off, they must deploy across the fields to reach us. But I did not really intend to use the ridiculous weapon at all – a lucky shot might penetrate a weak point in an armoured car – it might kill its occupants, but would hardly put the thing out of action, unless it cut a tyre. We have little confidence in the weapon, and our belief is that it is ineffective except against something like a Bren gun-carrier. Against a tank I think it would be quite useless – even against a light one. [I remember now (thirty years later) that my main reason for setting up our position right on the road, and by the level-crossing, was because I hoped, if the unit moved out of Caestre (as happened) a truck might be sent to pick us up – if so they were unlikely to linger to search for us off the road.]

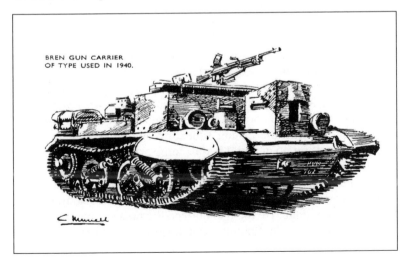

BREN GUN CARRIER
OF TYPE USED IN 1940.

But I had all the confidence in the world in my Lee Enfield rifle and in my own marksmanship; and I knew that if Jerry sent motor-cyclists towards me along that road without any preliminary bombardment of the level-crossing (or too heavy a smokescreen) I could see a few of them off; they would be easy meat coming straight down the road towards me, where it wouldn't be so easy to get them from a flank. I recceed a route by which I could escape to the flank under cover before the guns and MGs shot up the crossing – at least in theory I could. My battle plan was a bit vague from then onwards – heroically I thought I might take a pot from the flank at a scout, or armoured, car with the A/Tk rifle, if I made the flank and still had the nerve to fire. But this problem seemed a bit academic just then.

Absorbed in these speculations, I had forgotten the signaller. A small, bespectacled Scotsman of Brassard Exchange. He didn't look too happy. I asked him what sort of shot he was with a rifle – he had never actually fired one, but was willing to have a go, 'But ah'll no shoot yon elephant gun,' he added, indicating the A/Tk rifle, and I understood his feelings. I am a little scared of the thing myself. We had a bandolier of .303 ammo each, but there were no grenades in the QM stores, and anyway, I wasn't keen to sell my life as dearly as all that. The signaller was game, but nervous. So far I had amused myself with my first ever tactical problem but, with this settled, I laid down with him to wait, and then I too began to get a bit queasy in my stomach. The signaller began to purge a bit. He hadn't joined up to shoot anything, least of all tanks. I tried to console him with an assurance I did not feel. I was finding it hard enough to bolster my own courage without supporting his as well, and the strain of doing so began to get on my nerves and, after about an hour and a half of it, I found myself craving for solitude. I saw his point – he was in the Army doing a civvy job – he was really a civvy. He had no time for the bull and baloney, the spit-and-polish, the drill and display, the esprit de corps and all the rest of it.

Even if he could have used his rifle it wouldn't have been of much use as I discovered when, peering through his glasses, he admitted he could not even see the end of the road. Besides, if I was going to make a fool of myself, I preferred to do it in private; except for Jerry, I didn't want witnesses, and if my heroic intentions did not quite come off I wanted no witnesses to that either. I had another and less honourable motive still, for sending him back. Though the distant squealing and squeaking from the west seemed to be getting no nearer, I had become aware of a lot of revving of truck engines in the village of Caestre behind us. It sounded very much as though the Signals unit was moving out. I told the signaller that I thought the tank sounds were getting nearer, and that he was to go back and report this to the HQ in the village. He too had noticed the noise of motor engines in the village, and had come to the same conclusion as I. So little faith have

I in this unit that I quite believed we should be left there if they did move out. It seemed a very good idea to have someone to remind them of us. I told the signaller (I still do not know his name) to take ten rounds from his bandolier and leave the rest with me and, feeling a bit like Carruthers of the story books, I watched him as he smartly made his way back towards the centre of the village, with one or two nervous glances backwards over his shoulders.

I puffed at a cigarette and wished I had some tipple, and thought about Stella. I now had no audience, so there was no point in indulging in heroics. I felt sad to think how, if I snuffed it, she would grieve and never read this diary, for I had tucked it into a nearby culvert with all my other scribblings. I imagined the pitiable, rather sordid-looking relic I would be when the Germans kicked me over and went through my pockets, and I nearly cried with self-pity at the prospect of such an ignominious, lonely and futile end. And I cursed myself again for ever getting separated from my own battalion. All the while I kept my eyes skinned on the road ahead and on the fields on either side, but nothing came. I became aware of an ominous silence and stillness now in the village behind me. Apart from the distant rumblings, and the noises from the west, there was an uncanny stillness all around me. But I shall never know how near the Germans were to Caestre yesterday, or if they were miles away. I heard a motor engine behind me and turned to see a 15-cwt truck bounding down the road towards me at full speed. Joyfully I rose, retrieved my diary from the culvert, packed up the A/Tk rifle, and had it, and myself, on board almost before the truck had stopped.

In the truck were 77 Johnson, the Signals driver, and my late companion of the roadblock. Johnson was hopping mad, 'Those bastards have b******d off – they went out through our roadblock – none of them seemed to know where you were so we brought the truck back and found this bloke in the village, and he told us.' We tore back through the deserted

BREN GUN, STEN GUN AND MILLS HAND GRENADES.

village, killed a chicken as we cornered, and we caught up with the convoy and I promised Johnson a big drink the next time we found a café open (or one with liquor to sell). What we have left of French money is no good here, however.

***

We were on the road all day, often edging the vehicles past

13

and through crowds of walking refugees. These poor souls literally don't know if they are coming or going – many have turned round and are now trekking back the way they came as Jerry closes in now from France and the west. There was a lot of enemy air activity and we often jumped from our trucks and joined the civvies in the ditches alongside the road and conversed with them while Stukas screamed down to bomb the road and then they, and their fighters, swept low along the road machine-gunning. This experience is unnerving enough for a soldier to bear without his witnessing the terrible distress of women and children and old men sharing such ordeals with him. It makes me hate the swine who, with impunity and, I suspect, with sadistic pleasure, turn their guns on helpless women and children. Every now and then, after such a strafe, a body would lie still as the rest of us got to our feet, and we would hear the awful, harrowing cries of a mother lamenting the death or maiming of her child, or a child its mother; and sometimes a figure in khaki would not rise or would stagger, wounded, to his feet. And sometimes soldiers would go to comfort a woman, or a child, hysterical with fright and suffering. It is a shock to learn what war really is – to realize suddenly the full brutal ruthlessness that is war. And it seems so terribly one-sided. We sometimes potted futilely with rifles at the low-rushing planes, but we have no Brens, and as I looked up at other German planes flying serenely overhead – formations of bombers and giant transport planes and fighters all heading west or returning with empty bomb-bays to the east – I hated them as I have never hated anything before. And we hated the RAF and the French Air Force who allowed this to happen with such impunity to the Huns.

We now have nothing to give the refugees – we have had little or no food ourselves, and few of us have any cigarettes – mine have all gone now and I find myself regretting my generosity in giving so many away. Cigarettes have been so cheap and plentiful for the BEF that we find it hard to realize that there are no more. We scrounge and beg (those of us without). We seem thoroughly disorganized. Johnson summed it up pithily: 'The biggest bugger-up since Mons!'

There was at least one item of very cheering news yesterday. I learned that the Battalion is far from having been wiped out. We were waiting in the street at Caestre (and before I was sent out on the roadblock) when a staff car drew up beside me, and a staff officer (I suspect also a Guards officer) with a red band round his cap called 'Corporal!' and I went up to the car and saluted. He asked me what I was doing in Caestre, and I explained about Johnson and myself, and then asked him if he knew anything about the Battalion. He said that, until yesterday, they were in Arras but had now probably been withdrawn from there as the place was in danger of being completely cut off. This meant there were still some of the Battalion left and I told him of the rumours I had heard. He laughed and said they were very much alive and kicking. That the Battalion had done famously, and had held Arras practically alone against attack for three days and hadn't lost very many men in doing it. He wished me luck, and the car drove on, and I reported the good news to Johnson.

It has been a hectic day – raid after raid of bombers – high-level, and Stuka dive-bombers, have come over. The latter, though they carry smaller bombs, are terrifying engines of war. They seem to be fitted with some device that makes them scream as they dive down on their targets – and these devilish planes seem to be everywhere. I shall remember these Stukas till my dying day – a cliché not too apt, I suppose, for a man in my situation right now. It does not somehow conjure up the prospect of endless eons of time.

<u>26 May 1940 – 4.35 am</u>

Wonder what this day has in store for us? This must surely be unique. The GHQ of a large British Army, no more than gypsies and vagrants, chased out of it to live, and cower, in open hedgerows. Human riff-raff with less dignity left to them than the horses grazing in the field next to where I stand – because the horses, in their ignorance, betray no constant fear of death.

<u>27 May 1940 – 6.00 pm</u>

Again it seems that the British Army is smashed and a great retreat, if not a rout, is in progress now. It is incredible. Surely Jerry is not winning? And this after such good, heartening news. We, Johnson and I, were transferred yesterday to a sort of 'Foreign Legion'. A number of stragglers have now joined this outfit, mostly men from the Durham Light Infantry, and including a CSM of that regiment. We have been given two trucks, four anti-tank rifles, a Bren gun, two RAF .5 Browning guns, and bags of ammo. And we were to be a combined anti-tank and anti-aircraft section, and we operated thus for a time. We got the kit from a dump, and it was good to belong once more to an organized unit.

But now we have smashed the guns, and everything that went with them, and we have had to dump all 'excessive' kit we carried, and we have smashed up thousands of pounds worth of precious RAF kit under iron bars with any destructive tool we could lay our hands on. A terrible thing to do, but it couldn't be left for the Germans to have.

Barlow turned up here last night and brought with him hundreds of fags. Thank God! We have been gasping for them. We have fed on bully and biscuits – when available.

Today we have been bombed and machine-gunned almost incessantly and many signallers have been killed. I lay in a ditch at one time during the day and watched an RASC convoy on a converging road, and about 300 yards away, getting a hellish strafing from German planes. About ten German fighters suddenly swooped on the convoy and machine-gunned it. I watched the convoy halt, and dozens of men rush from the trucks towards the ditches lining the road, and I saw many fall as the MG bullets got them; and then, one by one, the trucks went up in flames as incendiary bullets hit the petrol tanks (or the cargoes of ammunition and petrol) until only a row of charred British trucks was left. How we wished the Hurricanes upon the Jerry fighters! But none came and, their job done, the German planes leisurely re-formed formation and flew off towards the east. But we saw a good dog-fight this morning, and have seen four Jerries brought down today.

I now have enough news from Barlow and the DLIs to know what happened around Arras after GHQ moved out. The Battalion did excellent work there, and I hear praise from many different units for what the Battalion did. Barlow was there until a few days ago, and all the rumours and counter-rumours about Arras having fallen (and been retaken) were hooey. The Battalion did not move from the place until it was ordered to do so on the 24th or 25th. It seems that the British and French made a counter-attack to the west of the town, with Arras held as the linchpin. The attack failed, and not until then was the Battalion withdrawn – its job was to hold the place which, by all accounts, it did superbly and it is good to hear them praised by other troops who were in Arras for a time with them.

So we are back where we were. It was good to be able to hit back at the German planes and only a little while ago (just before we were ordered to smash the kit) we definitely put Jerry off his stroke, even if we didn't stop him, when eight planes selected our own transport as their target. The CSM manned the Browning we were using – the AA (the other was with an A/Tk outpost) and we manned the two Brens, but the Brens were in a bad way – I suspect rejects – they kept jamming. But the Browning worked beautifully, and at last we abandoned the near-useless Brens, and I went up to help feed the belt into the Browning. He didn't bring any planes down, but I could see the bullets pumping into them. A number of bombs were dropped and these shook us a bit, but the Browning never stopped, and I am certain we put Jerry off his stroke and really drove him off, because he did not (as he generally does) come down to machine-gun us though for a while his planes were pretty low, and I admired the guts and determination of this CSM. He is almost too determined for as the eight Jerry planes flew off, another plane, flying very low, came towards us and we swung the excellent Browning, with a new belt of ammo, round to engage it. It seemed to be coming straight for us. We stood, unprotected, in an open field and I braced myself to take the shock of his machine guns when he opened up. But he didn't fire, and I saw our own fire plunging into his fuselage as he came nearer. Then he banked and circled round us, and I saw on the flank of the fuselage a blue, white and red roundel – in reverse colour arrangement to the RAF roundel – the plane was only a few feet above tree level and the CSM swung the Browning round and I saw tracers going into the side of the plane and the pilot gesticulating: 'Stop – he's French!' I shouted – 'A bloody Fifth Columnist more likely!' answered the CSM, 'so far as I'm concerned anything that flies nowadays is a f***ing Jerry.' And he continued firing at the unfortunate plane (which I believed was already in some distress) until it was out of sight, and the Browning .5 ammo exploded. I was relieved to see the plane kept going, though the bullets that we had pumped into the plane hadn't helped it much. I was relieved too to think we hadn't got the pilot – we must have seen him crash had we hit him.

We fired off the remaining ammo at anything in the air, even high-flying stuff. But the Brens would not fire for long enough to use up the magazines which we dumped into the truck to bury them in a pond when we came to one. Apart from superficial damage from blast and shrapnel the vehicles of the convoy were OK.

What a hellish day this has been, and still is! All around us fires are burning, towns, villages, dumps of ammunition, and petrol. At night, surrounded by fires, gunfire and bombing, the full macabre tableau of wax is revealed. It seems that everything around about is being destroyed. The scene is apocalyptic and one looks for the horsemen (in the rolling red-lit smoke clouds) as I saw them on the film as a small boy[1]. There is talk of an ultimatum from Churchill to Germany that we shall start bombing their open towns unless they desist in bombing those of France and Belgium. Sounds very grim, and this would surely mean that London will be bombed, which God forbid.

---

1. 'The Four Horsemen of the Apocalypse.'

2

Dunkirk

28 May 1940 – Sand dunes near Dunkirk – 6.30 am

We are now on the sand dunes just east of blazing Dunkirk. Some way along the beaches lies an enormous building that looks like a huge barracks but is, I believe, a hospital.

Here there are thousands of troops, mostly, I think, GHQ, Army and Corps HQ personnel – the long administrative 'tail' of the Army; though a more accurate description of a modern army would be to refer to the actual fighting troops as only the small 'head' of the lengthy beast. These men are dotted all about the dunes for as far as the eye can see, an untidy-looking lot many with dirt, and beards of several days' growth, on faces and chins – many seem to have no equipment, or rifles even, and many are sprawled unconscious in sleep, and few stir, even when the Hun planes come over.

Small boats are taking the troops out to steamers lying offshore from queues of men lined up on the beaches at the water's edge and I made a quick charcoal sketch of the dunes where we lie (see plate no. 4, 'Dawn at Dunkirk'). A British destroyer is patrolling the coast, and the sight of the Navy is a fine one for our very sore eyes to see. Guns are firing, and there's a lot of small-arms fire too.

A Jerry reconnaissance plane has just had a look at us so I guess we must watch out for the bombers soon.

Later

I had no sooner written the above, than an officer came along the dunes near the beach ordering us back further inland to avoid an expected bombing attack. As soon as we arrived here the three guardsmen flung themselves down on to the soft sand of the dunes and instantly fell asleep. We are all dead tired, hungry and thirsty – but sleep we crave most. Yet I remain awake out of worry, apprehension, or sheer excitement – I don't know which – I prefer to think excitement, and of the desire to record what I can of this amazing incident as it happens. We are looking a bit scruffy (for guardsmen) too, though (except for our big packs which we were ordered to dump) we are fully equipped and gunned; but we have not shaved since yesterday morning, and I must look like the others, red-eyed and haggard through strain and lack of sleep. But we are dandies compared to some of the desperadoes here. Men, some filthy dirty and with many days' growth of beard and no equipment or rifles – they look as though they have been fighting off Jerry in hand-to-hand combat every day for weeks – yet most of them wear the badges of administrative and ancillary units and corps – there are very few infantrymen here at all.

In addition to my three Welsh guardsmen I seem involuntarily to have collected quite a little army of my own, signallers who seek to stick to us like leeches, though their own quartermaster, the only unit officer now left, so far as I can tell, is here on the beach, and he still keeps the whole outfit together. Without him these men would now be dispersed all over this corner of France, many probably prisoners by now. Nevertheless, many of them stick with us. Apart from seeing that they kept their equipment and rifles, I have not attempted to order them about, neither have I encouraged them to join us. In fact I feel a little ashamed of them. Many of them are game enough, and cheerful enough. But they look such a weird outfit with their long hair and spectacles and beards (though only a few really wear glasses, and I am unfair).

Neither did I assume (as we came on to the sand dunes and realized that the rumours were, for once, true), that evacuation by sea was for anyone but the administrative troops of HQs of Army and Corps. I saw a staff officer (he looked spruce with his red tabs and cap band) standing on the south edge of the dunes, and I told the guardsmen to wait, and I went up and saluted the officer and asked him for instructions, after telling him how we came to be here. I was astonished when he told me to get myself and the three guardsmen onto the beach and queue up with the rest for a boat to take us off. I thought he hadn't fully understood, and I began to explain that my battalion was still somewhere to the south. He glared at me: 'Don't argue with me corporal, I've told you what to do!' Then, with less asperity, he told me that this was not just an evacuation of non-combatant troops, but of the whole British Army in France, and the sooner we, and all the other odds and ends, were got away the more chance there was for the fighting troops to do so. He became almost amiable, and half-smiled, 'Don't worry – your battalion's not far from here, with luck they won't be far behind you.' I saluted again and went back to tell the incredulous guardsmen his news and, though I still worry, I feel much easier in my mind so far as my own conduct is concerned; but badly shaken to hear it confirmed that the whole British Army is evacuating, or trying to evacuate, France altogether, and to realize at last that we are indeed beaten and routed – a defeated army – and that the Germans have virtually won the war! It is ghastly and incredible news. But now, thinking about it, this is not necessarily so, we shall be re-equipped and sent back to France again. After all, the BEF is only a small part of the French Armies here, though I find it impossible to believe that a British Army **can** be beaten by a German one. A bitter pill to swallow indeed!

I attempted to obey the officer's instruction to get back further inland, and I shook, and had to kick, the recumbent guardsmen to awaken them. When I told them the order they glared at me bad-temperedly and invited me to stop bobbing and to 'f*** off', and they dropped back into slumber. This was hardly the manner in which guardsmen are expected to address an NCO – even a lance corporal – when given an order; but, even if I had wanted to, there was nothing I could do about it, and they had put me on the spot by suggesting I was windy. It was a subject not to be pursued. We remained where we are now, and anyway it seems to me that these dunes, with their soft sand, are as safe as anywhere, and when the raid came (as I was writing) I realized that this was so. No bombs fell near us, but there were few casualties so far as I could see – the sand quite effectively muffles the bombs and they go deep before exploding. Nor did the planes machine-gun us here and that, I imagine, will be a different story, if and when it happens. The men on the dunes and beaches are sitting ducks for machine guns – there seems to be no shelling of this part of the beach either. Perhaps Jerry's not in range yet.

I rather maliciously looked for some stir and anxiety when the raid came, and anticipated being able to say 'I told you so,' but the guardsmen merely reached for their tin hats and put them over their faces, and dropped off to sleep again – as did some of the signallers with us – some in fact never stirred at all. The AA fire of the destroyer was terrific and seemed much more effective than the Army AA. An added hazard here is the amount of shrapnel that sizzles down upon us from this AA fire.

Though the vista of the beaches presents a scene of chaos and confusion and utter untidiness, littered as it is with cast-off equipment and clothing and ammunition boxes and general rubbish, there is obviously organization at work too. We on the dunes are not allowed to join the queues on the beaches until we are ordered to do so. And the queues themselves, though they would never be mistaken for participants in a Trooping the Colour ceremony, are orderly too – four, five, or six deep, the columns of men wait with apparently patient discipline, but it is a laborious business, and they scattered like mad when the raid came over and several of them never got up again and several more were wounded too. But the queues reformed more or less in order and they stand waiting on, as the small boats ply to and fro.

As I write now eighteen Spitfires are circling overhead. A most comforting sight, and away east over the sand dunes towards Belgium a fierce outbreak of small-arms fire is in progress.

What this means I can't tell. It can't be Jerry ground troops they're engaging, or we would be under shell and mortar fire right now.

***

We had a nerve-racking journey all night to reach here. The convoy left the Belgian village at about 11.30 pm. A DLI was driving our truck, and I think it must have been his first attempt behind the wheel. The night was full of sinister noises and weird lights – flares, searchlights and burning villages and towns, and we seemed to be heading for one particularly large conflagration, which I now assume to be Dunkirk itself. And all night long German planes droned overhead, to and fro, to bomb the stricken town some more, and each raid stoked the fires, and they flared up ominously.

The bloody fools over the dunes are firing at our own planes – fortunately they are too high for small-arms fire to have any effect. The destroyer has just let go some accurate AA fire at three Jerry planes over the sea. Wonder if the Spitfires will spot them?

We had been driving only about twenty minutes in the darkness when our driver ran the truck, with terrific impact, into the ditch at the side of the road. We were all pretty shaken up and I think Lamb broke his nose against the Bren gun tripod mounted into the deck of the open truck, and a newly-acquired A/Tk rifle fell across my leg and all but broke my shinbone. We scrambled out of the truck and the ditch and tried to stop other trucks of the convoy, but they were chock-full. At last one fairly empty one picked us up, and we began to run through an alley of ditched and abandoned trucks that lined the road for miles until we reached the sea.

Tons and tons of valuable equipment is jettisoned – whole switchboards of telephonic equipment – wireless sets – field guns and limbers, supply lorries, all the expensive paraphernalia of the Army's tail. Yet Jerry does not seem close. The zone we passed through was one of a complex system of waterways, canals, ditches and dykes, and these perhaps are hindering Jerry's advance? We actually passed some French tanks mounted on tank trailers going the other way. This did not look as if Jerry was very close.

I no longer believed that we were involved in an orderly withdrawal; all the signs about me pointed to only one hideous conclusion, defeat and rout. Somewhere along the road we were halted in a traffic jam – French carts and trucks and guns littered the area, and we went over to investigate shots that were coming from a wide canal, or river, with steep banks. We could hear the whinnying of horses, and sometimes terrible screams. It was still dark, but the fires and the flares and searchlights lit a ghastly scene. The canal seemed full of horses – many dead, and some still living – and these were being shot by British officers armed with rifles and revolvers. We were told that they were French artillery horses, dumped into the canal to perish so that the Germans should not have them. All the horror of war seemed to be along that road last night – and there were refugees on it too, and bombing by the light of the ghastly glow of flares dropped from German aircraft.

Many of the abandoned trucks were on fire, whether set alight by German planes, or by British troops, I do not know. We were at last ordered to get off our trucks and dump them, and we found that some of the already abandoned lorries contained NAAFI stores, including cigarettes – though there was no food to be had. I notice now that many of the troops here on the dunes have reversed the order given to dump big packs – they have retained **only** their big packs, which are full of cigarettes and have dumped the rest of their kit, including rifles. While most of the men I have seen retain some equipment and rifles, a great many have not done so, and it is a disgrace to see the rifles and webbing abandoned on the sand dunes.

And the conduct of some of the men lying on the dunes is no better. A couple of staff officers approached not long ago, and they stopped to confer for a moment or two. Jerry planes have been fairly constantly overhead for some time now and I heard, from about 15 yards away, hysterical screams of abuse at the two officers, and supplications for them to get down because the men nearby feared they would attract the Jerry planes to them and plaster the area. The two officers contemptuously ignored this unpleasant display of panic and abuse. But it left a hideous impression. There appear to be pockets of these live-at-all-cost fanatics as I found when I went to a higher hillock to view the panorama of Dunkirk and the beaches. It is not general, but this hysteria and panic has a bad effect upon others in the vicinity, and if these men imagine that by lying down, they are less in view from a Jerry plane than a man standing up would be, they are mistaken. The Naval AA fire keeps Jerry fliers at a respectful height, but even so they cannot possibly mistake the khaki-clad recumbent figures on the dunes for anything but British soldiers.

I still cannot believe that this is the end for us. This must be a nightmare. Has there been some terrible quarrel between France and Britain? Perhaps England has decided to wash her hands of France and Belgium, where spies are reported everywhere and where every move of ours is immediately known at German HQ.

What happens now I wonder? Will France capitulate and England continue the war alone? The only ray of sunshine is that I may be able soon to see my darling. Perhaps things will all turn out OK yet? Could go a mug of char right now.

30 May 1940 – Shrivenham

Am now here – actually here in Blighty! It seems absolutely, hopelessly incredible! It is like awakening from a ghastly nightmare in one's own snug, secure, familiar room at home. We are in a large modern barracks here near the small village of Shrivenham, and not very far from Swindon. The barracks are set in a large park full of magnificent oaks, chestnuts and elms – full-leafed in the sweet green luxuriance of an early English summer; trees that throw deep cool shadows over the lush grass and buttercup meadows. This is surely paradise? I can only repeat over and over in my mind those catch-phrases from Shakespeare: 'Earth of Majesty' and 'Sceptred Isle', 'This precious stone set in a silver sea.' Never before has England been so excitingly beautiful to me as now, with the chestnut flowers still in bloom, and the hawthorn too, and rhododendrons, and the long green grass, fresh and ready for its first cutting into hay. Serene, orderly, beautiful and, in spite of the danger that threatens now, infinitely secure. All day in this glorious sunshine the birds sing, and the insects buzz and drone over the grass in the strong, heady, country scent of this lovely summer; peace marred only by the droning of aeroplanes overhead. But these are friendly planes, though we still listen half-fearfully to the sound we have learned to hate so much. Just now a plane swooped low over the barracks and the men in the room winced and ducked, as though by instinct. I have rather lost the thread of events, of their chronological order, even of days and dates, since I last wrote only two days ago – but that time seems so remote now – could almost have been a month, or a year, ago.

***

We spent a wretched day on the sand dunes. It began to rain hard at about 4.00 pm and this was a blessing in disguise for it curtailed some of the enemy's air activity over the beaches. The low cloud ceiling made him vulnerable to the heavy and accurate fire of the naval vessels. Until the rain came Jerry planes were everywhere and, but for the soft sand, he must have killed and wounded many more than he did, and once I dug my fingers into the sand as I laid flat on my stomach and prayed when a salvo of bombs screamed down upon us. I was certain that I was about to die. But, though the bombs fell close, and killed or wounded men in the immediate vicinity of their explosions, the sand localized their destructiveness, as did the undulations in the dunes themselves and, except that I was blasted and shaken, I was not touched and neither were any of my party. But the sand and the hillocks provided less protection against machine-gun bullets. Even so, it was amazing how, after a strafing, so few men were hit by the streams of bullets that poured from the planes. But for the Navy AA and our own AA and even, to some extent, our own small-arms fire, Jerry would no doubt have come the acid a lot more with his MG attacks, but if little damage was done, these attacks were very wearing on the nerves.

Once or twice in between raids I went out on a foray to see if there was any food, or above all, a hot drink – or any drink – going. But I found nothing – only groups of grimy, unshaven, exhausted men – some no more than scarecrows – others fully equipped – many stretched out in the ungainly sleep of exhaustion, some playing cards and smoking and talking. Most seemed patient and calm, and I noticed a number of infantrymen, but stragglers, rather than organized units, I thought. Every now and then I would pass a 'windy group' who snarled at me to get down; but these were rare enough, and I wondered if men of a type collected together, or whether one man, who bobbed a lot, set those around him off. We were all windy enough under attack I suppose, but with some men it had become a phobia. But I noticed they were mostly older men of ancillary units.

Thousands and thousands of men were on those beaches and sand hills. Eight destroyers, and other smaller craft, kept Jerry planes high with pom-poms and 4-inch guns trained high. A formation of large German bombers, or air transports, I don't know which, passed overhead and an intense barrage surrounded them. It was exhilarating to see this determined hitting back after all the days when he just flew his planes to and fro with such contemptuous impunity. Good old Navy, they take it all in their stride! Suddenly one of the planes turned and dived into the sea and we on the beach cheered like kids watching a cowboy film. Only one parachutist fell from the plane, and he too landed in the sea. Some of the planes were bombers and they dropped salvoes of bombs on the dunes just east of where we lay, close enough for me to have my head well down, and when I looked up it was to see a thick cloud of smoke and sand overhanging the place where they fell, and then I put my head down again as sand fell like rain into my eyes. I wondered how many men had been hit. I could hear nothing for the din of the AA barrage.

I noticed later a group of men bathing in the calm sea and I admired their sangfroid – somehow to take off all one's clothes and stand naked under the threat of enemy bombing and machine-gunning makes one seem more vulnerable, though, apart from not wearing a tin hat, I suppose this is not so (and some of the bathers actually wore steel helmets). But, though a number of men seemed to be genuinely bathing inshore, I noticed that others were swimming far out to sea – no doubt jumping the queues on the beaches and swimming direct to the large vessels anchored half a mile or more offshore and I reflected that, with no clothing to hamper me, this swim was well within my own range – a piece of cake in fact.

I must have slept for a while. I was terribly tired. I seem to remember being disturbed once or twice by bombs, but when I awoke it was raining hard, and I welcomed the dampness on my face and hair after the dusty, gritty dryness of the dunes. I lit a cigarette, at least we had plenty of these now – a couple of days before I had been smoking anything I could get, including some black, strong, reeking Belgian cigarettes that made me cough like hell. The guardsmen were awake, and told me that things had got much quieter since the rain began. We wandered off in pairs and located the indefatigable QM of the Signals. There was no food or water, let alone tea. He said that it would soon be our turn to go down onto the beach and, at about 11.00 pm, we found ourselves lined up more or less in column of threes and part of a long queue that stretched down to the water's edge and right into the sea itself (in spite of my ducking at Dunkirk my notes and diary writings, in their oilskin wrappers, are dry and still legible).

Until we actually began to form up in the darkness on that beach, I don't think I really believed that I **was** going back to England (in spite of what the brass-hat had told me). Although the bulk of the waiting troops were non-combatants, I had seen for myself that there were many men on the dunes – infantrymen, gunners and sappers, who had weapons, and could handle them. There was ammunition in the abandoned trucks (not all of which had been set on fire) and the naval vessels must have had plenty of small-arms ammo aboard which could have been brought ashore with each empty whaler that returned to the beach to pick up more men.

I quite expected some officer with a megaphone to tour the sand hills calling for fighting personnel. Rumour has it that several such scratch forces (of fighting men returning from leave and in transit camps and depots) have been formed, and it is incredible that some such thing did not happen on the beaches, just as it is incredible that we were ordered to smash guns two days before, guns that could have been used on the beaches. Had the dunes and the beach been under shell and mortar fire, and in imminent danger of being overrun, it might have been difficult to organize this; but, except during actual air-raids (and these largely ceased for a while after 4.00 pm), we were left to loll about and sleep. I was not anxious to be dragooned into a scratch force and to be flung, as were the DLIs, with only rifle and bayonet, against German MGs and tanks; but after five years' service, I have grown so used to that wrath of WOs and NCOs who see men idle with the inevitable, 'What you on then?' that I still cannot imagine why we were not sorted out.

But once I found myself actually there, queuing in the darkness, awaiting the small boats to take me out to the dark hulls lying offshore and thence to England, my outlook began to change; and I know now that the change was not for the better. All men, I suppose, think base thoughts. But when I do so I have forgotten them before (even if I wanted to) I could record them. But what I saw and what I thought yesterday on the dunes and on the beach last night, remains very vivid, though jumbled in my memory. From the shame and hopelessness and despair of defeat on the dunes to the shameful, selfish thoughts that came into my mind once I began to hope only for self-preservation; as I did when I realized that the darkness (though this, in the glare of blazing Dunkirk was only comparative) gave me and my fellow guardsmen an anonymity we did not have by day.

We were unlikely now to be sorted out, and we were in the queue for England. Hope is generally lauded as a virtue. I do not now believe it to be a virtue in a soldier on active service. I suppose I hope, like others, to survive the war, but I have never believed, when so many infantrymen die, that I am destined to live. In a war such as the last one, it would be unrealistic to do so. I saw no reason why I, more than another, should be spared. If I did hope, it was a very cautious hope. But, once on the beach, I found myself hoping wildly that I should get away, and I began firmly to believe that I would. If I was windy before when planes came over, I now became obsessed with staying alive and reaching the boats. I found myself silently swearing and blaspheming obscenely, as flares were dropped overhead, flares that revealed us to the enemy. We flung ourselves down on the wet sand and awaited the bombs. But there was no attack on our queue, and in the din of the AA fire, and the glow of fires around us, I could not tell if other queues on the beach were attacked. The planes may have been only on reconnaissance missions.

As we slowly neared the water I felt I wanted to shout to those in front to hurry up (as some men were doing – until public opinion around them told them to pipe down). Some small-arms fire and other explosions sounded from somewhere behind the dunes. It was probably only ammunition going up from blazing and abandoned trucks, but to us it seemed that the Germans were closing in on the beaches. Even when the flames above Dunkirk flared brighter, as they did from time to time as more bombs fell, or fresh oil tanks took fire, the queue seemed to press forward, as though spurred by a new urgency.

I began, like the others, to watch jealously for interlopers trying to jump the queue in the darkness and, to my shame, I even grew impatient as the wounded were carried down into the water and given priority of embarkation, though I, and all the men in the queue, automatically accepted that this should be so, and none of the men around me breathed a word against this principle.

I even found myself resenting the priority of the men in front of me in the queue, and their alternating moods of optimism and depression, and the silly, childish jokes they made when a wave of hope took over. The little, unfunny jokes of fear and suppressed hysteria that were subtly and horribly different from the normal run of silly little jokes soldiers crack out of the sheer boredom of their army lives.

And I resented the stupid, irritating specimens of humanity some of them presented, though I knew that I myself was no oil painting to look at. They could not possibly have someone like Stella to go back to. They could not possibly have so much to live for as I had. Their lives were less important than mine, I was sure of it!

It is difficult to write this – even here in a private diary. I take no credit for the fact that I outwardly showed nothing of this hysteria and panic and selfishness – I thought it, and I was, and am, badly shaken to know that I did so.

But gradually decency and common sense restored themselves in my mind, and I was ashamed of what I had thought. We, the guardsmen, were the interlopers there. We were the ones who paraded our militarism under banners and behind drums in all the pomp and pageantry of military ceremonial in London streets in the days of peace – we were the self-avowed warriors, not those men about me on the beach – many of them nothing more than civilians in battledress, and most of them behaving remarkably well too.

Nevertheless, if I regained my sense of proportion, I did not fully regain the fatalism I experienced on the dunes. I was still desperately anxious to get away and continued to fret and fume inwardly, until some hero in front of us produced a mouth-organ and began to play the sad, haunting melodies that seem so suited to that melancholy instrument: 'The Londonderry Air', 'Loch Lomond', 'Mother Macree', 'Begin the Beguine' and 'Drink to me only with thine eyes' and other songs that soothed the nerves and dulled anxiety; and I began to look about me at the amazing tableau of a British Army in defeat.

It was a scene I think I shall never forget. On my left was an awesome spectacle. Dunkirk, blazing furiously, threw a savage, lurid glow on its own smoke and on the low hanging clouds, and it lit the beaches and was brilliantly reflected in pools of water and in the wet sand. The gentle breakers of the calm sea seemed almost phosphorescent as they lapped into the shore. Periodically an oil tank in the town exploded and a fresh, billowing blaze of fire soared heavenwards, silhouetting more vividly yet the long, patient columns of men waiting on the beach. Out at sea, their hulls and superstructure vaguely seen in the bloody reflection of the flames, the destroyers, minesweepers and other craft waited just as patiently and, if I heard the cry once, I heard it a hundred times 'Thank Christ for the Navy!'

Over on my right the beach was darker and even more menacing to us, for there was a rumour on the beach that the Belgians had capitulated and that now nothing stood between us and the German Army advancing from that direction; and it was to the east we looked whenever our minds dwelt upon the proximity of the enemy and it was to the east, though more inland, that other fires raged from the burning trucks and it was from the east there came the periodical explosions and crackle of musketry that suggested an engagement between the ground forces of British and German troops. To the south, and behind us, lay the dunes and the long brooding building they say was a hospital.

Sometimes, except for distant rumblings, the beaches were quiet – but not for long. Sooner or later the hated droning noises overhead would incite the pandemonium response of AA fire and searchlights, which never seemed entirely to fade, would multiply and add their quota of purplish-white light to the ruddier fascination of fire and the star effect of bursting AA shells against the backcloth of the night sky.

It was a grim, ruthless vista of war. Slowly but surely we reached the water's edge. The beach shelved gently and men, some way out, seemed to be in water only up to their waists. Now, as we neared the boats, I noticed that men's patience wore thin. There was occasional shouting and disorder when boats came in and some evidence of panic when the planes came over and later, when I stood deeper in the water myself, I appreciated the nakedness a man feels to know he cannot fling himself to the ground if attacked, and might well drown if hit and only wounded. I appreciated too the frustrating sense of being so near, and yet so far from, safety when an attack, or the threat of an attack, came.

<u>Continued 31 May 1940</u>

I could write no more yesterday. For hours I slept in luxury on an army bed and then went out into the sun to write. But I kept dropping off to sleep, even when I moved into the shade of a great tree. Some men just slept for twenty-four hours or more but I fought against it to write. But every time I did sleep I awoke to a delicious sensation of wellbeing and security as I realized where I was and that I was clean and fed and safe, and the present and the future did not worry me. I only longed to see Stella and Mother. Beyond that I was blissfully carefree, and I wrote on.

***

At last our boots were in the water, and I heard a couple of revolver shots up near the boats, and word was passed back that officers were shooting at men who panicked as a boat came in.

I shall never forget those three or four hours on that darkened beach. As men neared the boats the instinct for survival became dominant. The red glare from Dunkirk was sinister enough a backcloth for this macabre seaside dip without the off and on stage acoustics of exploding shells – the threatening, maddening drone of German planes overhead, and the searchlights, and other fires, and the threat of the Germans, 'lusty in victory', closing in, and the smell of defeat and the shame, and the undercurrent of panic that, except in a few instances, never came to the surface. But there were many optimists and brave men too; and few were so worried that they forgot to keep their fags (if not their powder) dry by hoisting their packs higher as they got deeper and deeper into the water; and the mouth organist started up again with some very appropriate naval airs, as he himself must have been very near his turn to go.

But I wished heartily that I was with regular troops under a firmer discipline. I kept my guardsmen with me and they behaved well, as did many of the signallers, and the DLIs who still stuck close to us. But some men in the queue got hellishly jittery as we got nearer to the boats, and they were a menace to the rest, and I found the tension mounting within me. Deeper we went into the sea, and I heard men gasp a bit, and I did the same, as the warmish water swirled about our sexual organs. Here the sea seemed as littered with debris as the beach: packing cases and oars and flotsam and jetsam from sunken boats; timber and garments; and once there was a commotion ahead and I saw men pushing away from them a corpse which had floated inshore.

As the whalers came in, manned generally by two sailors (naked but for a pair of ducks) so twenty-five men were detailed off to each boat – the Quartermaster of the Signals performing this office for his own men. I saw no other officers of the Signals' outfit there at all. The water came about my waist, up to the chests of smaller men. But, though only twenty-five men were detailed, more actually boarded each boat I saw loaded. In spite of the QM's threats, two or three (and more) men would rush forward and get lost in the confusion and darkness. As our turn came I told the guardsmen not to get split up but, if necessary, to await the next boat rather than do so. And so we were at the head of the queue when the whaler came in, and we found ourselves in the bows of it. We laid our rifles at the bottom of the boat, though it contained quite a lot of water, and between us we grabbed an oar, and I was amused to hear the two sailors trying, by supplication and threat, to sort out the chaos as oars waved about and the boat, with far too many aboard, was in danger of capsizing until the soldiers in it settled down: 'We've already had four duckings through you pongos[1] today – we don't want any more.'

But confusion was rife, and the water under the gunwale dangerously high and, just as we pulled away, another whaler came in and the matelots ordered four of us (who were not rowing) to transfer to it and, as I was not rowing, I did so. But first I made a desperate attempt to retrieve my (or any) rifle from the bottom of the boat; but the space was packed tight with the feet of rowers and with other bodies lying across them. I shouted to the two

---

1. Pongo – a seaman's term for a soldier, derived from the belief that they did not wash.

guardsmen (who were rowing) to bring my rifle aboard as, judging by the nicknames they used, the sailors of both whalers belonged to the same parent vessel. But in the din they did not hear me. So I went back to the beach and the matelots called 'Come on, a few more of you!' And this time there was a downright stampede, in spite of the bellows of rage from the beach officer, and the boat was nearly swamped as too many tried to board it. The matelots tipped some men back, but still there were too many – the whaler was aground astern and I, in the bows, found myself swinging round in an arc of 180 degrees, and the fires of Dunkirk seemed to be revolving too. At last the matelots yelled for some of us to get out and push. Obedient as ever, I complied, and so did a few others further astern, and the boat got going. But I kept pushing until the water came up to my gas mask and then I attempted what I discovered to be the most futile of pastimes – to climb into a boat from the water while wearing full kit and ammunition boots. With a tremendous effort I managed to get my respirator resting on the gunwale, but this rose up under my chin and pushed my head right backwards. The man nearest me (I was then amidships) was busily rowing but at last he heeded my bellowing and paused to hoist me further into the boat so that my stomach now rested on the gunwale, my face was down inside the boat, but my legs were still trailing in the water – at least I was half-aboard, and this seemed to satisfy him. He grabbed his oar and resumed rowing. Every now and then his (or another soldier's) oar went deep and caught my legs. I felt terribly weak after my struggles to get into the boat and I rested in that undignified position for a while to regain my breath and my strength, and then began to struggle some more. But my legs could get no leverage, and they just swirled away beneath me as I tried to use the side of the boat and push myself upwards.

I paused and rested again, and then an unpleasant thought struck me. If the whaler pulled in alongside the larger vessel on the side on which I was lying, my legs would be crushed to pulp. I could tell that we were nearing a vessel, and I yelled again for help, but the din in the boat as the enthusiastic rowers urged themselves on drowned mine and again I lay still, resigned to my fate as it were and quite exhausted. I was in some danger of losing my head and then I laughed, I would like to think in humour, at the indignity of my position – my head lay in the bottom of the boat that was swirling with sea water – my bottom was stuck into the air and my feet still dangled in the sea. But curiously enough my laughter, whether of mirth or hysteria, attracted the man's attention as my cries had not. He put his head down to mine: 'Wosser matter mate?' This, I thought, was obvious enough, but I told him to pull me in: 'You're a bleedin' nuisance, ain't you?' But he released his oar and got his hands under my thighs and jerked me into the boat so forcibly that for a second I stood on my head and then completed a somersault and my legs, as they landed, crashed on to the helmet of a rower on the opposite side of the boat. There was an aggrieved roar: 'Don't f*** about mate – this job's 'ard enough without you kickin' my teeth in.'

I collected my flying limbs and hunched myself up, sitting in the water at the bottom of the boat and trying to keep out of the way and not impede the oarsmen. There was no room on the seats. Someone found me useful to give him leverage, and rhythmically his boots pressed into me as he rowed. I was terribly weak after my frantic struggles to pull myself aboard, and I sat thus until we reached a minesweeper – the *Albion* I believe. I sat tight and prayed that the men would not capsize the whaler as they moved to the side nearest the large vessel, and the sailors shouted their warnings and tried to control the exodus from the boat. The water was almost over the gunwale and I knew that, in my weakened state, and in full kit and army boots, I could not have swum my way to safety. I was almost too weak to pull myself up the scrambling nets that trailed over the side of the ship, but hands grabbed me as I neared the top and pulled me aboard and I sprawled on to the deck and lay there for some minutes to collect my strength and my wits, and when I got to my feet I found myself trembling violently. Under the pretence of taking a farewell look at the Dunkirk scene I lingered on deck until the trembling subsided. I was badly shaken, but wanted no one to see how badly.

At last I left the darkness of the deck and went below sniffing gratefully (and almost nostalgically) the warship smells. I knew a feeling of tremendous relief not only to be safe, but to recognize, once more, discipline and order and efficiency. I looked for the guardsmen and they were OK. They were surprised to see me. Rumour, rife to the last, had it that the boat I was in had capsized and its occupants drowned.

My feelings of relief vanished, but not my overwhelming sense of gratitude towards the Royal Navy. And with gratitude went a greater admiration for it than ever. Those vessels lying static off the coast for so long were in deadly danger – as vulnerable as a ship can ever be – yet there was no sign of it in the cheerful, half-amused, half-pitying expressions on the sailors' faces as they played host to the mass of pongos who were their temporary guests. They gave us good hefty bully sandwiches and we wolfed them, but first I sucked down a few mouthfuls of scalding hot tea, my first meal for forty-eight hours, except for a packet of biscuits, but it was the hot tea we relished, and there was more. I burnt my tongue, but held my mug out for more when a sailor came round again with refills from a rather unusual container. It was a chamber-pot and we grinned as the man apologized for it. It seemed an unusual commodity to find aboard a warship – perhaps it came from the sick bay? 'Every jug an' can on the ship's in use, but this is alright – it's from the wardroom – 'ad only the best stuff in it an' it's been washed out!'

A Welsh voice sounded at my side: 'Let's 'ave your trousers Taff – I'll get them dried off for you.' He was a small, dark-haired friendly matelot and I felt terrible not to answer him in his own dialect. There seemed no point in surrendering just my trousers for drying – I was soaked through with sea water – but I did not wish to offend further, and he gave me a pair of blue bell-bottoms to put on and I took good note of the man's features to ensure I got back my battledress trousers.

The space we occupied was warm and surrounded by benches against the steel walls and bulkheads. Some men took off all their clothing to be dried and they sat and slept naked on the benches. Others had just thrown themselves down on the iron deck and fallen asleep, just as they came aboard, after eating and drinking.

Four men were drowned in one of the minesweeper's boats which capsized and another minesweeper was bombed, or mined, and sunk in the early hours of the morning. I retrieved my trousers and returned the bell-bottoms and inadequately thanked the little Welsh sailor for all he and the Navy had done for us, and we landed at Margate, though some later said it was Ramsgate – I did not see a designation board at all. We were bundled into a waiting train – the Southern Railway was running a shuttle service, a non-stop ferry of trains, to get the BEF away from the ports. It was daylight – the platform was crowded with women of the WVS with trolleys of tea and food.

I had expected to come back to a critical, censorious, if not slightly hostile, England after the awful lash-up we had made in France. The BEF of 1914 took just such a hammering, but did not come back. But there, at the station, was no sign of it. The kindly, cheerful, bustling, efficient women could not do enough for us, and I gorged myself on carton after carton of piping hot tea. And when the train started I was astounded to see the people in their back gardens giving us thumbs up and waving and cheering as though they were greeting a victorious army. I wondered if these people knew what was happening, if they thought we were in fact wounded men returning from France. It seemed impossible that a defeated army could be so acclaimed. And all the way up the line it was the same, wherever people lived near the railway they were the same, welcoming us with an absolute lack of traditional British reserve, back to our own country. Even if we did not deserve it, it was still a very touching thing. Gradually the men forgot the disaster and shame of defeat and waved wildly back, until sleep overcame them once more. I made my way to the lavatory on the train and washed as much as I could of my face and neck and arms, and pulled my razor painfully over the long stubble of my beard, and the other guardsmen did the same and once again we looked a reasonably presentable sight. Some men had not shaved or washed for many days, and some had real beards. I noticed the ladies at Margate making particular fuss over a few men who seemed to have no clothes but only a grey blanket wrapped round them.

Johnson shrewdly summed them up, 'I bet they're some of the buggers who jumped the queue and swam out.' And I suspected that he was right, but they may have been genuine survivors from a ship or boat wreck.

Although I wanted so much to sleep, I wanted more to relish this homecoming and to gloat to the full on this beautiful Kentish scenery through which the speeding engine drew us. The orchards and the blossom and the oast-houses and cottages and the green meadows, and cool woods, were Paradise after the Dunkirk beaches. And I have always felt that Kent was home to me, and Kent could never have looked more beautiful than then under that strong summer sun.

The train went on and on, and I wondered where it was taking us – and then I saw by the sun that our course was towards the west and not towards London and Caterham, and in the opposite direction from Colchester, where I believed the Training Battalion to be. I felt wonderful after my rough wash and shave, but later fell asleep and at last we ended up here. At Margate MPs brought about buff postcards for us to post to relatives.

More fellows arrive in batches – men of all units, and other camps and barracks all over England and Wales have been turned into reception centres for the BEF. Last night the troops on the dunes and beaches took a bad hammering from German planes which bombed and machine-gunned them mercilessly. Only thirty-eight men were saved from the minesweeper that was sunk and an RE told me that out of forty-eight men in his party which arrived on the dunes only six survived.

Apart from the beauty of the countryside through which we passed, we were particularly impressed by the peacefulness of it. It seems impossible to imagine that swine's planes destroying such peace and beauty – but I fear they will be over soon enough.

We were issued with any new kit we wanted – razors, soap, toothbrushes, mess tins, knives, forks and spoons – I still had all these things but gladly changed my underclothes and battledress for new, and we all were able to have as many hot showers as we wanted. And then we were left to sleep, as we were yesterday. The food here is good too. In fact everything is almost too good to be really true. We were given stationery and stamps and some pay, and I have written to Mother and Stella, and others, to let them know I am safe and well and giving my address. Roll on when I see Stella, and that should be very soon now – and then I shall know that I am really and truly home and that the nightmare is really over.

Even now, as our planes pass overhead, anxious eyes glance up. Jokes are cracked, but it is obvious that none of us will quickly forget the punishment we got from the air. And there is not a man here who tries to bluff his way and pretend he was not scared. Later, no doubt, we shall recount our escapades with bravado – but no one tries it on here – yet. All are bitter about the lack of Allied aircraft over France – they saw hardly any, and many men are savagely bitter against the RAF who, they claim, left us all in the lurch, and I felt that way myself. But, from what I have seen of the RAF flying over here, I suspect that they were deliberately not all thrown into the battle over France, and now, if England is threatened, as obviously she is, it is better that they should be here.

Everyone here is very friendly, all the old peacetime animosities of regiment towards regiment and corps towards corps are temporarily forgotten. All men agree on two things – the absence of friendly planes, and German atrocities committed against French and Belgian refugees when they bombed and machine-gunned them deliberately to stampede them and spread panic, and all are fiercely indignant about both of these facts. But I find myself doubting some of the stories I hear. Of German soldiers chopping off the right hands of French and British prisoners and then letting them go.

Everywhere men of many units are coming up to we Welsh guardsmen and asking after the Battalion, and I am abashed at finding myself basking in the reflected glory of the good name they have gained. Arras became a bastion in the battle and many troops passed that way and seem to know about the Battalion's performance far better than I do. At first I tried to explain that we were not there but, with everyone with a tale to tell, I found the explanations unheeded – I was a Welsh guardsman and that was all that mattered.

Last night we went down to the local pub in the village for a drink and Askew went up to get a round. But before he could do so the pints were there on the counter, and a man shouted: 'Make way for the good old Taffs – the blokes who held Arras alone against the whole bloody German Army!'

Before the war, in a place like Aldershot, any such compliment towards a Guards regiment would automatically be taken as vindictive sarcasm and would be the prelude to a set-to and a few broken heads. At least Askew can justifiably accept the drinks and the compliments; he was there, and was with the Battalion until he got shot up.

1 June 1940

Still more men turned up here last night, among them Lance Corporal Ray. He looked thin and haggard, and seems vague in manner and speech. He thinks that about thirty men got to the beach under the commanding officer, but other companies were possibly together and came off elsewhere. Our fellows took their places in the queue, though some others kept rushing the boats. But the CO kept the guardsmen in their right places to take their turn, but Ray managed to detach himself unnoticed and he waded out and got into a boat. I wondered if he knew what he was telling me – his eyes seemed to be staring right through me as if I was not there at all. He has been pretty badly shaken. He vividly described the conditions on the beach – it's very hot now with almost incessant air attacks and Jerry was shelling the beach as well. Let's hope the detachment, and any others, got away. He said the Battalion went into action at Cassel, and again at the Yser canal, after they left Arras.

This morning, at breakfasts, a man from the Tank Corps came over to me and asked after the Battalion. I told him all Ray had told me, and I felt proud of the tale the Tank Corps fellow told. They (the Tanks) were at Cassel, and he said the Welsh Guards held back numerically superior German forces for thirty-six hours and at last covered the retreat of the tanks and mechanized kit. The fellow was full of praise for the Battalion's effort, and even said it was his opinion that the Welsh Guards should have a memorial of their own in London's most prominent place for their action at Cassel. And from men who fought in other sectors I hear their enthusiastic praise for the Coldstream and the Grenadiers who have, by all accounts, fought superbly, though if reports are true, there are not many of them left. Our own 2nd Battalion was sent with Irish Guards 2nd Battalion to defend Boulogne, and both battalions are said to have lost heavily. There is also a report that the Rifle Brigade is making an epic defence at Calais, and has been practically wiped out.

Lance Corporal 68 Hughes is dead. He was in a trench and was showing those around him some trinket he had bought in Arras to give his wife when he got home – and Hughes was always supremely confident that he would survive the war. I have heard him say so over and over again – he seemed almost to be tempting fate. As he produced the trinket a bullet got him right in the heart. Several others of the Signal Platoon are dead too.

7 June 1940

Hawkers have been round the barracks and village flogging small worsted tabs that slide over the shoulder straps of a battledress blouse, and a number of men have bought them. They are lettered 'BEF'. There is something very distasteful about such exhibitionism, or opportunism, in a defeated army, or in a victorious one for that matter. The badges are quite unofficial, though the authorities have not banned their use. I was glad to note that none of the guardsmen here sported one of these tabs.

I am still astonished at the welcome given us by the people. Those with cars come over to the village to see us, and to buy us drinks, and to hear our stories. And it is irritating to see them taken in by what we call 'the scruffy bastards' and flock round them as iron filings are attracted to a magnet, buying them beer and lapping up their yarns. These are men who have been here, as I have, for days and who, though they were issued with all they required, razors, toothbrushes, soap, towels and so on when they arrived here, have made no attempt to shave their already lengthy beards and, by the look of them, little attempt to wash, let alone to bathe themselves. And most of them have hung on to their stained and torn 'Dunkirk' battledress and all these scruffs sport the boastful BEF badges; and they wear this stuff down at the village, and the civvies love it. It is what they expect to see from men 'snatched from the very jaws of destruction'. And these lads provide the local colour in abundance. They certainly look tough desperadoes. It is astonishing how the public associate uncouth manners and scruffiness with toughness – what looks tough must be tough.

But today, on parade, the Gunner RSM at last laid down the law and spoke a few home truths. He reminded us that we were still soldiers – that we had all been well rested, and would soon return to our own units – that we should not kid ourselves that we had won a victory – we had suffered a greater defeat than any British Army had suffered during the last war. He wanted a general tidying-up and a lot of shaving done by the next day. Some growls greeted this mild wigging and mutterings: 'Pity you wasn't there, easy for you to talk' – 'Take a running jump' – 'Get f****d!' But the RSM ignored the growls and muttering and dismissed us. But I, and the guardsmen with me, thought it proper order. There seems to have been a general tidying-up, though several hard cases are still knocking around and sporting their beards.

Shall not be sorry to get away now, though this break, in the sun, and in this peaceful countryside, has been like a beneficial convalescence after a long and serious illness. Yet, remembering the RSM's lecture, I reflected that the BEF of 1914 went through a similar retreat, yet it stayed the course, and the survivors of it did not come back here to England – they (if any lived that long) still had to face four years of trench warfare before their army was brought back.

3

England
June 1940–May 1944

After the Welsh Guards returned to England, the 1st and 2nd Battalions did not see any action for the next four years. In July 1940 1WG was stationed in and around Wimbledon and Putney and Charles Murrell and the Signals Platoon were billeted in large Victorian houses, preparatory schools etc in the area. This suited him well as he was able to see his new wife frequently. He could observe, experience and record the horrors of the Blitz at close range and admire the stoicism of Londoners.

There was a very real threat of an invasion and he had the prospect of defending places such as Chislehurst and Petts Wood which he had grown to love and cherish over the years:

> …and Stella and her family live in the Southern approaches to London; they live almost exactly in the centre of the Brown Line. 24 Guards Brigade has several defensive positions allotted to it, and one of them is this Brown Line covering the high ground overlooking the Cray Valley – from Sidcup, through Chislehurst, to Petts Wood. And, if the Germans get that far, and come that way, I shall find myself, with my battalion, defending that line, and fighting within a mile of the place where my own wife is living!! This is no hypothesis of fantasy. It could (and can) really happen! She lives precisely where the country ends and London begins. If the Germans break through the Brown Line, they are in London! There would be little point in my remaining alive to see that happen. (21 Aug 1940.)

1 July 1940 – Elstree, Middlesex

It was good to meet the fellows again; as I heard their stories I felt right out of it but no official comment was made about my coming off with the Corps of Signals unit. I and Barlow and Johnson were officially attached to that unit. I had, it seems, done the correct military thing by remaining with them. But this was little compensation for the regret I felt when I heard the men swapping their stories of Dunkirk. The majority of the Battalion eventually got back, but about a third did not do so, and many of my old friends remained out there dead or prisoners of war. [Note added later: only a quarter of the original Battalion failed to return to England.]

I think I was a bit of a disappointment to them when I arrived at Stella's home looking so pink and fresh and clean. When Stella first got my card sent from Ramsgate as soon as I got off the boat, she believed I had been wounded. The military policeman who crossed out the non-applicable words on the printed War Department card did so rather carelessly, so that it appeared rather as though I was well, but wounded also – a sort of true-blue British understatement. This misunderstanding I soon corrected in my letters to Stella so that, though they did not exactly expect me to stagger in with a bloody bandage about my head, I think they did rather anticipate more of a gaunt, hollow-cheeked, battle-weary warrior with a faraway look in his eyes; and I feel I rather let them down. It is true that many men, like Corporal Ray, turned up at Shrivenham looking rather that way, but sleep and rest soon restored them, more or less, to normal. And I had seen little enough, anyway, compared with some others.

There is so much friction between the Army and the RAF, whose very name is mud to the men who came back with the BEF. There are tales of fierce fights breaking out when angry soldiers find themselves among RAF men, and feelings within the Battalion run pretty high when the RAF is mentioned. But for the Senior Service there is only unbounded praise. The Navy's reputation is sky high with the British Army.

8 September 1940 – Southmead

It needs a great effort for me to write this at all. Yesterday the Germans switched their *blitzkrieg* to London. I think we all knew it had to come, but I lived on in hopes that it would not. People seem to think that this is the prelude to invasion and that Germany believes she has gained sufficient mastery of the air over England to make the attempt, though this is not what our propaganda has led us to believe. This then, is likely to be the end of my short but delightful idyll with Stella.

There was a somewhat sinister emptiness about the streets. It was Arras, and the fires of Dunkirk, all over again, and I was rather shaken to realize that so strong a force had broken through in broad daylight. There seemed a fair amount of noise and air activity around Southfields, though the raid was obviously concentrated against the East End. We walked back along Wimbledon Park Road to the flat and stood on the balcony gazing at the sad spectacle. And I wondered what the night would bring and whether I should phone the billet. The raid, which started about 5.00 pm, finished at 6.00 pm and comparative silence fell on the town, though even at that distance of 7 miles or so we could hear MGs mixing above the huge brown smoke cloud.

There was much damage caused, and many killed in the raid and in the one that inevitably followed as darkness fell. And at about 8.00 pm the sirens wailed again as the raiders swarmed over London once more. [Note added later: Goering sent 1,114 planes over London this evening and night – 372 bombers and 642 fighters.]

***

In the spring of 1941, the Guards Armoured Division (GAD) was formed. This included the 1st and 2nd Battalions Welsh Guards. It was initially conceived to meet the threat of an expected invasion in 1942. The 2nd Battalion was converted to the 2nd Armoured Battalion and the 1st Battalion was to provide part of the infantry of the Division and it went to Midsomer Norton in September 1941 for training under the command of Lieutenant Colonel Vigor.

The 1st Battalion remained in Midsomer Norton for a year. They then moved to camps in Wiltshire followed by a spell in King's Lynn. In July 1943 they went to Scarborough and the surrounding area for the final training period in the build-up to D-Day with realistic battle exercises such as 'Blackcock' and 'Eagle'.

During this period there is an underlying feeling of frustration and impotence, shared by his comrades, and a self-awareness that while they were drilling and shining, others were fighting – in North Africa, and then in Italy and Burma. This was somewhat lessened as the training became more intense and operation 'Overlord' approached.

> A new inscription, recently scrawled in pencil on the door, caught my eye. A poignant message that obviously came from the depths of a human soul racked and tortured by his own inadequacy and by the inadequacy of a regiment that went on lapping it up in Blighty while their comrades in the Fourteenth Army fought it out tooth and claw with their Nipponese opponents in steaming, fever-haunted jungles. Said the scrawled message: 'The Guards blanco while Burma bleeds!' (Jan 13 1943 – Knook Camp, Wiltshire.)

I like this town, but things are damned dear and fags almost unobtainable in the shops. One day I entered a small tobacco-cum-sweet shop where I asked for ten cigarettes and the shopkeeper, a worried-looking, thin, more than middle-aged woman, produced a blue packet of the detested Churchman's 'Tenner' brand. I asked if that was all she had, and she rounded on me furiously, saying that it was high time we stay-at-homes got abroad and did some fighting, and she reminded me that the 'Boys in the Desert' would be glad enough of a few cigarettes, 'Tenners' and all. Abashed, I slunk out of the shop and have not been near the place since. What she said was true enough to hurt a bit, and I wondered if she had someone, husband – or son perhaps, abroad and fighting, and I understood her feelings well enough. (7 June 1943 – King's Lynn.)

Murrell was always a reluctant NCO and returned to the ranks. After completing a course in early 1941 he joins the Intelligence Section. With his background in draughtsmanship and knowledge of military history and tactics, he seemed well suited to the job. He was able to put his artistic abilities to use in making models of tanks, armoured fighting vehicles, guns, aircraft etc and the 'I' Section exhibitions and sand-table layouts were valued and admired. Part of the Section's duties involved drawing up plans, maps and diagrams for lectures: 'worked on enlargement of Libyan battlefield for lecture' is a fairly typical entry. Another entry reads: 'I bless this job that is given me – it does much to take my mind off the depression of leaving Stella.'

They were at times a privileged section with better billets (often in civilian homes) than most. Other privileges allowed them to be struck off fatigues, parades, route marches and other duties, much to the annoyance of NCOs. Additionally Charles Murrell was excused duties to paint, among other things, murals on mess-room walls, the Adjutant's carriage and assorted crests, pennants and insignia for officers.

MEMBER OF
SIGNAL PLATOON
WITH 38 WIRELESS
SET.

Charles Murrell, together with the rest of GAD and, indeed the entire Army, had to come to terms with the changing character of war. With the increasing importance of aircraft, wireless, armour and mechanized transport and with rapid advances in engineering science and equipment, it was a very different army from the one he joined in 1933. There were also the arms, equipment and ammunition (not to mention men) lost in France in May 1940 to be made good.

In addition to the rifle ('we pine for the old U-sighted Lee Enfields') there were Bren, Sten and machine guns, PIATs, various types of grenades, mortars, mines etc to be mastered, or at least understood. As a signaller and member of the Intelligence Section, he had to learn the mysteries of wireless and other methods of signalling. The 1st Battalion practised new roles as an armoured division and though Murrell developed a certain expertise on tanks and armoured fighting vehicles (many of his later sketches feature these) it was the 2nd Armoured Battalion Welsh Guards who actually trained on them.

The feeling of inferiority compared with German AFVs slowly disappeared with the build-up of armour over the next three years. In the early days training was done on obsolete Covenanter tanks – then Crusaders and Centaurs and finally the excellent Cromwells.

***

THE FAMOUS
"CROMWELL" (30 TONS)

There were plenty of lectures, demonstrations, manoeuvres and exercises (or stunts). The larger the exercise, the greater the tedium and discomfort for the men and though good experience for the higher echelons they were less instructive for the troops, though as a test of stamina, hardening and maturing exercises they were more effective. Later exercises in the Yorkshire Wolds in 1943 were more realistic.

The Intelligence Section 'stunts' were more interesting and enjoyable and allowed the men to use their own initiative to a greater extent, though at times it seemed more like a game of Cowboys and Indians. These exercises, large and small, are recorded (as with everything else) in some detail. They were often dangerous affairs and he records fatal accidents, blinding, amputations, etc along with the humour that is ever present in the Guards.

They finally moved to Brighton and Eastbourne for their last weeks in England. Their training finished with the waterproofing of their vehicles and the arrival at a sealed concentration area. The 1st Battalion was now under the command of Lieutenant Colonel G.W. Browning and formed part of 32 Guards Brigade commanded by Brigadier G.F. Johnson.

It is interesting to compare the addresses to the troops of General Montgomery, Lord Gowrie (Colonel to the Regiment) and General Eisenhower in 1944.

9 February 1944 – Scampston, Yorkshire

The boys all very browned off and there was much muttered criticism of Monty. They cursed his guts and wished him back to the Eighth Army. But I doubt if Montgomery really knew the bull he has caused. This included a meticulous inspection of battledress – greatcoats creased, vicious haircut, shows and so on. As the C-in-C arrived we turned inwards and, after talking with the COs of the various units, the General walked between our ranks. He wore a black beret decorated by two badges and had rows of ribbons, including the Mons Star. He wore plain battledress, but no gaiters. He looked very fit, his complexion very brown but with a strangely malt-like texture of skin – almost as though some artificial acid had been used to emphasize the healthiness of his face. The same effect I had noticed in the face of King George V during the Troop in 1935 and on the complexions of other members of the Royal family on state occasions. Yet he looked

41

older and more wizened that I'd imagined, and much shorter too. I think our fellows would rather have seen Alexander their C-in-C – not because he's a Guards officer (rather, in fact, in spite of his being a Guards officer) but because we all feel that it was Alexander's brain that was behind most of the strategy in Egypt even if Monty planned, and won, the tactical victory of El Alamein. But the more spontaneous and brilliant strategy that led to the sudden collapse and annihilation of Von Arnim's and Rommel's Armies in Tunisia was, we feel, Alexander's doing. As for our officers, they are openly letting the men know (without actually telling them) their disparaging opinions of Montgomery.

It may just have been Montgomery's fame and record, but there seemed to be something arresting, almost hypnotic, about his eyes which seemed to stare right down into the very depths of my murky soul as he passed, and others said the same thing later. He told some Grenadiers (we were all standing stiffly at ease) to relax. He then climbed onto a jeep and told us to crowd around, though he spoke into a microphone. Unfortunately we were badly placed and the acoustics of the great hangar were bad, and I couldn't hear much of his talk at all, though the voice sounded clear and crisp, and very decisive and confident. Whatever our opinion of the man as a show-off we all desperately wanted to hear what he said, and what some of us missed we got the gist of later from those who had heard perfectly. It was that he'd had a Guards brigade with him in his 1st Division in France in 1940, and two brigades of guardsmen had fought under him in North Africa. He praised them all as first-class soldiers, and he asked us for our confidence in him, and he affirmed his confidence in us. But still one could sense the almost hostile attitude of his listeners – nothing obvious, but it was something that went much deeper than the usual irritation we know after being b******d about TFO for hours and days, before a big inspection, and I think this was due to three things: a) Montgomery's showmanship and ungentlemanly exhibitionism; b) the adulation accorded him by the press; c) an unconsciously envious resentment of those of us who have not fought in the desert, towards the renowned Eighth Army.

We do not deny them their hard-earned laurels, but we do, perhaps, feel that the Eighth is really Monty's Army, and that he will never feel the same way towards another army, and will be liable to undervalue the worth of the Second Army which, though lacking actual battle experience, must surely be the best trained, best equipped and most efficient force, as an army, ever to be raised in Britain, including even the superb BEF of 1914 which though composed of excellent material and units was never trained, as ours has been, as an army, as corps, and as divisions. Compared with ours, theirs was an ad hoc organization. And Eighth Army, because it has been fighting, has had little opportunity to train, though plenty of time to learn its stuff from actual battle experiences. Lastly, we all wish Alexander had been made our leader, though it would actually mean demotion I suppose – he is really an army group commander. American armies too have been raised and trained over here. They too must be well trained by now, though how they compare with us I do not know. The Yanks flopped badly at first in Tunisia, but this seems to have been only a temporary setback. Under the eccentric and dashing Patton, and with their go-getting ways, they seem to have done pretty well since then.

Perhaps too, the barely-concealed contempt of our officers (I think of most of them anyway) has had some influence on us. Talk doesn't really mean much – neither does grousing, and I've heard the Prince of Wales (who was popular enough with us) called some shocking names prior to one of his official inspections of the Battalion in peacetime, even on St David's Day.

25 May 1944 – Eastbourne

At 0845 we were paraded to hear a sort of farewell lecture by Lord Gowrie VC, the Colonel of the Regiment. His array of medal ribbons was proof enough of his valour and service in the last war, but I don't think the Battalion was much impressed by his talk. He seemed a dithering soul. He rather gave us the impression that we, the Welsh Guards, supported by the Bill Browns, Coldies, Jocks and Micks, were really **the** invasion. He didn't say so, but I got the impression that we couldn't rely too much on the rest of the Army, or on Canadians, Poles, Americans and Free French. Not that he mentioned them, and perhaps 'I got him wrong' as the Yanks say – maybe he, as Colonel, was speaking only domestically, but it was not too reassuring, however flattering, to think that Adolf was over there just waiting to annihilate the Brigade of Guards so that he can deal at leisure with the smaller fry, fling them back, and so thwart the invasion. I doubt if there is a man in the Battalion who, given the opportunity, would back out of the invasion now. For four years we have had it easy here in England, I think we all feel that we owe it to our own people, the munitions workers, the firemen, the bombed and homeless, to the Russians, to our own armies abroad on active service, and above all to our own conscience, to do our stuff now. It 'takes us' and we know it.

But the Colonel's approach was faulty, and, to me, irritating. This, he told us, was the chance for which we have waited so long. Now was the time to get a crack at the Hun – our thirst for battle would soon be assuaged. These were not his actual words, but the implication was there. 'Once more into the breach!' Now, in this sixth year of war there is no place, except in retrospect, for Shakespeare and rhetoric. There is nothing, I think, wrong with the morale of the Battalion. Perhaps the Colonel is right, we **do** know that we are the finest battalion in the British Army, but none of us is prepared to say so. We know that Hitler and Nazi Germany must go, and that we must help get rid of them, but we cannot kid ourselves that we are ardent crusaders – we still have a sense of humour. Curiously enough, the Colonel beseeched us not to lose our sense of humour, as if one could, in this mob! We had to give the old fellow three cheers – these were not too enthusiastically voiced, I thought. As we cheered I thought of the gladiators' cries in ancient Rome: *ave imperator morituri te salutamus*! For the Colonel will be sitting pretty at RHQ while we battle it out with the Hun: though I know, in my own heart, that he would go with us if age did not debar him from so doing. It is cheap enough to sneer, but anxiety and reasonableness hardly go hand-in-hand, I suppose.

We paraded, in a lot of fuss, at 10.30 and by trucks to Brighton where General Eisenhower addressed the Division, or at least the guardsmen in it. And what a contrast this was to the Colonel's talk earlier in the day. I was, against my will, much impressed by Monty's address to us in Yorkshire. In his cold-blooded way he inspired every man of us with confidence in him, and in our training and equipment.

But my own will did not come into it with Eisenhower. We were ranged in a three-sided square in a Hove park – a jeep occupied the fourth side. As soon as he climbed onto the jeep and greeted us with a wide friendly smile, international prejudice vanished. This big man's friendliness was infectious. Beckoning us with his hands to come nearer to him, he told us to break ranks and close on the jeep. We looked, he said, too much like a firing squad, standing there in a three-sided square. Nobody moved, and then our officers order us forward and we grouped informally around the general's jeep. His American drawl was full of confidence and his words inspired tremendous confidence in us. He stressed that we were going into action an essential part of a superbly trained and equipped team. Where the Lieutenant Colonel had given us the impression that we were, more or less, the invasion – Ike reassured us that the men alongside us, in the air above,

"CHURCHILL" INFANTRY TANK.

on the ships that will transport us, will all be efficiently trained and expert at their own particular jobs. He said just the right things, in just the right way. He spoke to us not as if to children and inferiors, but as man-to-man. We had been

"HONEY" LIGHT TANK (10 TON):
BEHIND ARE A HUMBER SCOUT CAR
AND WHITE HALF-TRACK.

pushed about, as usual, and after the Lieutenant Colonel's address, few of us, I think, wanted more propaganda speeches for that day. Yet Ike's speech to us almost worked miracles and something happened that I've never known before. When Ike had finished the men broke out into a spontaneous burst of handclapping and they would have cheered lustily had anyone set them off. But, of course, Ike, like Monty, is not of the Brigade of Guards, and so there was no official cheering for the general.

15 May 1944 – Eastbourne

Sometimes on my way to the town from our billet, I am diverted from the most direct route (down the steep hill) by the lure of St John's Road, into taking this route – 'Tank Avenue' and going via the sea front. This broad, tree-lined avenue of large, if sometimes rather ugly, yellow and red-bricked houses, is packed tight, along its fringes, with armoured vehicles. Sherman, Churchill, Cromwell, Centaur and lighter Honey Tanks and Greyhound and Staghound armoured cars, and M10 self-propelled guns all lying head to tail beneath the two lines of trees.

The scene is busy enough, and noisy enough, by day when crews maintain and paint and cosset their vehicles, and the powerful engines roar. But at evening time all is quiet. Our short stay here is a kind of interlude, a lull between the concentrated training on the Yorkshire Wolds and the battles to come, though the infantry continue training, the tanks remain and, while their crews are regaling themselves in NAAFI, dance-hall or bar, these engines of war lie grim, but silent, the muzzles of their guns sheathed in canvas hoods. Patches of bright orange red-lead paint show vividly against the grey-green or browny-green disruptive camouflage paint of the armoured vehicles. These bear no divisional or battalion or squadron signs now. I believe new ones are to be painted. Only the white Allied Star, common to all the armies taking part in the invasion, decorates them now.

I think we rather resent this ubiquitous and impersonal star. It has about it an American flavour, and civvies take us for Yankees, and when the Grenadier tanks came in, the British squaddee's bitter envy of his affluent American counterpart, who can afford to drink himself stupid in our bars, and who bears off so many of our women, was expressed in white chalk on the grey flank of the Bill Browns' tanks: 'Don't cheer, girls, we're British – not Yanks!' or 'Sorry girls – no gum – we're only British!'

It is a strange, almost surrealistic, experience to walk down the middle of this wide avenue, that could well be a road of an exclusive London suburb, complete with its council drains, peacetime lamp-posts, its letter-boxes and its once well-tamed trees, and to pass between rows of silent, sleeping lethal monsters (created only to kill and destroy, as they will surely do when they are awakened). Along a man-deserted road that will end suddenly in nothing except a precipitous, nightmare drop into the sea. Only as one clears the crest of the hill to see the cliff promenade and the coastal road, is this illusion dispelled. I know it's illusion; but time after time, I am lured that way to prove it.

PART TWO

NORMANDY,
20 June–28 August 1944

4

Landing in Normandy
20 June–29 June 1944

The Guards Armoured Division was made up of 5 Guards Armoured Brigade and 3 Guards Brigade – the infantry of the Division – and consisted of the 3rd Battalion Irish Guards, the 5th Battalion Coldstream Guards, the 1st Battalion Welsh Guards and 1st Independent Machine Gun Company, The Royal Northumberland Fuseliers. The 2nd Battalion Welsh Guards formed part of the Divisional Reconnaissance Units along with the 2nd Battalion Household Cavalry.

The two Welsh Guards battalions crossed to Normandy in various detachments between 18 and 29 June 1944, landing at Arromanches in the shelter of an artificial harbour.

Commanding Officers – 1st Battalion Welsh Guards from 20 June 1944

20 June 1944	Lieutenant Colonel G.W. Browning	Commanding Officer (CO)
" " "	Major M.E.C. Smart	Second-in-Command
29 June 1944	Major Smart	Wounded
" " "	Lieutenant General Browning (CO)	Wounded
" " "	Major J.E. Fass	Takes over as CO
30 June 1944	Major Fass	Killed
1 July 1944	Major C.H.R. Heber-Percy	Promoted to Lieutenant Colonel – takes over as CO
4 July 1944	Major J.F. Gresham	Promoted Second-in-Command
4 Aug 1944	Lieutenant Colonel Heber-Percy	Wounded
5 Aug 1944	Lieutenant Colonel Gresham	Takes over as CO
Oct 1944	Lieutenant Colonel Heber-Percy	Returns as CO

Landing in Normandy, 20 June–29 June 1944

Intelligence Section and Signals Section from 20th June 1944

Robertson	'Rob'	Captain	Intelligence Officer
Herepath		"	Signals Officer – wounded 29 June 1944
Graham	Andrew	"	Signals Officer from 1 July 1944
Wilcox		Sergeant	Sergeant in charge of Intelligence Section ('I' Sec) – wounded 30 June 1944
Murrell	Charles	Corporal	Sergeant in charge – 'I' Sec from 1 July 1944
Degville	'Deg'	Guardsman	Promoted Corporal – 'I' Sec 8 August 1944
Hoare	Brian	"	" " "
Church	Trevor	"	'I' Sec
Stacey	Herb	"	'I' Sec
51 Davies	Dai	"	Signals Despatch Rider
25 Williams		"	Signals Despatch Rider – killed 29 June 1944

Other members of the 1st Battalion who feature in the diaries

Major J.M. Miller	Officer Commanding Prince of Wales Company
Major H.E.J. Lister	Officer Commanding Support Company
Captain J.M. Spencer-Smith	Adjutant
A.R. 'Snowy' Baker	Regimental Sergeant Major

Murrell crosses to Europe in an LST (landing ship, tank), and to be under American command and to sample American food was a new experience and not to everyone's taste.

20 June 1944 – Tilbury

A sunny day, but the water's a khaki-grey colour. The beach had tides reported to be very high. A Yankee officer on our LST commanded, as we began loading, 'C'marn – let's go – we're an hour late already!' And I knew a tinge of resentment at the foreign command. He was, presumably, the LST's skipper. I could see only a silhouetted figure high up in the gun platform at the bows of the ship. American sailors look scruffy and sloppy by Royal Navy standards – garbed in any old rig, they wear tiny white caps atop, at the back of masses of untidy, uncut hair. But they seem efficient enough. For a troopship the vessel is almost luxuriously appointed – hot and cold water, modern lavatories and wash basins, and heated closets. The food is strange to the point of being exotic to us. It's all tinned stuff – eg supper – a meal more or less unknown in our army. No tea to drink – a dead loss. Some kind of spaghetti, pickled cabbage, rissole (hamburger), chopped vegetable, about seven different concoctions altogether – all tasting rather sweetish it seemed – then jelly and coffee – first time I've ever seen guardsmen eating jelly, and it's not often we drink coffee. I half looked round for a liqueur and a cigar. Except that there was no tea, this pappy, artificial-like food rather suits my effeminate stomach, and some other fellows lapped it up too. But some of our John Bulls moaned, craving plainer fare, even army tack, and I think we could all tire of this effete diet in time. I notice that the Yankee sailors don't look too healthy or robust, but they're a cheery crowd. Except when orders are issued through its loudspeakers, the Tannoy system seems devoted exclusively to swing, jazz and jive music. We sleep in bunks – very luxurious too. Rather hot and stifling atmosphere down below. The ship's captain inspected this morning. I like the smell and feel of a ship.

We finished loading about 5.00 am. I overslept, and so had no breakfast and no wash and shave until after inspection and felt dead self-conscious and nervous until I had removed my beard. There was unlimited milk and sugar on our table at dinner time. British civvies would go spare to see how these Yanks live. But the RSM soon stepped in and put an end to that, and he personally rationed our supply of milk and sugar at suppers, saying that these animals (us) would scoff the ship empty otherwise. Snowy's concern for the American war effort was most commendable – he has probably pinched more army sugar than any man in the Army, but even Snowy can hardly send Mrs Baker purloined sugar from an LST lying off Sheerness. Could spend hours sketching here. Not much chance, but have made a few roughs.

21 June 1944

Raw, crude, syncopated music blares TFO from the loudspeakers – these

Yanks never seem to tire of it, and the sailors' feet and shoulders are eternally twitching to the mumbo-jumbo din, and there is no escaping it. These Yanks aren't dumb of course, but one could be excused for thinking them so.

There's something horribly artificial about this ship and its men, yet their system works. …and this artificial way of life is obviously the pattern for the future, but here there's something disturbingly unnatural about the canned food, the canned music, the canned warmth of quarters, the coffee that pours hot at press of button from a hole in the wall. The RSM soon stopped that lark too. Free and unlimited coffee for guardsmen obviously outraged his principles. We hate his guts for this repression, yet I have a grain of sympathy for his bewilderment, and perhaps fear, of this automatism that threatens to make life too easy for us. The softer a man lives the harder it must be to come literally down to earth and stick it out in a slit trench or shell-hole under constant strain of bombardment and fear of death and where the only benefit he can derive from automatism is in his weapons.

After the landings, the 1st Battalion went to St Martin des Entrées, to the east of Bayeux. On 28 June they took over a quiet sector of the line near Bretteville l'Orgueilleuse while south of their position the battle for Caen and the nearby Carpiquet airfield raged fiercely.

28 June 1944

There's much banter going on among fellows – to hide this slight nervousness we all feel, I suppose. The officers, in particular, seem unnaturally gay – though all ranks seem extremely unconcerned – at least on the surface. I don't think we're going to do much this time anyway – just holding the line – but there's bound to be shelling, mortaring and patrolling. We are all browned off not to be going into action as a division, but this is no attack. We shall, I think, only be holding the line in a more or less reserve role. What we all fear, I think, is that 32 Guards Brigade could be half wiped-out before our tanks arrive, and that GAD, after all its training, be committed piecemeal, rather as Jerry's armoured divisions are being committed now.

1400 hours

We move off now. I in the office-body. Strange riding to war sitting at a mobile 'desk'. Never has been quite a war like this one, where a soldier can write of a battle as he goes along – traffic jams – men seem to drive more recklessly on active service. All mobs mixed up on the road – some 3-tonners standing in cornfields and (a touch of romance) women threw pink roses to us.

29 June 1944 – Bretteville l'Orgueilleuse

Eventually we pulled in off the road yesterday and into the orchard of a large, deserted château – the orchard full of deep slit trenches, two-thirds covered by timber or corrugated iron, piled with earth, against shell and mortar fire.

We're inside our gun-lines now. We had not been installed here for more than three-quarters of an hour before we suffered our first casualties. We heard a low-flying plane and AA guns chattering madly at it and we heard the swish-crack of a bomb landing close by.

Sergeant Fletcher of Support Company killed and another bloke's leg blown off. The bomb just missed the CO's scout car – Fletcher was actually leaning on the vehicle, talking to the CO's driver – bad luck!

We stood down at 2330 hours last night, and we stood to again at 0400 hours this morning. I felt pretty tired – everyone feels tired I think, and all are moaning about headaches from the deafening symphony of the British guns all around us. My head almost hurts from the din. This we shall get used to. With little sleep we smoke more, and this doesn't really help. But this is nothing to what must come.

This typical French château has, even in its present misery and desolation, much charm. Built of a dusty, floury-looking stone – not quite as deep as the golden stone of Bath in Somerset. This village really has been roughened-up. Curtains have been dragged from windows, and the shops looted and defiled. A costumiers and a shoe shop turned quite upside down. New shoes lie in broken glass and heaps of plaster dust. A female wax dummy, indecently dressed – or undressed, and standing in the rubble of the street, made one stare for a moment – she wore only a bowler hat, and some Canadian artist-cum-pornographer had nippled her breasts with chewing gum, coloured pinky-red, and had stuck, between the dummy's

GERMAN "PANTHER"
KNOCKED OUT.

C. Murrell.

legs, a triangle of fur from the looted furrier's shop. She stands, obscenely exciting, ankle deep in this rubbish and waste of war, and near her lies the gruesome remains of a half burned-out Panther tank, reeking already from the charred, decomposing bodies within it. The carnal desirability of women was horribly emphasized by this 'Beauty and the Beast' complex that the vision of the naked dummy produced in my mind – a thought I was ashamed to entertain.

This Panther, smashed by a Canadian PIAT, lies close against a shattered cottage. Telephone wires and electric cables festoon its turret, and around it lies a heap of rubble from this shattered building – this massive, roasted-steel coffin is a grim, fascinating study in two colours, black and orange-red. Sergeant Wilcox stood with me, and he climbed to look into the turret, and I had almost to nerve myself to do the same. The stench of death coming from the tank told of human occupants. Some disgusting thing still occupied the driver's seat, but in the sinister blackness, I could not make head or tail of the burned corpse, and I lingered above the turret only long enough to convince the Intelligence Sergeant, and anyone else who might be looking, that there was no trace of squeamishness in an old soldier, and hardened campaigner, like me. As I climbed down from the tank I let out my breath (held in my lungs since the first whiff of overpowering putrefaction hit my nostrils as I leaned over the turret) and I had a job not to show that I wanted to be a bit sick. I do not envy the men of the Pioneer Corps, or those whose business it is to cleanse battlefields, the job of handling these grey and rotting carcasses from the bowels of the Panther and preparing the grisly remnants for burial.

This is the first Panther I have seen at close quarters – they are massive beasts. I made a sketch of the tank, tinting it later while colour was still fresh in my mind. Near the Panther lies another burnt-out enemy tank – a T-38, and in the fields immediately outside the village lie five more knocked-out German tanks, Panthers and Mk IVs. In all, eight smashed enemy tanks lie in this small area.

A French 'suspect' was brought to us. The IO was not around, so I, as the only French-speaking member of the Section questioned him. Took him along to the gendarmerie and was charmed to see the gendarme courteously shaking the hand of the suspect as the latter introduced himself. A short thin Norman, the man wore a black beret. Under his arm he carried half of a long French loaf and in his hand he clutched an empty suitcase. He had tried to pass through the British lines. He didn't seem a bit scared, or worried, to be under suspicion. After some gruff questions he was OK'd by the gendarmerie, followed by much handshaking all round.

I walked him back towards our cooker hoping to get him some food, for this was the object of his dangerous mission. He lived at Rots, now a front-line village recently captured by the Canadians and still held by them. This man, hearing that Rots was liberated, had walked from Bayeux (where his wife and 28-day-old baby were now) with the intention of returning to his village and home to get food for them. But, with the Canadians still fighting there, he was turned back under arrest, and he was ordered back to Bayeux. He seemed so cheerful about it all that I blushed for our army, knowing too well what sort of home he'd find on his eventual return to Rots. I asked Sergeant Buchanan if he could fix the man up with a scoff before he went back to Bayeux – the poor swine must have been starving. Buck heated him a tin of steak and kidney pudding. The sergeant has the reputation of being a hard case; but, (either because it amused him, or because he was genuinely touched by the courage and devotion of a man who walked all the way from Bayeux to a front-line village, 2 miles from here, to collect some clothes and food for his baby) he fed the voyager up on all kinds of scoff – plum duff, then more meat, and so on. At first the Frenchman refused to eat the tucker – saying he would rather take it for his wife; but Buchanan assured him, through me, that he would be given food to take away. So the man ate, and we stared fascinated as he wolfed the meal. His appetite seemed insatiable. Buck loaded the man's case with tinned food, and we were embarrassed as the fellow burst into tears over a tin of evaporated milk – for his baby, he said. The Sergeant stuffed sweets and cigarettes into the man's pockets and at last he departed. His gratitude was pathetic. He promised that, if we were still here when Rots was at last clear of fighting and he could return to his home, he would kill a couple of the chickens he had left there and bring us these, and some eggs as well. His naivety was shaming and touching. The shambles of Bretteville l'Orgueilleuse had not, apparently, registered with him. The only living creatures he'll find at Rots when the Canadians and the SS have finished their business in the village will be mice, rats and maggots. My eyes feel heavy.

We put up our tent last night, but I slept in the open alongside a slit trench. The infernal artillery barrage went on all night. The ground shuddered beneath me, and the flashes from the muzzles of our guns lit the orchard with weird, flickering light, and even the sky seemed permanently alive with lazily-soaring red tracer shell. For some time I could not sleep for the noise. The vicious whip-crack of the massed guns – the whistling and rushing of their shells over my head, the wail of shells going the other way, the crack of Bofors firing, and bursting of AA shells. The roar of our own bombers high overhead, and the nearer roar of strafing German planes – the whistle of their bombs – the dull crack of their explosions and, when the din lessened for a moment, the husky click of mortars firing, and the long bursts of machine-gun fire 2 miles away in the front line. These, and other unidentifiable noises, tautened my nerves and, in spite of my tiredness, kept me from sleep.

Once, I experienced a wave of sheer terror. The full realization of what all this meant made me feel defencelessly naked, utterly exposed to the enemy's wrath. I was tempted to throw off my blanket and to run away from it all. What the hell, I wondered, was I doing here? They didn't really need me. One man, more or less, could make no difference in a battle involving thousands, and millions. I knew a terrible loneliness – though other men lay near me, it was no help and I longed for today's light to come. It was like my first few weeks at Caterham when I would waken daily into a nightmare world of savage discipline, unbelieving, at first, that this could possibly be happening to me. Only this was worse. It was sheer terror that I knew for those few minutes last night. Whether it was the whine of a German shell, or the hate and ruthlessness that inspired the shocking din all about me, I do not know. Suddenly I realized that this was war – real war – and that I hated it. Strangely, I found myself thinking of the Guards Depot. 'If,' they said, 'you could endure that, then nothing else in life can shake you.' And as I listened to the din of war around me I remembered that this was what the grim barracks at Caterham was really for – to train men to withstand this kind of thing, and I, as a regular and volunteer, had less right than most to fret that I was here. The mood lasted only a few minutes and thoughts of Caterham led to thoughts about Stella. My panic passed, and I was glad that I had not, as I was tempted to do, taken to the slit trench alongside me – for none of the others around me had done this. I fell asleep and heard no more until I was roused to stand to at 0400 hours. The blessed day dawned, and I felt much better this morning.

Afternoon

On the move again now. This time to meet the expected German counter-attack of five or six Panzer Divisions. We pass some burnt-out German Mk IV tanks and some smashed British Bren-carriers. Over the top of my 'desk' I see the Adjutant's head and shoulders in front. He has started to sing his macabre 'CRE' song once more. As we passed two dead and rotting German corpses alongside the track, he grimaced and pressed his handkerchief to his nose as the stink of the bodies reached his nostrils.

Soldiers of that Pioneer Corps are digging graves here. We all ducked futilely into the vehicle just now as a shell whirred low overhead and exploded beyond us. We are now travelling along tracks and through more of our gun lines. The guns seem countless. Gunners, not actually firing, sit around, but all near their trenches. Every now and then they duck or disappear into their hidey-holes when a shell, or airburst, explodes nearby. At such times we feel very exposed perched upon the seats of this weird, unarmoured wagon. More airbursts explode about us – dead loss. Some of our guns fire, others rest. Our rifle companies have de-bussed, and are marching forward now. Don't feel unduly nervous, but wish the Adjutant would stop his ghastly singing.

5

Caen: Cheux
30 June–11 July 1944

One of the key objectives of the Allied forces after D-Day was to capture the strategically important city of Caen. In simple terms the plan of the High Command was as follows:

- PHASE 1. After the initial landings the ground gained was to be extended as quickly as possible until it included Cherbourg in the west and Caen and the Orne estuary in the east.

- PHASE 2. Once they were firmly established, they were to threaten to break out of Caen on the eastern sector in order to draw the main German reserves to that side.

- PHASE 3. Once that had been achieved and the main enemy reserves were committed to the eastern flank, then to break out on the western flank driving southward, then east and up the Seine to Paris.

By the end of June phase one was still incomplete. On 29 June the 1st Battalion Welsh Guards along with other battalions of 32 Guards Brigade were detached from GAD and sent to hold a line behind some newly-won ground not yet secure. The 1st Battalion was posted to the half-destroyed village of Cheux, about 8 miles west of Caen and joined the battle area for the first time.

They dug in on the reverse slopes behind the Orne Valley where British and Canadian forces were fighting their way towards Caen. They were not called upon to take part as the fighting in front of them was successful and they held their position for twelve days. They were heavily shelled and mortared, however, and lost their three senior officers (two wounded and one killed) and a number of guardsmen before they had even seen the enemy. The Intelligence Section lost its Signals officer, sergeant in charge (both wounded) and its despatch rider (killed). Major C.H.R. Heber-Percy took command of the Battalion and Charles Murrell was promoted to sergeant in charge of the Intelligence Section.

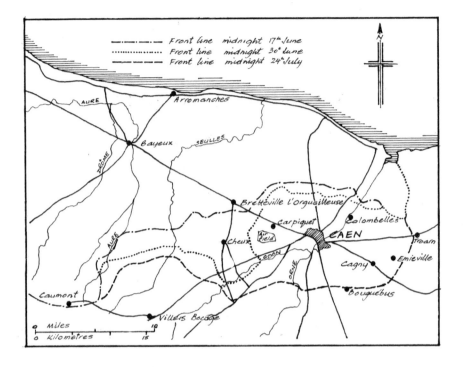

30 June 1944 – Cheux

Had to dig in upon our arrival here last evening. During the afternoon we had moved on through our own artillery concentrations of wheeled guns – a continuous barrage of fire. Then into this field which was full of our self-propelled 25-pounder guns firing like mad, non-stop. Traffic jams on our way down, very unpleasant as enemy shelling increased in volume. The CO said that SS Panzer divisions were counter-attacking, and urged us to speed our digging. I dug three slit trenches, all of them confiscated by officers for their own use, or as command post trenches – dead loss. I marvelled at the sangfroid and unconcern shown by our post-Dunkirk fellows. I later realized it was another case of ignorance being bliss.

SP artillery in the field stepped up its firing rate to maximum. The din terrific and drowned the noise of German shells and mortars which were landing intermittently in our field, but in the orchards on our right, mortar bombs were falling thickly and regularly about 150 yards away, and we watched them fascinated whenever we paused from our digging which, for me, was not often. I needed no spur other than the mortar bursts. A drop of 100 yards in range would put us in the thick of it with precious little chance

— VEHICLES WILL BE DUG-IN AND SANDBAGGED —

of living for any man still above the surface of the earth. Only the post-Dunkirk fellows around me took it more casually and I felt a right windy bastard by comparison – but the bursting mortar bombs were too close for bravado and comfort. The Intelligence Section truck and trenches were about 200 to 250 yards from Battalion HQ and only a sunken road separates us from the orchard where German mortar bombs were falling so regularly. It was a nasty spot, but the section slits were well-dug, I sharing one with Sergeant Wilcox, and the 'I' truck was sandbagged against shell and mortar splinters.

After I'd finished setting up, and marking, maps in the command post dugouts, the IO told me that I could go over and join the section and get down to it for a while, and I selected my route carefully via groups of men where I knew there were slit trenches, and I hastened my pace as I neared the sinister orchard. Some British soldiers lay huddled against the banks of the road, or in shallow grooves in the ground – two of them lay dead, slain by the mortars. These men looked rough and dazed and seemed to be leaderless, stragglers from the battle. I was told that they were men of 44 Brigade of 15 (Scottish) Division Platoons of Royal Scots and Black Watch who had been overrun by 12th SS Panzer Division tanks, and by Panzer Grenadiers who used flame-throwers on them. Presumably all their officers and NCOs were killed or wounded and these men had streamed back as far as this sunken road, but, trapped here by the barrage of mortar fire in the orchard beyond, they could go no further. Their attitude seemed entirely passive; beyond cowering into the bank of the road for protection, they made no attempt to help themselves. In their eyes was only the blank stare of the idiot, or of the punch-drunk boxer. For the time these men had had it. The horror of their experience was obvious in their eyes. It is 15(S) Div that is taking the brunt of this German Panzer attack and the IO says they are fighting very well; they must be, or the Panzers would have broken through to Cheux last night and I would be too busy trying to stay alive to be writing this in my trench now. Another brigade of 15(S) Div was defending Cheux from the west and, unless Jerry switched his attack, would engage the enemy before we would. We are in fact merely a long-stop here at present. Some of our officers began sorting out the stragglers, and collecting them into a unit.

Meanwhile it grew dark. The SP guns in our field suddenly ceased their hectic shooting, packed up and retired through our lines. An ominous sign that heralded the near-approach of the German Panzers. Sergeant Wilcox came over to the 'I' Section trenches to tell us that a cooker truck had driven up to Battalion HQ and that there was hot tea here. Having just come from Battalion HQ I wasn't too keen to return that way, even for a mug of char; besides, the section had brewed its own tea, and I'd had some of this before settling down in my slit trench.

With all the anxiety and excitement, constipation is not a problem, and before I settled down, I set off to find somewhere where I could relieve myself. I came across a square slit trench about three feet deep, abandoned by some unit, and I huddled against the lee side of this. A shower of shells or mortars came over and burst between me and the road – I cringed against the wall of the trench and then, as the rushing whistle noise of more projectiles came (nearer it seemed) I flung myself flat on the earth floor of the trench. These were very close, and metal zinged about me and clods of earth showered down on me. Not until this spate of hate lightened did I realize that I had fallen on my own excreta and fouled the leg of my BD. Brigade summaries came in useful and I used water from my bottle to cleanse myself as best I could. Felt wretched and thoroughly disgusted with myself. I was alive, but wondered if a gentleman should prize his life so high – a conceit. Such is the glamour of war, but at least it raised a laugh when I told the blokes, who were a bit ruffled by the pasting we'd had, but were otherwise OK.

Back in my deep slit trench, half covered with earth at the top, I felt safer, and brooded upon the indignities of a soldier's life. Thought of the immaculate tunics we wore. Seems ages ago now – the speckless white 'buff' equipment we had to blanco – the gleaming boots, rifles, bayonets, a speck of dust could lose one's name. The knife-edge trouser crease and the glittering brass of buttons, curb chains, of anything that could be made to glitter with metal polish – even to the tiniest brass stud on buff equipment or webbing. The fastidious inspection of hands and fingernails after shining parade – the fetish against dirty flesh. Yet here I am, in the same mob, the same job, already larded up to the eyebrows in unmentionable muck, and thus must I live (I hope) and feed TFO for days – or even weeks! And we're not even properly in action yet!

By this time it was completely dark. Machine-gun tracer bullets seemed to be coming from a corner of our field on a fixed line. We suspected that this might be a guide to Jerry's mortars and arty [note added later: artillery]. Several fires were burning in our neighbourhood – some haystacks I think. Got down to it, and then Wilcox came about the tea, took his mug, and went back towards Battalion HQ and the cooker truck. The time then was about 12.30 am. Shells and mortars were landing fairly consistently in our area now. Another salvo of shells fell not far from our truck, and I sunk deeper into my trench – it seemed the 'I' truck must surely be a write-off. Hadn't the slightest idea what was happening, but, whatever it was, it must be fast reaching its climax. The crescendo din of the battle reached nerve-racking impact. Then from somewhere above me, I heard Sergeant Wilcox shouting to us: 'Come on – the CO's been hit, and there are dead lying everywhere!' He sounded a bit hysterical. I stood up in my trench and, when the din quietened a little, I could hear shouts for our stretcher-bearers to get over to Battalion HQ. I asked Wilcox if there was anything we could do, but he kept repeating 'The CO and Second in Command have been hit – 25's killed. They're lying all over the place!' He quietened down, and I yanked him down into the trench – he seemed unaware of personal danger just then. I wasn't sure if W was just telling us news, or ordering us to go over to Battalion HQ to help. I didn't at all want to go over those 200 yards of open ground unless it was necessary. W said that men were there – stretcher-bearers and ambulance trucks were alerted. I did not see that there was anything much we could do. To my relief he agreed. W seemed pretty badly shaken.

Not until this morning did we learn the full casualty roll. Crassly (in view of the shells and mortars falling so regularly only 200 yards away) a cooker truck had come up, and men had gathered round the tailboard to get their mugs full of hot tea. Until then nothing had fallen within 100 yards or so of Battalion HQ and as it was then dark, and unlikely that a Jerry OP had spotted the truck, it was ill luck that a salvo of shells should land right among them at that time. The CO and Major Smart (the 2-in-C) badly wounded – Bill wounded and Wacky, driver of the office-body, had his left hand shot off – I'm told he just stood staring at the stump by the light of the blazing haystacks and buildings, saying 'effing Hell – look at my bleedin' hand!' Several wounded. 25 Williams killed outright, and Pritchard, Drummer 18 Davies and several others. Captain Worrall and Captain Herepath (the Signals officer) badly wounded. A right sort-out all round. Battalion HQ has now moved over here alongside the 'I' Sec dugouts, though this is not a whit safer, as I found out last night. I went over with Doug Marsh, to fetch my kit from the office-body this morning, and there Doug and Ianto, their faces chalk white, carried out their task of lifting the blankets and identifying the bodies – almost impossible with some, and only their identity tags told their names. Drummer Davies was hit in the act of drinking tea from his mess tin which was still embedded deep into his face where the blast had forced it – his legs, smashed, lay doubled beneath him. 25 Williams lay in pools of blood, his arms shot clean away – his left one. from the shoulder. 77 Johnson was taken away by ambulance, cut almost in half by the shells, but still alive. Mercifully he died en route. The ambulance brought him back and we buried him with the rest. I remember, with gratitude, Johnson bringing a truck along to get me back when I was left on my tod at Caestre in 1940. Pritchard seemed untouched. He lay on his side, his legs bent up as a man might sleep in his bed, his cheek rested in the palm of his hand – he just seemed to be sleeping peacefully – killed perhaps by blast. By far the keenest emotion I felt towards these bodies was pity. They looked so weak and frail and puny – the life and the vigour and the toughness ripped from them, and only this left.

Just as, when I spurred myself forward on the school cross-country run by repeating over and over in my mind some words from a banal song: 'I don't mind being all alone, when I'm all alone with you,' so now, in my bewilderment, and perhaps slight shock, the words of another song, Ianto's brave, deep-voiced 'Trumpeter' repeat themselves over and over in my brain today. And these words are not at all inappropriate now:[1]

I'm calling them home – come home, come home!
Tread light o'er the dead in the Valley.
They are lying around, face down to the ground –
and they can't hear me sounding the Rally.

A SELF-PROPELLED 17 Pdr. ANTI-TANK GUN (M.10)

---

1. Ianto Evans sang 'The Trumpeter' at Battalion concerts to great acclaim.

We are tired, frightened, a little slap-happy. Childishly perhaps, I associate this shallow vale we're in with Tennyson's 'Valley of Death', but I cannot keep the words of this song from my mind. This is very different from my experience in 1940, and what worries me is that we have not properly started yet! Everyone's a bit shaken up now – the banter and gaiety and adventure of yesterday has gone for those who are witnesses to the little massacre of last night.

Further along the hedge from where Battalion HQ lay last night, more bodies lie under grey army blankets – the crew of one of the 17-pounder anti-tank guns attached to our Battalion – the whole lot killed in the same bombardment that sorted out Battalion HQ last night.

Major Fass now becomes our commanding officer. Last night the fixed line tracer bullets ceased as the farm whence they came caught fire. I believe our own carriers went in to fix the Jerry's duff. This new blaze, with its attendant acoustics of crackling timber and exploding ammunition added, during quieter moments, a new horror to the stark grimness of the short June night, though to me the night seemed eternally long – like the Dauphin before Agincourt, though less poetically.

So far there is ample time to write this stuff, though I should be trying to kip now, but I get many visitors dropping in to see the situation maps that I maintain in the 'I' trench. But at least the RSM, drill-pigs and CSMs are too busy staying alive themselves to think up the usual irksome parades and shows with which we are normally burdened on exercises.

Now about 7.30 pm and we're all set to meet the expected super counter-attack of three, or more, Panzer Divisions against Cheux and the 'Corridor'. General opinion of summaries etc is that last night's affair was only a reconnaissance in force to feel out the strength of our defence. Even so some tanks got here at Cheux before Jerry withdrew. The battle din died down last night not long after Battalion HQ was hit, and the shelling and mortaring died away to what is generally termed 'sporadic' or 'desultory' fire and, by comparison with last evening, things are relatively quiet at present, but none of us is complacent about it. There'll be hell to pay when Jerry opens his attack and no one wanders far from his slit trench.

Tales of the fanaticism of these SS troops now facing us. Practically all his Panzer and SS Panzer divisions in this theatre are massed against the British sector, and against this particular bit of it. We, and the other brigade in Cheux, hold this key position, in more or less a reserve role. We are the base of a triangular trap – the cheese in fact. Who wants to be cheese? But it is again 15 (S) Div that will take the brunt of the attack, as before, and the blue circles (each a Panzer Division, on the talc of my situation maps) look grimly formidable. One's stomach doesn't feel too settled – one doesn't want to look as pathetic as those this morning. War's a nasty business, though it did not need the corpses of friends to teach me that. They were good fellows, particularly Pritchard, whose passionate loyalty to his young wife was well known.

I write and write to keep my mind off this impending attack. Just cannot shut my mind to the tune and words of that wretched 'Trumpeter' song. It's childish and melodramatic, but it persists. I can't get rid of its theme. Find myself unable, or unwilling, to think of Stella during this battle and this shelling, except to worry about her safety and wellbeing under this new flying bomb attack, and in her pregnant condition. Thoughts of Stella do not go with the degraded lives of soldiers on a battlefield, or with the reek of rotting human corpses in ditches, and of bloated cattle that lie, their legs still and ludicrous, on their backs in the fields. British dead are buried as soon as possible, but German dead (except those near our own positions) are left, presumably until the battles die out and they can be interred without undue risk, or until the Pioneer Corps moves in.

Strangely, a few cows are still alive around here, and, in the comparative peace of today, some have wandered into this field, but, not having been milked, they are in great pain, and one limped into our lines this morning, dragging with her a leg almost severed after the night's shelling. Corporal Coles led her away from our lines, and then shot her where the carcass will not be an added offence to our nostrils. He, and some guardsmen, milked the unwounded creatures and tried to drive them back to safety behind the lines, but the stupid beasts ambled into this field again, seemingly undeterred by the carcasses of other cows, and began feeding. They must have grown accustomed to shell-bursts – they flinch, but do not run, from them. All must be slain soon – kinder to shoot them now really. It surprises me that our Army has not some kind of organization for collecting and salvaging these animals, even from the front line. Staring at these calmly grazing creatures in this field where bursts of shell and mortar fire

GERMAN FIVE-BARRELLED
ROCKET MORTAR *NEBELWERFER*
OR " MOANING MINNIE."

occasionally fall, I almost envied them their insensitive ignorance – they seemed, absurdly, incredibly brave (they have no trenches) – and other men have wryly remarked upon this also.

Never heard arty fire like this last time. Mostly bombing then. Thank heaven, not much of that so far – except for Jerry. There go his mortars ranging now. They have been at it all afternoon. These are his six or eight-barrelled things, I believe – 'Moaning Minnies' or, as the Russians call them – 'Sobbing Sisters'. Wonder when this attack will come in. Feel a bit nervous. I wonder what the others are thinking?

News just come through that our armour is now in Normandy. This has cheered us all – we shall be a division again when this do's over. Spitfires flying almost contemptuously through German flak. A commander, or artillery spotting plane (an Auster) seems to cruise round and round leisurely, and with impunity. There are Gunners' armoured OP Shermans here. They move up in turns to the OP. We seem to have drawn all the German armour from the American sector onto the Caen front here.

Clotted blood from the mouths of Phil and 77 Johnson – they were buried with the rest today, in army blankets. Am dying for sleep. Barely dozed last night. Might have a chance of a kip soon. That damned Trumpeter song through my brain again – Blast! Like a nursery rhyme to a child.

1 July 1944 – Cheux – about 9.00 am

We are, at present, being soundly shelled – or mortared – I'm not fussy which. And stuff is pouring back non-stop in the opposite direction from the muzzles of our 25-pounders and we all moan because our own Gunners make such a din that we can't hear Jerry's stuff coming until, or unless, it's right on us. The expected German attack did not, apparently, materialize – our own guns, going like mad TFO may have discouraged it, but German shell and mortar fire was stepped up to almost a continual bombardment, as heavy as (and more protracted than) the previous night's shelling. Had rather a ghastly night last night. Many shells fell upon us from the newly arrived Panzer divisions – mostly 88mm and 105mm calibre I think, but there were mortar bombs too and I came nearer to death than I cared for.

Sergeant Wilcox and I shared a trench [note added later: this was my domestic, or 'sleeping' trench. The Intelligence trench was our 'working' trench and housed the situation maps and was manned permanently by roster – one man by day and two men by night] alongside the sunken road, and near the hedge on top of the bank lining this road. We were out of the trench stretching our legs during a lull in the shelling, but we dived into it again as the rushing, howling, screaming sound of shells [note added later: mortars – not shells] coming near, struck our now attuned and sensitive ears. The Sergeant beat me to it, hurling himself to the back of the slit trench, and I (only a second behind) crouched up against him, getting as much of myself under the roofed half of the slit as I could. This was a particularly spiteful burst of hate. Battalion HQ was being thoroughly pasted. The scream of shells came alarmingly close, and one burst within a foot of the edge of our trench. I was stunned – the roof of the trench seemed to come down like some huge, powerful fist striking the top of my steel helmet, and punching me hard in the face and nose as well. Indeed, examination of the shell mark later indicated that my head was barely a yard from the explosion. But I had no time then to consider my reactions. I realized that, miraculously, I was alive, and I shouted to Wilcox, asking if he was OK. But he was shouting that he had been hit, and for me to get him out of it. I remember disbelieving him and suspecting him of yelling out of fright, since I was between him and the explosion. Didn't waste any time however, I pushed away some tin sheeting and other debris that had descended upon us, and got the Sergeant out of the trench amazed to find that he had, indeed, been quite badly hit in (of all places) the nape of his neck!

Only today have I worked out how this could happen. Wilcox wore a motor-cyclist's steel crash-helmet. As he hugged the wall of the trench he must have turned his face to the back wall of it for protection, leaving the back of his neck towards the opening of the slit. The shrapnel that hit him had whizzed over my head and cut open the back of his neck. Wilcox kept his hand tightly over his wound, and blood was pouring from it through his fingers and down his back and soaking his BD blouse. The time was about 10.45 pm [note added later: Double Summer Time]. It was dusk, but in the area of Battalion HQ it was night.

The shells had created a black cloud of dust and pungently acrid gunpowder smoke through which dimly-seen figures ran to and fro, and men shouted for stretcher-bearers, and orders mingled with the cries of badly hurt men. Supporting the heavily-built Sergeant as best I could, I made my way towards the sunken road and the RAP. A slight figure loomed out of the fog and haze and supported Wilcox on his right side. 'Who's this? Sergeant Wilcox?' Gratefully I recognized the absurd, lisping voice. Captain Miller, with his nose for dangerous and troubled spots, was, as always, on the scene. Even before we reached the road Wilcox was begging us to drop him and leave him there. He knew, he said, that he was done for. I tried to reassure him, saying that he'd soon be fixed up OK at the RAP. Shells were still falling in the area. Again Wilcox proclaimed that he was done for, and begged us to drop him, leave him, and take cover ourselves, and again I tried to soothe and reassure him.

The Sergeant's rather heroic babblings seemed to be getting on Captain Miller's nerves. With authority and asperity, he said 'Now come on,

Sergeant Wilcox, pull yourself together!' I marvelled at (was even amused by) the result. Wilcox undoubtedly believed he was dying, yet an officer's voice could still call him to discipline. 'Yes Sir – I'll try Sir – thank you Sir!' Bloody marvellous! More shells fell as we reached the sunken road, but this gave us some protection from shrapnel and fragments. Halfway down the road to the RAP another salvo of shells almost blew me over, and as I neared the dressing station, I felt some wet on my right arm and realized that I'd been hit mildly in that arm. The RAP was full of casualties, the MO, Padre, Sergeant Dobbs, Warner, all were hard at it, jabbing people and patching them up. As though I were half-drunk, I saw things with startlingly vivid clarity, or perhaps it was only the sharp, incandescent glare after the blackness outside.

An incandescent lamp, attached to an ornate brass chandelier suspended from the ceiling, shone down upon a white tablecloth laid over a round table. The cloth gleamed and glittered, in that harsh light, bottles and jars and shiny steel medical implements, and steam rose from boiling water that stood in a receptacle on a methylated-spirit stove. I observed the cheap but richly-patterned wallpapers against which, on either side of the polished, ornate and heavily be-vased mantelpiece, hung large, framed sepia photographs, one of a man, one of a woman, presumably the owners of this small villa, and who are now God knows where.

But the harsh light did not penetrate into the corners of the room, where they were working by torchlight. We laid Wilcox on a palliasse in the corner and his blood drenched the bed. If possible, I wanted my arm dressed, so I waited and sat beside the Sergeant until the MO could deal with him. Wilcox kept begging me to get the MO to him, and I tried to reassure him that the doctor would come over as soon as he could. Wilcox asked for water and I gave him some. The MO came over and examined the Sergeant's wound. He jabbed him with a needle, morphia I supposed, the whole room reeked of some kind of anaesthetic. Then I held a torch while the MO groped inside a large hole that lay, like a volcanic crater, in the centre of a large bump that had arisen on the back of the Sergeant's neck. From the blood and mess of the crater the MO found the two ends of the severed white pipe of what I assumed to be an artery – to each end he clipped shiny, scissor-like tongs. Wilcox kept pleading with the MO to stop the blood, and this, I think, is what the scissor-like objects were for. This done, the MO left these implements dangling from Wilcox's neck and returned to a more seriously wounded casualty. The Sergeant asked if the rest of the section were OK, and I said I thought so – I remember listening, in a detached sort of way, to shells exploding somewhere outside, and a building shaking to their impact, or blast; but they no longer scared me.

I was past caring and felt only that I wanted to be a bit sick. Even after the needle, Wilcox seemed to be in great pain. I could do nothing more. The

Padre was attending to the fellow in the opposite corner who had had it in the groin and testicles. In the other corner the MO and Dobbs battled for the lives of badly mutilated guardsmen. The walking wounded, patched up, went off by ambulance, and, seeing Warner temporarily clear of patients, I asked him if he would dress my arm before I went back. A hole, between quarter and half an inch wide was all that was there. Said I felt OK except that the arm felt pretty stiff. Warner said that the shrapnel would work its way out [note added later: not so – the stuff is still somewhere inside me now (1968)] and advised me to see the MO when he got a break.

I walked back to that ghastly field not caring what fell, or what might hit me, and I was deadly tired. The rest of the section a bit shaken but OK. I learned that the salvo of shells that got Wilcox also ripped away half of Major Fass's face. Poor old Doug Marsh, standing in the slit trench alongside the officer, had his greatcoat drenched in the new CO's blood. Fass died instantly. So now we have a new CO, our third in our first two nights in action – and our three senior officers are hors de combat, killed or wounded. At this rate 'Corporal Lace'[1] will be commanding the Battalion next week, I think.

Got back into the now lonely slit trench and tried to sleep. I did doze, and awoke suddenly as the dreadful rushing and whistling betokened the arrival of more shells and mortars on our positions, and earth and stuff showered me again as another shell exploded only a yard or so from my trench. By the law of averages I felt that one must eventually land in the trench itself. At least I wouldn't know much about it. I felt quite terrified, and began to believe that Jerry was picking on me, could see me, knew exactly where I was, and was determined to get me. A little later I heard two of our signallers (one of them, I think, Gus Pennington) above my head blaspheming, and cursing all gunners, German ones in particular, as they searched for breaks in their signal cable. I admired them, and felt that I would never dare climb out of my slit trench again. I thought gratefully of the half a mug of hot, sweet char, traditional perquisite of wounded men, I had drunk at the medical bunk. Felt horribly scruffy and mucky.

I am now thoroughly larded in gyppo. Dried sweat, dirt, mud and grit, my own excreta dried into the BD trousers after I'd fallen in the stuff the night before, and now my BD is smothered in the blood of the wounded Sergeant, as well as in my own from the hole in my arm, which is stiff and almost unusable. We clean ourselves as best we can – rubbing off caked dirt when it dries, and we wash and shave – eight or nine of us using a petrol tin of water in which we later rinse our mess tins after eating food. But a wash, when one cannot strip, merely means pushing tide marks of dirt down one's neck and up one's arms. Nevertheless, it makes an amazing

1. Lieutenant Mitchell.

difference, and morale and optimism soar after a crude toilet and with the taste of toothpaste on a tongue fouled by too much tobacco smoke.

We show weapons and mess tins and the rest as well as wash and shave each morning, but these inspections, though adequate, are almost perfunctorily performed, by peacetime standards. The ever prevalent threat of enemy fire speeds proceedings a great deal, I find. But, however unpleasant the conditions, we are not allowed to 'go native'. And a good thing too. We naturally moan about it. It needs an effort for a tired man, dying for sleep, to get out of the foetid comfort and safety of his slit trench in order to wash and shave in a tin of scummy water, and to spruce himself up and do what he can to clean his boots, but I, and the others, feel much better for it afterwards.

Another activity that is much speeded up here is the attendance to calls of nature. No luxurious lingering, or savouring of the situation, now. One feels horribly vulnerable sitting on a thunder-box in the middle of a field, or orchard, under enemy fire threat, with only a hessian screen as a shield, and the unholy din of one's own artillery constantly banging away all about. At such times men emulate the jerky movements of the chicken as, with ears cocked, their heads twist from side to side listening for the rushing wail of approaching shells, and no man lingers there a second longer than is necessary. I think we all have a particular dislike of being caught with our trousers down. Actually we don't at present run to the luxury of a thunder-box – but the whimsical fancy demands it. Except for this, and the shelling and the presence of blood on my clothing, this is no worse than any of the 100 stunts we have done – and very much better than some we did in winter months. In fact this is better in some ways than any stunt as we don't get b*****ed about, except by Jerry, and he, with laudable impartiality, democratically b*****s about officers, warrant officers, NCOs and men alike. Jerry is no respecter of persons.

<u>8.30 pm</u>

Few of us have really slept for three nights now. I'm on my knees. More mortaring and shelling this morning and a tank battle developed – there was much 'sound and fury', and the battle approached very near our own positions and we stood to. Solid armour-piercing (AP) shells whirred and rushed through the air. The din gradually receded. We stood down and only the desultory enemy fire continued – find this writing tedious with my arm so stiff, but I've nothing else to do.

With Wilcox wounded, Blanchette still in England with rheumatic fever, and Carey posted to Brigade HQ, we now have no NCOs in the section, and I am to be promoted to Sergeant I/C Intelligence Section. I never wanted promotion, but the IO won't make up anyone else from the section and he threatened that, if I refused the tapes, he would have no alternative other than to bring in a sergeant from outside. Only hope I can live up to the good opinion they all seem to have of me. Felt a bit sorry for Sergeant Wilcox, who may by now even be dead. Technically, I have been running the section for some time. But Wilcox was more a man of the sword than the pen – he was courageous, and had been given no chance yet to show his mettle out here. Even if he lives I doubt if he will ever rejoin a fighting battalion now. [Note added later: Wilcox lived, and later wrote us a letter from hospital in England. But I never saw him again (1968).]

So far no one in the rifle companies has been hit. They are dug in on the reverse slope of a ridge facing east, that overlooks 12th SS Panzer Division in the area of Carpiquet aerodrome, but, unlike the Coldies and the Micks, our companies are not actually in contact with the enemy. Although I had personally marked enemy positions on our situation map on the night we arrived at Cheux, I seem to have misunderstood the situation, believing that the enemy attack came from the south-east, and that 12 SS were attacking also. In fact, I learn now, the deepest penetration was made by 9 SS Panzer Div and their attack came in against 15(S) Div salient from the west, or south-west and this attack reached a point only just the other side of the woods and orchard that were so liberally mortared and shelled, and only a few hundred yards from Battalion HQ. I realize now also that the Scottish soldiers in the sunken road were not trapped by the wood from going back any further – they had in fact been forced back through that terrible wood in retreat and had 15(S) Brigade not held them, the Germans must have come through the wood and debouched from it at the point where Battalion HQ lay, and we would have been the first company in the Battalion to engage them. A closer study of sit map also explains why Cheux village is getting such a pasting. It is the focal point in the salient for German gunners firing from south, east and west. Only from the north, where our own guns are amassed, are we not being shelled, and even from there, if a careless gunner miscalculates the range, we could be shelled too. We wouldn't know. A tragedy indeed, to be killed by one's own side.

Battalion HQ is now desperately short of personnel, especially of signallers. One often hears very long bursts of MG fire from, I think, enemy MG 42s. These are good weapons, but it is said to be dangerous to use captured models against the enemy. He resents these liberties, and vents his spleen on the spot where the gun is sited. MG 42s also annoy (as they are meant to do) British soldiers, who are also liable to let rip at the sound of this weapon being fired.

This 1914–18 'Journey's End'[1] dugout business is exasperating to men of an armoured division. It's very messy again here – raining hard, and

---

1. A play by A.C. Sheriff – 'A moving portrayal of life in a dugout on the Western Front in 1918.'

masses of mud. Mud gets into everything, waterlogs the floors of trenches and renders the sides oozy and sticky. But at least my hands are beautifully clean, they look as though they'd had mud pack on them, which, I suppose, they have had, and a drop of rain will help purge my BD of its more offensive soiling. But I'm grateful enough for a slit trench after last night.

A good sight at about 8.15 pm last night. Some 200, or more, British bombers blasted some place to the south-east near Caen. This is the nearest I've been to the receiving end of a massed British air-raid. An awesome business, and I found savage exultation, mixing it with a degree of pity for the SS warriors, or whoever was being blitzed. A huge black cloud of smoke and dust rose above the stricken area. Slowly it drifted our way until (though the sun shone brightly then) we became engulfed in a fog not unlike a London pea-souper. Intense German flak greeted our bombers at first, though I did not see a plane brought down and, significantly, the AA fire slackened as the bombers set about their business.

2 July 1944

Our signallers are constantly busy repairing signal cable cut by shellfire. A linesman's job is no joke in the war. No first-line reinforcements to replace the heavy Sig Platoon casualties yet, and the survivors are much overworked. The situation maps are the devil to maintain in wet weather. Could do with a good bath.

War, today, seems to be fought mainly with largish lumps of dull-grey jagged-steel shrapnel – a lousy bizz. Jerry is very good with his mortars – three of the section's greatcoats have been ripped to pieces by shrapnel. An 88mm armour-piercing shell whizzed clean through the signallers' store truck yesterday, smashed up some number 19 sets and other gear, emerged from the other side of the truck and passed on through the thick stone wall of a farm outhouse. Where it went from there I do not know. The projectile missed Ted Edward's head by about a foot. He stood near the truck, and men laughed at the comically surprised expression on his face as the truck alongside him shuddered and swayed.

We're all getting pretty quick on the uptake now. Still no Jerry attack. It must come soon, our bridgehead must get stronger each day – he can't afford to wait now. It is cheering, after a severe strafing by Jerry, to hear the Irish Guards' pipers in the next orchard, wailing their sad, but stirring, music. There is history and reassurance, in the sound. They seem to say 'To Hell with Hitler and his jumped-up Nazis – the pipes led the Micks to victory before Hitler's Germany was born, and they'll go on playing on battlefields long after Hitler and Germany are smashed!' As a mob the Micks aren't all that old but, as Kipling says, the Irish Brigade 'had the honour at Fontenoy, of meeting the Guards brigade'. Now the Micks are with us – a good mob indeed – they have their bugles with them here too.

3 July 1944

Poured with rain all morning – up to our necks in mud – slithering everywhere. I am now a sergeant. Hope people don't expect too much of a bloke. The air-raid we watched the other night was on Villers Bocage. A quiet night – at least so far as Jerry was concerned. Our own batteries were very noisy banging away all night, but no shells or mortars fell near us. Still no attack. Jerry's not biting. A Coldstream patrol penetrated 12 SS Territory and had a nose round Carpiquet aerodrome.

I was handed the pay-book, wallet, letters etc of an SS man whose corpse lay in front of 4 Company's position. He came so high that they had to bury him. His name is, or was, Sommer – born 21 June 1926. He was 18 years old then, only two weeks ago! He is in 26th Panzer Grenadier Regiment and no rookie – he has fought in Russia. It is said that there are even some boys of 15 in 12 SS facing us, and an artillery officer said a boy of 12 was found sniping from a roof. These SS are undoubtedly very good troops, and a boy of 15 can be as deadly behind a gun as a man of 30. In a way it is flattering to the British that the SS divisions are concentrated in this sector, but exasperating to know that there are children among them. These are the exception, but the fellow whose pay-book I had was really only a child when he joined up – if, that is, SS men do join up – they seem to belong, body and soul, to the Nazi war machine even while they are at school. There are stories of badly wounded SS men refusing British, and other alien, blood transfusions and dying for lack of it – of men refusing the Last Sacrament, saying that they know of no god other than the Fuehrer. Inevitably there is the story of Allied doctors deliberately, and ironically, injecting known Jewish blood into the veins of SS men, wounded too badly to know, or care, about it.

In his wallet Sommer carried newspaper cuttings and maps of all the war battlefronts – a twenty-mark note, and a smaller one of lesser value and a driving licence. Many snapshots of his family – farming people I should think – pleasant, homely-looking folk. Some pictures of himself in SS uniform – having a haircut in the field – of himself with his mortar detachment – with his Company on a captured block-house – a photograph of a girl – not pretty, but vaguely attractive. Incredible how Hitler and his Nazis had bred these creatures, from the age of 7 or 8 or 10, into these fanatical warriors we face today. They are said to know, and to care for, nothing but war and their beloved Fuehrer. These are the cream of the German Army, but the scum of German civilization. Pity that such blind faith could not be diverted into decent and proper channels. So now Sommer lies 'in some corner of a foreign field' and I suppose these relics of him, impregnated now with the stench of death from his corrupting body, will one day find their way back to his home and to his people.

4 July 1944 – Cheux

Fine morning. The expected British barrage from 600 guns, plus 16-inch shellfire from HMS *Rodney*, to cover the Canadians' attack on Carpiquet aerodrome didn't disturb my short sleep. Apparently the field guns never stopped – their detachments must be very tired. Just after stand-down this morning, and while we were brewing tea in the cover of the ditch, some heavy stuff came over from the Carpiquet area. We went quickly to earth. The shells fell some distance away, but their explosions were exceptionally loud and scaring – 15cm or 17cm stuff I think – what it must be like for Jerry with *Rodney*'s 16-inch shells whizzing around, I can't think.

It has rained today, though it's sunny now but there's still much heavy cloud about. Watched our rocket-carrying Typhoons attacking 12 SS on Carpiquet aerodrome. These are deadly weapons of war, and the awful, belching sound as they discharge their rockets sounds like a German *Nebelwerfer* firing its 'Sobbing Sister' mortars, and is frightening, even at this distance away. The flak from the 'drome and from Caen, was terrific. The cost of war, in cash alone, must stagger the imagination were it revealed. The Canadians attacked, and BBC says they've captured the aerodrome – don't know how true.

Some first line reinforcements arrived yesterday and with them, to replace Captain Herepath as Signals officer, came Captain Graham, bringing with him a spot of colour onto the drab battlefield in the shape of his enormous orange whiskers. He seems a decent bloke, with a great sense of humour, and extremely cool and nonchalant; though, of course, he ''ain't seen nothin' yet'. We go out on Thursday – we hope!

Major Heber-Percy is our new CO. He has the reputation of being a fine soldier, and a quite fearless man. But he gets around, and gets a heave on us, and on the rifle companies – inspection of arms, mess tins and slit trenches etc at regular hours. In return (rumour has it) he sees that the Battalion gets plenty of pack ration food and fags, chocolate and sweets and rum – anything that is going. The quartermaster's admin is good indeed.

Major Lister delighted by a report that thirteen Tiger tanks are approaching our positions, and heading for PoW Company. He's itching to use Support Company's A/Tk guns. I doubt if these are actual Tigers – if they are, then our 6-pounders will need luck, as well as good shooting, to stop them. Jerry has some independent Tiger tank Battalions in Normandy, but I believe men mistake the massive, though less powerful, Panthers for Tigers. Not that I sneer in contempt of thirteen Panthers heading our way. But 6-pounders and PIATs have a chance against a Panther if they hit one in a weak spot. I don't think the 60-ton Tiger has a weak spot – even its tracks are nearly a yard wide. There definitely are German tanks in the offing and solid AP shell has been flying about our area, and one has just landed near our trench. Someone said an 88mm, which would indicate Tigers, but it might well have been a 75mm projectile. 3 Company had three casualties today.

Marvellous scoff in these fourteen-man pack rations. Individual steak and kidney puddings, veg, spuds, fresh fruit salad, and tea. Cost 5/- anywhere in the Smoke, and civvies would gape to see it. I have fed more comfortably, but never better, in the Army. The cookhouse, in a corner of the orchard, is not so far from us now – only about 30 yards. Nevertheless it is always a relief to have got there and back, and on the return journey one prays that Jerry will lay off for a minute or so – one cannot hurry so much, and it is exasperating to have to throw oneself flat and risk losing one's scoff in the mud.

The RSM moaning about the tight squeeze it is to get into the signal exchange dugouts – a disadvantage being as massive as Snowy on active service, and he's massive even for a guardsman. He presents an outsize target to the enemy, and needs an outsize trench for protection. Snowy's OK out here – quite cheerful. But Sgt X is suffering hell – never see him – just sits in his trench and sends someone over for his food, and whatever he wants.

A young Gunner officer from our Divisional A/Tk regiment comes here most mornings – ostensibly to see our situation maps, and to get the form. In fact he comes really for moral support. He climbs down into the trench and literally pours out his heart to me. A smallish, dark-haired, rather sensitive middle-class fellow from a smallish public school or grammar school, he got his commission via the ranks. He is going through hell now – and I feel sorry for him, though I find his confidences embarrassing coming from a commissioned officer. The most emotional remark I can recall hearing from one of our own officers is: 'For God's sake wake up, you dozy man!' This Gunner officer and his men have now been dug in around Cheux for eleven days and nights, and I believe his nerve is going – has nearly gone in fact. Apart from the gun crew slain when our own fellows got sorted out on our first night here, he's had a number of casualties, including more of his men killed last night, and they haven't seen, or engaged, enemy tanks yet! One of his men shot away his own foot last night and another has gone clean off his rocker. He just huddled in a trench all day and all night with a blanket over his head, and today they wheeled him off in an ambulance. Lightnings just going overhead and heading north, and being heartily shelled by Jerry AA fire.

Not that the Guards are immune from fear, shellshock or bomb-happiness. Corporal Y has been busted down to guardsman, and, it is said, the man is petrified, and can do nothing. Poor swine – an old regular soldier, before my time, and called back as a reservist. It is cruel to keep such people in the line. Amazing how Sergeant X gets away with it; I bear him little love, but feel sorry for him – he too should be sent away out of it. For the Adjutant I have a sneaking admiration. He is coping, but it must be hell for him. He, I know, would fight like mad to avoid being sent back. The rest of our officers carry on more or less in traditional guardee style, underplaying the whole affair as a huge bore; either out of habit, as a superbly controlled act (or as some men unkindly put it) out of sheer bovine stupidity – on the 'where there's no sense there's no feeling' principle. In this they are wrong, but it makes us feel good to think it.

The sun is catching the underside of white AA shell-bursts making them look like miniature clouds. It is hard to believe that these pretty-looking puffs of cotton wool were composed of the same razor-edged lumps of jagged steel that have ripped away men's faces here at Cheux. Feel stiff and damp from our soaking yesterday. Had my arm dressed at the RAP. The MO said I should have shown it to him on the night it happened, and told me to see him with it each day. But it seems such a trifle compared with the ghastly wounds some men get. The arm, I think, has turned a bit septic and is painful – makes writing a dead loss too.

Roll on a more mobile and interesting kind of action – then peace – and then Stella.

My feet permanently soaked and clammy. But we're in fine fettle – and all seem very fit.

5 July 1944

Caen lies in a dark-bluish misty mass as a backdrop to the ochre-grey, dry, dusty-looking aerodrome and hangars in the middle distance, except for the figures that move near the German tanks, distant shell-bursts from our own guns, and white and black puffs of AA fire – there is a deathly stillness about this sinister landscape as seen through binoculars. Seeing things magnified, one almost expects to hear the noise of them. The dirty-grey hangars are ripped and holed by shells – concrete pill-boxes litter the 'drome area. We had no telescope up there today, but glasses revealed a great deal.

Our OP is about 700 yards in front of our Company outposts, and is in no-man's-land with nothing but standing corn and barley between us and 12 SS we are watching – all mildly exciting. Much quieter, and safer, up at the OP than here in Cheux.

We all well down in our trenches. RSM is producing a daily 'newspaper'. A finer day, but still some cloud. Typhoons getting at Jerry on the Carpiquet 'drome again. Must be terrifying things to be under, these aerial rockets. Although Jerry still holds Carpiquet, the front line generally is receding from Cheux, and some Pioneers, or gunners, are now busy digging 25-pounder gun-pits in the field before us. Some fellows are now showing the strain a bit. Jerry's shelling us again now. We hear the long approach whine – suspense mounts in me as I write – they're falling short – others fall closer – pray not too close. Shelling seems to have stopped! Now our own guns have opened up – so cannot now hear Jerry shells coming until they're right on top of us. Most unpleasant. Our counter-battery fire is, indeed, terrific. My hands sweaty and trembling a bit. On my tod here – no one to impress. Don't feel too secure tonight. Don't know why. Nervy I suppose – most of us seem OK though. Amazing how quickly the Company can vanish from view once Jerry starts shelling.

We are all very dirty, but officers see that we keep shaven and as clean and spruce as possible. Since the shelling of the first two or three days here died down, we can strip a bit and make more elaborate toilets, but water is valuable here, and the petrol tin of water gets horribly hairy and scummy by the time we've all had a go.

Trevor and Dai have just returned from the OP. The Jerrys on the 'drome are shelling the track near the OP whenever our convoys use it. Sounds cheerful. Dug-in Panthers from Carpiquet are doing the shelling. One has to admire the sangfroid of these SS tank men – they seem to take very little notice of our shelling and mortaring, and generally they sit calmly on their turrets observing their tank's fire. Only in quite concentrated fire will they deign to get inside their tanks and close the hatches.

Deg and I go up to man the OP in the morning. (One very close then, and some Micks, washing themselves in petrol tins, have just disappeared entirely – into their trenches I think – if hit they must all be dead, for there's no sound from them, though I can't see much for smoke dust from the shells. Rumble of SP arty – unpleasant. Micks all seem to be OK. Can hear them swearing horribly as they, presumably, resume their toilets. Dust cloud settling, but still too thick for me to see them.) Smell of dead cattle, or people, from the burnt-out house and farm near our trenches, seems particularly vile today. A full moon is rising. More heavy fire on us at present – looks like being a dirty night – at least (shells bursting just short of us and one brute screamed right through us, but does not seem to have exploded). Hands sweat and tremble after each near miss, or near hit (as one sees it) and the effort to appear nonchalant after an undignified dive into a slit trench is amusing. The only thing that's not amusing is the pathetic lump of seared flesh and torn cloth when a man gets hit.

6 July 1944 – Observation Post – 2015 hours

Slept OK, but a mix-up with Drill Sergeant Blackmore who roused me for stand-to. 'Who's there?' he shouted down into the damp, earthy blackness of my trench. The words registered, but not their sense. People ask me this kind of question when they drop in to see the situation maps, as they indicate a red or blue chinagraph disposition whose designation we don't, perhaps, know. And, in my somnolent daze I thought this was what the drill-pig was asking me. I could only answer 'Where Sir?' He obviously didn't recognize my voice, which was probably as thick as my head. 'Why, down there where you are, you bloody fool!' I could think only of the German unit on Carpiquet, and, knowing I was making a wild guess, answered '12th SS Panzer Division, I think Sir.' There was a bit of a pause, and this gave me time to think more coherently. 'Eh – have you been at the bloody whisky?' It was my turn to wonder if the drill-pig was going a bit bomb-happy himself. 'No Sir.' 'Well – get out of it and stand to.' I did so. He recognized me, and went off grinning. There seemed a greater alertness and awareness on the part of Battalion HQ big shots than usual on this occasion, and later I discovered the cause, and also the reason for the Drill Sergeant's strange question. Corporal Coles and Drummer Gregory, on sentry during the night, got at the officers' whisky and were both blind drunk at stand to. Hell of a stink and commotion. Both are under close arrest, but God, how I envied them their condition then!

Over on Carpiquet, British shells are falling now behind the three great hangars. Quite an arty blitz from Jerry at about 9.20 pm last night, shelling the track about 150 yards from here. 3 Company OP here gloomily prophesy that Jerry might well sort us out here at any moment – they have an OP about 150 yards back down the hedge. Hope not – don't think we've been spotted here yet – at least not from Carpiquet. The ride up here on Deg's pillion quite exciting – odd how one cares less about what comes over when moving at speed and in a din of one's own making. We leave the motor-bike about 200 yards back down the hedge, and cautiously creep up here along the line of the hedge, using this as a screen against OPs on the aerodrome, when we relieve the OP personnel. Jerry tanks are still dug in there.

The Divisional Commander, General Sir Allan Adair, and the Brigadier, came up to our OP for a dekko at Carpiquet today. But they're a dead loss visiting OPs like this – their field-craft leaves much to be desired, and it's likely that Jerry spotted them. The general seemed interested in our doings and adventures and seems a decent fellow.

From this ridge we can see the barrage balloons flying from ships on the beaches. They seem homely somehow. Very worried about these flying bombs now blitzing London. Hope and pray that Dearest is OK. Militarily these freaks seem useless at this stage of the war – but they can do much damage.

Battle generally drifting away from Cheux – some REs and Pioneers are road-building near the village, though there's still a fair bit of shelling. Fellows looting knocked-out Jerry tanks and robbing the bodies, foul and black, a grizzly pastime. A few more casualties in Battalion, but not many. Shrapnel in my arm hurting rather – hope it's not turning too septic. German flak pretty hefty against our planes. Even a couple of birds in this hedge – trilling now – sounds incongruous, nice to hear them. A few birds still visit our orchard – sound a bit scared though.

7 July 1944 – 9.00 pm

A big do tomorrow – some excitement I should think. My scar dressed again today. Feels rather painful now. It's damn-all, of course. Doesn't look

GUARDSMAN OF
RIFLE COMPANY
AND SIGNALLER
USING 18
WIRELESS SET.

Fighting order and no.18 wireless set

now as if we shall go out tomorrow – dead loss. Seems we're stuck here for the duration.

Degville is back – it seems that some of our mortars, from 3 Company, fell a bit short and shook them up in the OP. A good crowd of fellows in this Intelligence Section. Hope I can live up to my job, and look after them OK. More rain – roll on!

Shells landing quite near now! Too near – quite a barrage – it's lifting – no, stop! Nearer yet! Very unpleasant – heart beats too fast – hands sweat a bit. Has stopped! Odd how one experiences fear. Wonder if there really are men who don't? Futilely stupid to record running commentary under bombardment. Perhaps I think, if I get away with it, that I can read these words and re-live the frightening experience, and savour all the more the security and comfort then about me?

But I doubt if words alone, even if written by a master of descriptive writing, could do that. How could one verbally recount so that a reader could reconstruct in his own mind the conditions under which a man knows such fear? The nervy tiredness from lack of sleep and chronic anxiety of a mind that half-senses that its body is condemned to death, and the flashes of hope – of extravagant optimism, never long-lasting, that convince him he'll live and survive the wretchedness of his body's state, dirty, sweaty, sticky, aching from the cramping confinement and dampness of the earthy hole in which he lives; the smell of wet earth, charred timber, gunpowder, rotting cows and human corpses – the ever-there nagging ache between the eyes of a head stupefied by the almost incessant din of half-a-thousand guns – the naive reliance on good luck – the constant dread that it may run out – by the law of averages alone. The loneliness and ennui of an unshared trench and above all, the hopeless uncertainty of the future – to say nothing of the craving for peace, security, comfort, and the love of women, and the tenderness of home. The writer of genius must first bring his readers to that state of mind and body before he can even begin to frighten him into the state of mental fear of a man who is terrified that the next shell may land smack in his own trench. A hard thing indeed to try on a reader clean, warm, dry, comfortable, un-tired, well loved and well fed and as secure as a man may be, and with a limitless future stretching before him.

Later

The signal cable from our OP to command post went dead after the shelling and mortaring on the ridge. So Dai and I up on an M/C to find out if Herb and Brian were OK. Called in at CP en route to see if they had heard anything more from OP. They hadn't and we prepared to continue our journey. But Colonel Heber-Percy and the IO wouldn't let us go on for a while because the shelling had recommenced and was pretty heavy then. Still no report came in from the OP, so Dai and I mounted the bike and he fairly raced it up to the ridge. Felt mildly heroic, yet rather stupid too, as we belted through, and beyond, our company positions.

The field had that ominous emptiness of a zone under bombardment, and I was acutely conscious of the fact that hundreds of eyes of our Battalion, as well as the Colonel's and those of others in CP, were watching us from ground level as they stood in their trenches. It was a bit like one of those ghastly situations I so much dreaded in peacetime when I found myself out on my tod before the whole Battalion, and I think now that fear of ridicule was as strong in me as fear of the German shells. We seemed to be the only living creatures above ground. I had a momentary, but vivid picture of how dashing we must look to the multitude, and how comically absurd as we disappeared for all time in the blinding flash and the dust and smoke of a direct hit. But, as before, the din of the machine drowned the noise of falling shells, and its immense speed over the bumpy field, roused in me an uncharacteristic reckless exultation and fatalism, and in the end I didn't give a damn, until Dai stopped the engine at our destination, and other, more sinister, noises again struck our eardrums. The fire was comparatively light – mortars I think, and nothing fell very near us at all.

They were OK at the OP – the shelling had cut the signal cable, and the Sigs had the unpleasant task of finding, and repairing, the break in the long length of wire. They are great chaps in this section, and Degville and Trevor Church were almost fighting to volunteer to go up to the OP when communications went dead. I didn't relish the job, but knew that it took me to go – if only on the grounds of *noblesse oblige* as a sergeant. We relieved Brian and Stacey, told them to report the break to the Sigs. An OP's not much use without communications, and line is the safest thing – wireless gives the game away too soon. It occurs to me that men, well trained in field-craft, could approach our ridge through the standing corn and barley in large numbers, though I suppose they would be unsupported, and would be massacred by our companies as they topped the ridge, nevertheless we keep a wary eye on the barley, two of us wouldn't stand much chance against a surprise attack by a Jerry patrol, and the 'I' Section would never live down the disgrace anyway. Our sole communication, until the wire was repaired, was by motor-cycle.

8 July 1944 – 1500 hours

Up to OP after breakfasts. Day dawned wet – only with the utmost difficulty could I keep my eyes open during stand-to. Dog tired – far too little sleep. It's getting the hell of a job now to rouse men in their slit trenches. We all sleep like men drugged on some tremendously powerful dope, and some men refuse breakfasts to get down to it for an extra hour's kip after stand-down. The Adjutant and RSM often sleep on. But Captain Graham, a fastidiously clean man, always, at stand-down, strolls over to the cooker where he politely asks the cooks if they can spare some hot water. He uses the tail-board of a Sigs truck as washstand, carefully laying out his washing and shaving kit as though he were at a hotel. He washes, and then very carefully shaves all around his enormous orange whiskers.

We laughed our heads off the first day he arrived from first line reinforcement, knowing that he would soon forsake this leisurely and fussy toilet for a quick wash and shave from a tin in, or near, his slit trench. But this has not happened. Even a solid shot hitting the truck at which he stood shaving (while everyone else was in his trench) seemed only mildly to surprise him. He is not foolhardy, and takes cover when it's wise to do so – but always calmly, and always with that slight, almost apologetic, smile that suggests that the whole war is a bit of a farce really. We notice too that he allows his own servant to get down to it again after morning stand-down and does all his fetching and carrying himself. I doubt if any other officer in the Battalion, except Hugh Lister, would give his servant a break like this. Graham has brought with him a touch of refreshingly whimsical humour to the grim and sordid village of Cheux. His unruffled coolness under enemy fire is fantastic, even in a Guards' officer. He never, I think, sleeps by day and he, like myself, is passionately fond of his morning mug of char, preferring it, as I do, to a bit of extra kip.

Deg and I went up to relieve Dai and Trevor on the OP. We dumped the M/C as usual, and, as we neared the OP, two columns of black smoke arose near it. We approached, as usual, along the western side of the hedge. The OP had obviously been observed – probably given away by a careless visitor. The other two went off and five minutes later Jerry let fly at us with about twenty-five shells from 15cm guns, judging by the size of the shell-holes. One fell about 3 yards from the shallow slit trench, providentially dug by 23 Hussars during the first attack on Caen and in which I had flung myself for cover. With quick-beating heart I wondered where the next, and the next, and the next shell would fall. Fortunately, of the twenty-five shells fired, only seven or eight seemed to explode, and they with seemingly less noise than some smaller calibre shells that have come our way. Never known so many duds. We assume that the slave labour exploited by the Germans in conquered countries, is responsible for manufacturing dud shells, and Redman, I was told, taking cover in 3 Company slit at their OP, said, every time a dud fell – 'Good-oh! Well done the Czechs and Poles!'

The CO and Major Lister came up to the OP today to observe our mortar and MG fire on the aerodrome. This is only a diversion – a feint – to support the main Canadian attack coming in from the north-east. It looked colossal, but most of it fell on the forward slopes, where we have seen no enemy for the past twenty-four hours. Both the CO and Major Lister took trouble to approach our OP sensibly under cover so as not to betray us any further to the enemy. We are sure now that the shelling this morning came, not from Carpiquet, but from the high ground on our right where we have established a bridgehead over the River Orne. High ground we assumed was British-occupied. But obviously not all of it is. The Germans in the Orne bridgehead battle must have plenty to worry about, and plenty of targets, in their own zone. Our front faces east against Carpiquet and 12 SS. It is irritating that German gunners from another battle cannot mind their own business, and not poach targets outside their allotted zone. Rather disconcerting to think that we may have been under observation every time we approached this OP. Today we met, and led, the CO and Major Lister upon the Carpiquet side of the hedge but keeping to the ditch as much as possible, and nothing came over while they were at the OP. I was particularly anxious that no one should be spotted while our mortars were firing.

Two things seem to bring out the worst in all gunners. One is enemy mortars, the other enemy troops attending to calls of nature within full view of an OP. Once mortars start firing the Gunners immediately counter-fire at the suspected mortar concentration and at any OPs that might be directing the mortar fire, and mortar platoons are trained to come into action quickly, get off their shoot and be packed up and away before the indignant enemy can register his own counter-battery fire against them. A mortar platoon in action is about as popular, even to its own side, as a moggy at a mouse's tea party. It's the poor devils in whose area the mortars fired, who must remain and take the can back for the departed M platoon's action. We, in turn, searched the high ground to our right for likely Jerry OPs, but could find nothing. Also, we made a very thorough and detailed search, using a telescope, of the front we are watching, and I elaborated a sketch I made of Carpiquet.

At rare times, when our guns and Typhoons are silent, an almost siesta-like Sunday afternoon atmosphere of sinister, brooding peace and uneasy quietude descends upon the panorama we view from our OP. The distant towers and chimneys of Caen appear blue and undamaged, until the amber and Vandyke brown buffs start again and the click of their explosion disproves the illusion. Our guns, and especially the SPs, are like huge mortars pounding the earth, and vibrating and thudding the sides of our slit trenches. Trying to get some sleep. Flattering, though frightening, to be sniped at on OP by German 15cm guns, and so wasting twenty-five rounds on Deg and me, when they're already reputedly short of ammo!

<u>11 July 1944 – 0600 hours</u>

Another day. Grey skies again – but no rain yet. It's chilly, and I'm wearing my greatcoat. Can hear the cheering roar of our petrol cookers and the clanging dixies as breakfasts get underway. We make tea in our trenches on our little Tommy cookers using solid meth tablets, and I shall never forget the stinging, though rather pleasant, smell of these tablets. They are good and can boil a mug of water very quickly – the art is to put the powder into exactly the right temperature of water (it must not be actually boiling or the dried milk element congeals) and then, almost instantly, to bring water to the boil in order to brew the tea element in the powder. This stuff makes one's mug messy and one sips the brew from an enamel mug crusted around its rim with crystallized browny-white powder – it's OK though, if properly made. Add a few saccharines and it's fine.

Feel more jumpy in evening than in the morning – more tired perhaps – or maybe some primeval dread of the coming dark? This is our fourteenth day here. Roll on! It seems an eternity. Must get washed and shaved and rouse section for breakfasts.

Jerry's 'Sobbing Sisters' are frightening things – we seem to fear these more than we fear ordinary mortars and shells.

Am concerned what I can do with these diaries – mustn't bring them into the line again – too stupid. Have only been here in Normandy three weeks and already I've written more than I thought I would write in two months. Trouble is there is so much daylight now and so much time to write that I do not (as I planned) keep diary to essentials and however much I abbreviate, however small I write, the notebooks fill too quickly.

6

Caen: Cagny and Colombelles 12 July–28 July 1944

The Battalion came out of the line on 11 July to rejoin GAD at St Martin des Entrées – to the great relief of all:

> and it is paradise to walk about free from the constant threat of German shells and mortars…marvellous to be away from the perpetual pounding and racket of our own artillery. How good last night to stretch one's legs and back – take off one's boots and to sleep soundly for nine or more, hours!

However, the major requirement of guardsmen – alcohol – was in short supply.

12–13 July 1944

Allowed to walk out tonight to Bayeux (now in bounds). Went with Tony – but it was a waste of time – just a teeming mass of dreary khaki. Most cafés closed – those open were packed out, and men were even drinking soft drinks – very little alcohol about at all. But loads of dairies and other shops were open, and there the Norman shopkeepers were selling hundreds of boxes of Camembert cheese at eleven francs a box – not bad either. And, though this is not stuff squaddees go for much, men with money and nothing to spend it on, were buying the stuff TFO. The Normans cannot get rid of their milk any other way. But no chance in Bayeux of a drink and we envied two Yankee matelots who were as drunk as coots. The cathedral is impressive, but we were too thirsty for tipple to bend our minds to culture – and we did not go inside. Think we're in for some bull here. So back on a tank-transporter loaded up with men, and each man, sober as a judge, clutching to him a round box of Camembert cheese. Brewed some char, ate our cheese and army biscuits, and to kip. Very tired still – more so than ever.

Cheered by a very delightful letter from S. All well with her. Blokes coming back on crowded transporter: 'Mind my f*****g cheese then – take yer bleedin' boots out of my bloody butter!' Strange fare for guardsmen –

even more strange to see them drinking lemonade and stuff in absence of harder tipple.

13 July 1944

Blokes laughing over 39 Phillips who accidentally let off a burst of Sten in the orchard at Cheux, just after stand-down one night – the shots hit a tree and just missed another signaller's head. I remember the incident, and the furore that ensued as Snowy, believing a Jerry sniper to be at large, ordered Battalion HQ to stand to once more and organized a man-hunt through the orchard and beyond. But I did not know then that 39 Phillips was the culprit. But Phillips says he was nearly wetting his trousers with suppressed mirth as he also, as solemnly as he might, stalked the mysterious sniper through the night. Snowy at last gave up, but posted double sentries that night – and the last joke is that 39 Phillips was not stung for this duty and got down into his trench and squatted there laughing like mad, until he at last dropped off to sleep. And this is where the excessive discipline of Guards regiments becomes nonsense. It was more than Phillips dared do to own up to his offence.

16 July 1944

A pint bottle of English beer each tonight – had Herb's as well. Each sergeant is entitled to a free bottle of whisky per month – but as I have only recently joined this freemasonry, I don't yet size. Not having tasted beer lately, the stuff seems more potent and I feel almost happy.

This has been a day of constant work – no break at all until now – distributing and sorting maps – mounting air photo mosaics[1] of our advance and annotating them. Everything possible is done to ensure that we know the country over which we must attack, and it's all very efficient. Buzz-bombs[2] came over last night and I believe some long-range shells fell around the place – roll on!

Many of our sergeants, off duty, lie around out to the wide – dead drunk on gin and whisky. I envy them their temporary oblivion, but not their heads tomorrow morning at reveille. Seems wrong, when men can get only a pint of beer each – but I am a sergeant now, and this sympathy is hypocrisy. But I am not really sergeant material – a complete phoney.

Cherbourg was captured on 27 June and all of Caen to the north of the Orne by 8 July. Phase one of the plan was complete and phase two could now begin. The British were to threaten to break out from Caen on the eastern side, while the Americans made the real breakout on the west. This was known as Operation Goodwood and started on 18 July with Field Marshal Montgomery attacking with

---

1. Mosaic – a term applied to the technique of aerial mapping by which photographs taken from the air are fitted together like a jigsaw puzzle.
2. A one-ton jet-propelled bomb – used in the bombardment of England.

strong forces of armour and infantry east of Caen, preceded by an enormous air and artillery bombardment. The Division moved slowly forward into choking clouds of dust. Most of the fighting was done by 5 Guards Armoured Brigade and after they had dealt with the main opposition, the 1st Battalion Welsh Guards, while not being engaged in the confused fighting of the 18th, was sent in to clear the village of Cagny where many prisoners were taken. The following day they captured the village of Le Poirier, three-quarters of a mile SW of Cagny, where they stayed until late on 22 July when the Division was withdrawn. The weather changed and they had four days of continuous warm rain which turned the thick dust into a quagmire. Their slit trenches were half-filled with water, which were difficult to leave because of almost continuous mortaring and shelling. A plague of mosquitoes completed their misery.

Although the Germans just managed to hold the British attack, the major object had been achieved and six Panzer divisions and all three battalions of Tiger tanks had been attracted to the British (or west) sector of the front, leaving only two Panzer divisions on the east, which greatly helped the planned breakthrough which started on 27 July. The British forces (which included GAD) were switched from the east of Caen to Caumont, west of Bayeux to assist in the breakout and both 1WG and 2WG crossed the Orne on the night of 30 July and entered the *Bocage* country.

It was time for phase three and though the fight in the east was still raging, the Americans were ready to break out on the west, having conquered the whole of the Cherbourg peninsula.

18 July 1944 – 0600 hours

Moved off from Bayeux concentration area 0300 hours. It is now 0600. There's a railway on our right and an aerodrome on the skyline to our left. It is just dawn, and the sky's a mass of colour. A blue-grey, steely-looking ridge of cloud lies just above the skyline sandwiching, between it and the dark and dusky horizon, a narrow strip of gorgeously striped orange, gold and red and yellow that heralds the advent of the sun and of another, for us, most dramatic day – the 'Baptism of Fire' for the Guards Armoured Division. Above this dark ridge of cloud the sky merges gradually through translucent purples, mauves and blues and light greens into pale azure against which, high above the horizon, lies a mass of pink-tinged sheep clouds. But there, in the sky, the beauty, if not the drama, of this perfect dawn abruptly ends.

A long, black, grim line of stationary tanks and vehicles lies, expectant and menacing, and nearer, a mass of tanks in single file are silhouetted black against the eastern sky. Men are standing on these tanks, as a sort of grandstand, to view the work of the enormous phalanx of Allied bombers that now roars above us. Other men cooking breakfasts near their vehicles. Now German flak goes up to engage our bombers – 2,000 of them in this awesome aerial armada, and we watch in silence until someone says (apropos Jerry) 'those poor bastards must be sh***ing themselves over there'. Heavy four-engined bombers now – one is hit, and down in flames – terrific sight – the mass of planes seems endless – our coastal barrage balloons silhouetted behind the 'drome look almost homely to a Londoner – we travelling on a 'wheeled' track of wire laid across the plain – two 6-pounder armoured cars in our column and some armoured half-tracks. Many Bofors gun-pits dotted over the plain. The German flak is only moderate. And still the bombers come – some Spitfires overhead too. I travelling in CO's car and dozed during night approach march. Small

ONE OF THE ANTI-TANK PLATOON'S
6-POUNDER GUNS AND A DESPATCH
RIDER.

haystacks in these fields – crump of AA – 17-pounders and A/Tk guns – to rear mostly.

<u>0815 hours</u>

Emieville reported overrun – battle now in full swing – thick brown-black clouds of dust hide most of it – some German shells falling – a few unpleasantly close to us – had a wash and shave during our long halt – we're halted still now. Annoyance when one's wet soap falls into gritty earth when washing. So, spick and span, into the battle, and I travelling and writing this, in the most luxurious vehicle in the Battalion, the CO's saloon car – a luxury I would gladly forego for the discomfort of a half-track or carrier that puts some armour-plating between me and the ever-thickening enemy fire, and I am uneasily aware of the twenty-four gallons of petrol stowed in jerrycans on the roof of the car, and directly above my head. We in here will be blazing torches in seconds if anything hot hits those cans. The tanks on the track on our left have started up in a racket of snorting – revving and backfiring, and are now on the move, each tank raising its cloud of Vandyke dust, that fades to amber higher.

0850 hours

Guards armour now moving up on our left – constant gunfire – the nearer crump-crump of German shells. Most men wearing still their GS caps (khaki berets) – our latrine screens have been taken down by the sanitary squad. Loads of anti-radiation strips of silver paper (dropped by our bombers to confuse enemy radar) litter the area. Our air-raid is still on, and another bomber is afire. This new raid began about fifteen minutes ago. The brown dust clouds linger – the sun shines brightly through their pall – the skies are clear – answer to the RAF's prayers. Guards armour now goes forward to match its strength and skill against that of the élite 1st SS Panzer Division – or so intelligence summaries suggest.

1000 hours

Our worst time is to come – forming the pivot. So on again. Now passing the gliders of 6th Airborne Division who landed here on D-Day – some badly crashed – some OK, others appear to have been dismantled, and the perspex windows and domes broken – a fascinating sight. So on through Benouville – our artillery very active – it's getting hot now – on, through ripening corn and red poppies. All the Battalion, except officers and WOs, wearing canvas order, a sartorial revolution for the Guards. Our gliders seem to have landed here in spite of the poles erected by the Germans to stop this happening. Bofors gun-pits dug all over the place – the sun shines through the dust in rays of golden and bronze monochrome, and our DRs look like ghostly apparitions covered, as they are, from head to foot in the fine, powdery grey dust.

Sappers, stripped to the waist, still at work on their Bailey bridges thrown across small streams, ditches and depressions. We pass over York bridge (class forty) and we are now travelling along Palm route – on, over three more bridges – pontoons – and now Airborne and Commando troops, wearing their pride of red or green berets, stand about a bridge and watch us silently as we pass – fine-looking soldiers these. By the bridge a casualty being treated on a stretcher – reminder that, for all its efficiency so far, this is no exercise. Can barely see the next vehicle ahead for the thick brown dust. Our artillery spotter planes (Austers) look absurdly tiny and toy-like below the great Lancaster bombers – passing more gliders than ever – we are not yet actually beyond our original front line, I suppose?

1445 hours

A few minutes break – our first prisoners – a Czech and a Hun – both very helpful – both seemed very scared and they smelt a bit – both of 125th Panzer Grenadiers' Regiment of 21st Panzer Division. We halted once inside a concentration of our own artillery – self-propelled 25-pounder guns, and we spent a very uncomfortable half hour sheltering at the edge of a quarry while German 'Moaning Minnies' thoroughly plastered the area, and I heard no more pity for, but only invective against, the 'poor bastards' who were giving us such a pasting. Yet I couldn't resist a sneaking regard for the courage of men who will fight back so hard after the drubbing they got from the air this morning. Was glad when we moved forward again – very hot and sultry now – feel tired out already – but cooks dished up a mug of hot char for every man – and this did us much good. We seem now to be bang in the middle of the battle – seems chaotic, and crazy to be sitting here in a limousine car and writing this – whizz-bangs flying about all over the place – no one seems to know a bloody thing – tanks everywhere, many hit and belching smoke – our infantry mopping up just ahead and to my left.

<u>19 July 1944</u>

Am 32 today, a right old birthday party this is – spent in middle of an armoured infantry battle.

During the late afternoon and evening the section busy with prisoners – and there was little time to watch our tanks nosing cautiously up to the high banks and hedges on the outskirts of the village of Cagny – there they opened fire with their machine guns while our infantry, which had advanced through the open cornfields in extended order, moved up each side of the hedges bordering the small fields in single file – these hedges are planted in tall banks and are very high and thick, and plentifully interspersing the hedges are the odd lop-topped trees peculiar to Normandy – and, for the first time since I joined the Army, eleven years ago, I watched guardsmen, Micks and Taffs, advancing in real battle. Yet, in spite of the German fire and the occasional casualty, the whole thing seemed almost stunt-like to me – so realistic had been our training in the Yorkshire Wolds.

Fortunately most of the German shelling went over our heads, and their mortars seemed more interested in what was happening behind us too. But enough muck fell around us to make it an effort not to duck as we lined up our captives by the right and searched through the pockets of their grey-green flimsy jackets or camouflage smocks. They were utterly exhausted, and stank strongly of the peculiar German smell mingled with that of sweat and fear – and some were near to becoming gibbering neurotics, and all were desperately anxious to be gone from here, and away from the menace of their own fire; and I admired the sangfroid of Brian and Deg and the rest as they snarled *Nicht rauchen* at any who looked like getting cushy and thinking of smoking. I solemnly called the prisoners to attention and saluted Mr Koppel (the only fluent German linguist at Battalion HQ) when he came up to interrogate them briefly.

A ridiculous pantomime in the middle of battle, but thus have we been taught, and the German mentality obviously reacts advantageously to this kind of disciplinary charade, because Brigade HQ sent us a congratulatory message on the ripeness of our prisoners for Brigade interrogation. But I suspect that some of our act was also due to a kind of grudging respect (mixed strangely with contempt for their condition) for these stinking scarecrows who had endured so much since our air and land attack began that morning. We paid them the compliment of wanting to appear in their eyes cooler, calmer and braver soldiers than they – however unfairly. It seemed cruel to keep them there, and they obviously bobbed as much on Snowy's ferocious glare and 6ft 7ins of bulk as they did on the dangers from their own shellfire. The RSM speaks no German – he didn't need to. But I was glad as each batch of prisoners was doubled away en route to Brigade HQ, and I could unostentatiously amble off to stand nearer the safety of my own trench. The prisoners needed no spur as they went; and the most exhausted, and even those with superficial wounds, kept up with the rest as they were run back to the relative safety of Brigade and Divisional HQs and the prisoner-of-war cages further back still. Nearly all these prisoners (fifty-four of them) were of 21 Panzer, or 16 German Air Force Divs. It was a day of heat and hunger, dust and thirst, disgust and fear.

After dark last night we moved again and started digging new trenches soon after midnight, and we were on the go all night – digging slits, and pits for vehicles, and then sandbagging them. Mortars and 'Moaning Minnies' fell plentifully during the night. In the dark one can actually see the 'Minnies' going up from their multiple barrels – they look rather like flak

MINE DETECTOR
USED BY
PIONEER PLATOON.

ACHTUNG MINEN

tracer shells at first. If they go up at an angle they fall left, or right, of one's position, but if they go straight up, then it's wise to take cover – it's only a matter of range if they get you or not.

Night brought the *Luftwaffe*, like giant bats, into the air, and it was an unnerving experience travelling through the dark in the CO's car with all that petrol above, and not knowing what undetected mines remained in the fields we crossed – with Jerry's mortar and shells falling in the area, and in our ears the roar of low-flying German planes – the short scream of falling bombs and crack-lash of their explosions. Two blazing Sherman tanks we passed seemed to be drawing a lot of the enemy fire, and I was tempted to give way to panic and jump out as shrapnel struck the car, but the vehicle, unharmed, moved on just as someone blew up one of the burning tanks – or perhaps its ammunition exploded. It seemed that my end had come at last. Only the flares, dropped by German aircraft, and blazing tanks gave any light, and that only a weird, macabre and confusing light. I had no idea where we were when we were halted and ordered to dig in. Tried to find the section and our own 15-cwt, but all I could see, once we got away from the blazing tanks, was a great electricity pylon close by, and the star-shells and flak and gun-flashes – a rather dreadful night.

Mr Graham, cool as ever, hailed me – how he found me I don't know. He wanted eight copies made of defensive fire (DF) task traces, and so I was with him in the car as I drew these. He referred jokingly to the shindig going on all around us – he was reassuringly cool but, like all of us, very tired, and he dozed as I drew – and sometimes I found myself dropping off too and kept starting up to carry on with my task, but I felt very sorry for the officer who had to distribute the finished traces, one to each of our companies, one to the CO and one to Brigade HQ, and he as lost as I had been until the traces showed on the map where we were. But he showed no sign of being perturbed – polite and amusing as ever – danger is a good test of a man's character. I would have preferred to make the traces by torchlight in the relative safety of my half-dug trench, but he suggested we black out the car windows and use the interior light (still working) and sat in the car, and I felt jittery for a while when mortars fell and I could hear lumps of shrapnel hitting things in the vicinity, but his coolness and light-hearted banter, and his 'if we must die – we die in comfort' mood was infectious. Lack of sleep frays the nerves and makes one a bit light-headed, and there was something dream-like to be sitting in a comfortable car and drawing, isolated by the blacked-out windows, from the crazy and dangerous world outside, and occasionally exchanging pleasantries with a man who looked, and spoke, as though he were taking his ease in the lounge of some swagger hotel in London, and not in a car rocked by high explosives.

Later

We moved at 5.00 pm – to attack beyond Cagny – was glad to leave that cabbage field – though we're still among cabbages here – felt very exposed and naked at the last place and the soil there was inhospitable, gravelly and damp. Here we are dug in on the outskirts of Cagny. Fifty yards away, along a row of tall trees, lies a battery of four abandoned 88mm guns, and strewn about each gun, a pile of the yard-long shells that are so deadly to our tanks.

The shelling didn't seem to cause us much damage, except for holes in our vehicles, and a few put out of action. It's amazing how much HE is needed to kill or wound men once they are dug in. And even after our huge air-raid and artillery barrage, and in spite of the enormous bomb craters all about us, this orgy of destruction seems to have killed few Jerries – what it did do, I think, was temporarily to shatter their nerves and diminish their morale, and some of the prisoners we had in yesterday were just nervous wrecks – and understandably so – they had, for the moment, 'had it'.

88mm dual-purpose gun

20 July 1944 – 1415 hours

The RSM's trench lies only a short distance from mine – suddenly I heard him let rip in a full-blooded barrack-square roar, and I peered over my trench, and through the cabbages growing all around it, to see what was afoot. A driver had dug in only a few yards from Snowy's trench and was busy (during a lull in the shelling) half-covering the top of his trench with earth laid on a very firm roof foundation of about a dozen live 88mm shells that he had laboriously carried from the abandoned German battery. Snowy went berserk, called the driver a 'dozy man' and press-ganged as many guardsmen as he could to carry the lethal monsters back whence they came, and well clear of his, the RSM's, slit trench. Whether or not live shells, hit by hot shrapnel or by incendiary bullets, will explode, I do not know. Snowy, obviously, was taking no chances.

About 6.00 pm

No line from Dearest – am worried. Unreasonable, I suppose, to expect the postman to call just now – but so well-organized is this campaign, compared with the shambles of Dunkirk, that we half expect a daily newspaper left in the porch each morning.

There go his foul-sounding rockets again – like a cow with whooping cough. 'Whoo-whoo-whoo.' Hope not coming our way, though it is the rifle companies, ours and the Micks, he's plastering, and we only get their overthrows – but a lot of metal is flying overhead on to targets further back – on our guns I suppose. There's going to be some picnic if we're relieved tonight – anything on wheels must surely get bogged down in this morass

– and that, right in the open, will be unpleasant.

Blast the rain! It shows no sign of letting up. Constant whine and whizz of shells and mortars and incredibly long bursts of fire from Jerry's MG 42s. There's some kind of attack coming in, judging by all this din and activity. The only vehicles that seem able to get around in the quagmire are Bren-carriers and a few jeeps. The former cause many misgivings as they approach one's position – the whine of their mechanism sounds very like incoming shells and mortars destined for one's own trench.

…Snowy appeared after his ducking, and during a lull in the bombardment, carrying a spade and obviously en route to attend to a 'call of nature'. Round his legs he has wrapped some empty sandbags, and tied these crosswise with cord, and looks a bit like some Saxon warrior from 'Hereward the Wake' (see plate no. 12, 'RSM Snowy Baker').

All my bones ache now with damp from the slit trench walls – and I, like the others, am soaked through from head to foot. Thank heaven this rain didn't come during the night while I was digging in. Must deepen this trench – it's dangerously shallow. More 'Moaning Minnies' on their way. One detests the gunners of both sides. Life's a sheer misery (with all this rain) without their interference. 'Minnies' fell on the Micks, I think.

21 July 1944 – Cagny – 0700 hours

Well, here we are, another day – my bones and my back aching – my sodden clothing sticking clammily to my tired body. To add to the miseries of mud and waterlogged trenches, constant strain, and all the other miseries of this place, whole squadrons of viciously buzzing mosquitoes have appeared, biting and tormenting us. But here we are still. A rainy, misty, chilly dawn – dumped vehicles lie dotted over the cabbage and corn fields – here a long 17-pounder gun sticking out, at an odd angle from (aesthetically) an unsatisfactorily traversed tank turret – there a group of Bren-carriers, or Carden-Lloyds – the captured German half-track used by our REME[1] and fitters. The odd, lop-topped trees that line the hedges rise blue above the mist. It is as though all things are just hanging in the air, for the low-lying thick white mist obliterates everything at ground level – the dreary puddles of brown water among the cabbages, and always this dreadful, bumpy, shallow and waterlogged trench.

The only cheering sight, or sound, at dawn comes from the glow, and roar, of our petrol cookers preparing breakfasts. Our cooks have had rather a bad time of it and 24 Thomas nearly caught it yesterday when a mortar exploded almost in his trench. He was duty cook this morning and had switched on the petrol burners and was about to light them when another salvo of hate came over – he dived for his trench and the other gyppoes

---

1. Royal Mechanical and Electrical Engineers.

'ALLENGER'' (OVER 30 TONS)
H LONG 17-POUNDER GUN.

were laughing as he tried lighting matches and throwing them at the burners in the hope that they would ignite. Another cook got out and switched them off and then lit them when the fumes had dispersed a bit.

The cooks are dug-in on the rim of an enormous bomb crater, legacy of the RAF raid on the 18th. This crater must be 60 or 70 feet in diameter and about 20 feet deep. It is considered a good joke when German projectiles are heard coming our way just as two men, each clutching a mess tin of stew and a mug of char, are making their way back from the cooker to their trenches (only two men at a time are allowed at the cooker). Already walking gingerly to avoid spilling food and drink and to avoid slipping up in the mud, the two men look a bit as though they have had an accident in their trousers. But it is their air of comic indecision as their well-attuned ears catch the sound of something nasty coming their way that is so amusing – whether to risk losing half their scoff by doubling to the nearest slit trench – or carry on and chance it, or get down flat in the mud and cabbages. I watched Davies caught this way, and the stuff came near enough for everyone to bob down in his trench, and when we looked again, Davies and his companion were lying flat on their faces in the mud, mess tins and mugs flung aside, and at first we thought they had been hit, and only as they got to their feet did a roar of laughter break out from the audience in their trenches – and hopping mad they both were at this – but the gyppoes refilled their mugs and mess tins this time. But only when stuff seems coming down right on them will men risk losing precious tea and food by falling flat – because, next to mail from home, tea and food and our issue of seven cigarettes, are the only events, the only things to look forward to – during these seemingly interminable hours and days and nights we spend here doing nothing.

8.40 pm

The shelling and mortaring is now almost incessant, and it's very unwise to leave one's trench for anything less than food or easing the bladder and bowels, and we get very few visitors at present to view our situation maps, which we maintain somehow in the 'I' trench – in spite of the rain and mud. Our own guns and mortars hammer back at Jerry, but now, for the first time since we have been in the line in Normandy, it is the enemy who is putting down by far the heavier concentration of fire in our zone.

Some prisoners, once they have been looted of a watch or trinket of sentimental value (they expect their money to be pinched) will toot again at Brigade or Divisional HQ and are useless for questioning, and for this reason riflemen are forbidden to take such articles from prisoners – but some still do. We already have here quite a collection of field glasses, compasses, army watches etc, and even weapons, so blasé are the rifle companies now about the innocuousness of thoroughly scared prisoners. Surprisingly enough, many of us have had our hair cut to stubble in the interests of hygiene, but most of our prisoners – Germans from the Fatherland of the legendary close-cropped military skull – have comparatively long hair, hence the combs, when they think they are safe.

Have never felt so thoroughly wet in my life. At least in peacetime – at places like Clanfield Camp in 1935, we marched, and the heat from our bodies helped dry our clothing – but here we just wallow, like hippopotami, in water and mud all day. Those damned mosquitoes again! Shall never forget this little picnic, and if I live to enjoy once again a civvy bed, I swear I'll recall this every night before I drop off to sleep. We need just two hours of sunshine for us, and the tracks, to dry out a bit – but it's too late now. Roll on!

<u>24 July 1944 – Colombelles – harbour area</u>

Did sentry until 0400 hours. Tony[1] the corporal of the guard. We dug a shallow sleeping trench for the NCO off duty, and the six guardsmen of the Battalion HQ guard dug theirs a little way off.

…I understood well enough what Tony meant as he indicated, by gesture, what lay all about us – a nightmare of absolute chaos, periodically illuminated by the macabre, yet sometimes beautiful, pyrotechnics of war. The mauve-blue whiteness of searchlight beams, their lower edges merging through mauve and purple, into the deep royal-blue of the night sky. Questing beams holding captive, for a few seconds, the frail white moth of a higher-flying German plane that attracts to itself other hostile beams and the orange-red blobs of ascending tracer shells that explode prettily in bright white star-clusters – like a child's sparkler firework on Guy Fawkes' night. And lower, the night sky glowed with the ghostly blue-white halo of abortive incendiary bombs burning themselves out where they found no combustible targets – or the sulky, dull-red glare of exploding bombs, or

---

1. Tony Hibbott was an old friend from his Army days in the mid 1930s and the only one who kept in touch after the war. He lost a leg in the 'Island' in early October.

shells, on the skyline. Very rarely do these lethal fireworks concern us personally, and then for only brief and frightening moments. But they are a fairly constant feature of the night life around here. And here, if his aesthetic nostrils were not too much offended by the prevailing stench of corruption, artist Salvador Dali, with his penchant for the crucifixion in surrealistic form, might linger, fascinated, and perhaps inspired. For on the crest of the hill that rises from the south bank of the Orne, and only 100 yards from here, there still stands, dominating a small, ugly, bomb and shell-shattered cemetery, a life-sized effigy of Christ on the Cross. And, as Tony spoke, the Calvary was vividly and dramatically silhouetted against a cluster of parachute flares dropping low, like molten gold, over the Colombelles factory.

More heavy shells whistled overhead and burst well beyond us – somewhere on the other side of the river; and the shifting night breeze was foul and heavy with the smell of sewage and of death and decay from bodies trapped inside German tanks and other AFVs that were tossed, like discarded soup tins, into the gigantic bomb craters created by the RAF in their raid on 18 July. Foul too with the smell of bodies entombed beneath the awful debris of the great factory demolished in the same massive raid, and with the smell of older death that seeps from the ravaged graves and disinterred coffins in the nearby cemetery.

And especially horrible and pungent is the smell of decomposing flesh from the bodies of men killed in the wood that borders our harbour area when the Canadians attacked Colombelles a week ago. This splintered and blasted wood is a sinister, evil place – for all I know still plentifully strewn with mines and unexploded booby traps. The Battalion, true to form, has had us out tidying our own area and cleansing it of the more offensive, or lethal, rubbish in a grim parody of the family area fatigue of old, when innocent matchsticks, dog-ends and fallen leaves were the offending material. And our fellows have felled saplings and small trees from the wood and the sanitary squad has established their latrines there. But the place gives me the creeps, and I go there only when nature compels, and I do not envy the Pioneers whose job it is to cleanse the wood, and the tanks, of their grisly remains – nor the Sappers who purge the place of its lethal contraptions. And we were glad when the wind veered from the north and brought to our nostrils less pungent odours as we stood on guard.

Went for baths today to a Canadian bath unit, operating in a quiet back area on the south bank of the Orne Canal, whence the unit drew its water supply. The bath units are very efficient, and I revelled in the hot water of my shower; and sheer *joie-de-vivre* set the Welshmen singing their guts out as they bathed. Except for our BD and berets and boots we left all our soiled clothing in the bath-tent, and we emerged, naked and wet, to draw up clean shirts and underclothing and towels from another marquee, and we dried and dressed ourselves on the grass of the canal bank. It seemed strange to be standing there stark naked in sight of the civilians, mostly women, on the far bank, and I hid myself behind other men as a group of peasant women and girls approached, walking along the other bank on their way to, or from, work in the fields; and some men turned their backs, and sat down, to finish drying and dressing themselves; but other men carelessly stood their ground…but the French women did not squeal or run away. Some of the younger ones kept the eye down at first, but the older women eyed our fellows curiously and, I thought, approvingly, and they laughed as men gave them wolf-whistles, and the younger women looked up and laughed too as bawdy, though largely unintelligible, badinage flew to and fro across the canal. We, having had little contact with women lately, would gladly have reversed the roles and have gazed admiringly at the nudity of some of the women in the party. But, as proof that the male derives some erotic pleasure in displaying himself naked before feminine eyes, one of our riflemen turned his back on the women and retired, running and chuckling like mad, to hide himself in the crowd. His own nudity and sight of the women had combined to cause him a temporary, but fairly obvious, embarrassment. And a burst of laughter from the far bank followed him, confirming that the women also had fluffed to his discomfiture.

All bridges over the canal are blown. The devastation around Colombelles is terrible – this is a blighted area. The eyes of many of our men, including officers, are puffed up, and almost closed, from the bites of gnats and mosquitoes. Mild surprise that blue blood even is not immune.

25 July 1944 – 0900 hours

At dusk last night Corporal Plow came over to us for a chat and said 'Goodnight' before getting down to it in his trench. He must have been killed by the blast of a 'butterfly bomb' because, it is said now, there was no wound or mark on him. Tough luck – a decent fellow. Beginning to feel quite a veteran – a word, I think, much misunderstood in the past. To me it once suggested a lean, hardy fellow, with nerves of steel, whom nothing and nobody could frighten. Yet he would well be a near gibbering and useless idiot who survived (and so became a veteran) partly by luck, and partly by cowering, for as long as he was allowed to do so, at the bottom of his slit trench, and then only because of chronic neurosis and because he would starve rather than leave his trench to eat. I suppose this Battalion would soon rid itself of such a wretch. But Sergeant X was pretty near this state all the same and many of us must verge upon it at times. A veteran may grow more wily, I doubt if he ever grows more brave.

27 July 1944 – Colombelles

Colombelles is, or was, an odd sort of factory village – the ruined houses were like a series of pill-boxes made of grey-brown cement – in fact this is what at a distance, I thought they were. A co-operative store the main shop – all now hideously blasted – toy-like box *maisons* – closer to the factory the stench of death is ghastly, almost unbearable. The factory itself looks deathly still, except for the brown dust of German shells exploding there among its torn girders and sagging roofs. Rusty conveyor tube and trucks thrown everywhere. I thought, under the blue, half-storm sky and in the sunlight, that the buff of the cratered road made an Orpen[1]-like picture. Wish I could have four hours, and no intruders, to draw all this to show future generations the horror, filth and futility of war. Fat lot of good it would do, and I'm not technically competent anyway to try. Not a single hut or dwelling of Colombelles is left undamaged. A sordid sight, though I imagine it was no beauty spot in the first place. I suppose this gunfire is coming from 111th or 346th German Divisions near the coast?

28 July 1944 – 1210 hours

This part of Normandy has not been blasted by our bombers. Here were some troops about – mostly men of the recce unit of 51 Highland Div and an artillery Air OP unit, and it was strange to see their Austers dug into the field, up to wing level, all round the hedgerows and covered with camouflage nets. Passed a troop of 25-pounder guns – all well dug-in. Passed through a peaceful orchard full of 51st H Div recce personnel. Radios broadcast dance music and crooning, and I envied them the wholesome peace of their bivouac. Like 7th Armoured, 51st Highland is another division that has an unjustifiably inflated opinion of itself. Except for the hard-fighting 50th Division, the veteran desert divisions of Eighth Army do not seem up to the standard of other Second Army Divisions. Much was expected of them – but perhaps they have had enough, though there was no sign of their knowing this as we passed them. We marched at ease and our fellows matily enough greeted them as we passed, but they got only silence, or surly growls in reply, and one man shouted after us 'You shower would run a mile if you ever saw a bleedin' Jerry!' There was nothing our fellows could do about this – but it seemed an uncalled-for insult from men so pleasantly and comfortably installed – especially as we had stayed on for two days at Cagny to let their Division take over in comparative dryness and comfort. So back from the fresh green orchards, lush meadows and golden stubble and stooks of unspoilt country that reminded me of England, to the dreary, dangerous and dust-laden Hades of Colombelles. Better than the line though.

---

1. Sir William Orpen – First World War official War Artist.

Only at times, usually in the line, do I experience moments of acute depression and fear when I realize that we are stuck in a dangerous spot and kept there by the will of other mortals, and where another crowd of mortals, whose business it is deliberately to kill me, and who do their damnedest to perform this task at the will of yet another batch of mortals. And only at times like this, when I realize fully the absolute ruthlessness of war, am I tempted to panic, and to get out of my trench, and to run away from it all. The mood passes, but not I think, for all – and one is sorry for those for whom this panic is more or less chronic – and Sergeant X was one of them. He was much disliked, but I heard no one say 'Bloody good job' when he was hit – unless it was in sympathy. Yet how often, back in England, did not men crave that X should 'stop one' when we got on active service? Perhaps our not knowing when we might not 'stop one' ourselves includes some charity towards others? Even to those we do not like? It doesn't do to dwell too much upon the subject anyway – but cool analysis can do no harm.

7

The *Bocage*: Montchamp
31 July–8 August 1944

While 2WG was deployed elsewhere, 1WG was ordered to clear the villages of St Denis Maisoncelles and St Pierre Tarentaine which they did on 2 August. The gruelling battle for Montchamp began on 4 August. Having taken the village they were heavily counter-attacked and German tanks overran some of the positions of the leading companies and it was not until the following day that it was completely won. There were heavy casualties, including Lieutenant Colonel Heber-Percy, already their third commanding officer in Normandy. By the end of 9 August they had captured the high ground north of the Vire-Vassy road.

Murrell does mention at one stage, 'Seem to have got mixed up in days, nights and dates.' I have not checked these for accuracy and they remain as originally written in his journals.

<u>31 July 1944 – 1900 hours</u>

On the move again in great clouds of brown dust. Peaceful country – civvies looking, and waving, from the houses. There was an interesting Norman farm and church at Sallen (see plate no. 17, 'Norman Farmhouse at Sallen') – our harbour area last night – made a sketch, as we, the 'I' sec, were sent on to recce the harbour area. Battalion arrived at 0500 hours. IO told me to kip when possible, as there was much work in the offing for our section. Two more of our fellows stung today – they've had very little sleep. Advance seems to be going well. We are now in XXX Corps.

This countryside is charming and a wonderful break from the stinking ruins of Caen and Colombelles. But it's very bad tank country – though the Yanks seem to be doing OK. This is the *Bocage* country – wonder if we shall ever return Caen way? If the German front can be extended beyond Avranches then his line must begin to thin out somewhat. His 376th Infantry Division must be in a bad way by now. Wonder if 9th SS Panzer will come over to this front? Expect so – 10th SS too, I dare say. The Russians are going great guns – roll on!

Should be beer night tonight. Looks as though we've had it – the sorrows of war – could do with a drop too. One snag about advancing all the time is that armies run out of essential supplies, like fags and beer. The farm at Sallen was a sort of flakey grey-brown and very pleasant on the eye.

We pass through the Sherman tanks of 1st Battalion Coldstream Guards – and a young French civvy, with a pretty girl on his arm, has just waved us a friendly greeting, and Roberts, our driver, mused a while and then voiced, in his North Welsh accent, just what I was thinking: 'Here we are, fighting to liberate France, and all the Froggies iss out enjoying themselves an' taking the missus for a walk! In Bayeux yesterday morning all the blokes wass walking out with their tarts – Blotty goot issn't it?'

How refreshing to see this green, compact, countryside and these villages, untouched by war! People here seem happy to see us – and they wave to us – unlike the unfortunates of Caen. This is the nearest thing to a stunt-like English atmosphere so far – guess we'll soon discover it's no stunt!

Yankee troops passing in their lorries, and we greet each other cheerily enough. They travel, even in this peaceful area, clutching loaded weapons lying across their knees. Only the darkies seem to stare straight ahead – taking no notice of us. All American troops seem to wear steel helmets, even well behind the line. Must be an army order, I think. On through Balleroy, where, in the main square, stood a loudspeaker van relaying martial music to quite a crowd of rather gaily-dressed French civilians. This pleasant, hilly town is liberally hung with patriotic and Allied bunting. Noticed the Free French symbol – the Cross of Lorraine.

The dust raised by our column is terrific – it is (when we are on the move) like driving through thick fog.

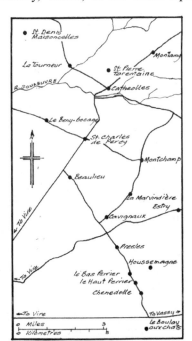

THE *BOCAGE* COUNTRY

2 August 1944 – 0600 hours

In this *Bocage* it's a bit like being in a jungle – everything is close and confined – it's not like a battlefield – we here see nothing of the enemy – or even of our own rifle companies – the orchards and woods and tiny fields bounded by trees growing out of 8 feet high banks – just seem to have swallowed up, not only our own battalion, our brigade and division, but the whole German and British armies on this front.

This makes life much safer for us of Battalion HQ – we can hardly be under enemy observation in such thick and hilly country – except on the narrow roads – and they are death-traps – German guns and mortars have got them taped, and vehicles, even at crawling pace, raise great clouds of dust as they go, and anywhere near the crest of a hill in the vicinity of a road is very dangerous. But I doubt if this close country is very safe for our rifle companies and for the attackers generally. It is ideally suited for defence – one is right on top of the enemy before one realizes it, and tanks in attack are pretty useless, though in defence they can be deadly. It is infantry country that demands good reconnaissance for success. It is 'cat and mouse' terrain, and all the advantage lies with the mice.

Even our air superiority does not count for very much here – except against enemy-held roads and even they must be mostly invisible from the air – they are virtually 'tree-tunnels' and the enemy can use the roads in the *Bocage* on more or less equal terms with us – they are just as dangerous and dusty for him as for us, but it must seem almost a holiday to Jerry to be more or less free from our constant air surveillance and assault. Relatively, he can come and go as he pleases – hence our abortive attack of last night against expected opposition from 21 Panzer Div. Jerry simply withdrew, unknown to us, and left us flaying empty air.

Another strange feature of this *Bocage* 'battle' is that many French civilians have stayed put in their homes and farms. We have bombed the bigger towns in the zone of operations – but no attempt has been made to create a 'bomb corridor' through the *Bocage* – it would be futile anyway; and so the civvies stay and take their chance of getting mixed up in some localized action where two opposing units meet and Jerry decides to hold on and fight it out in a rearguard battle for, generally, Jerry seems to be carrying out a slow withdrawal on this front, conforming, I suppose, to the threat of an American breakthrough on the left flank of the German front in Normandy. But some civvies, their homes and farms shelled and ablaze, are trekking back north and it is appalling to think of their trying to do so by using these deadly roads on foot, and these narrow thoroughfares are often half-blocked by knocked-out Sherman tanks and by German armour and vehicles destroyed and overturned in the adjacent ditches.

At about 2230 hours, just as we were digging in last night, we heard the now-familiar, but ever-frightening 'Whoo-whoo-whoo' of 'Moaning Minnies', and their sighing, sobbing whine seemed interminable as they came our way and we, like ostriches, pushed our heads down into our partially dug trenches, leaving our backsides in the air, to take their chance. But the shells went over our heads and burst among 3 Company who had just arrived, and were preparing to dig in. Lieutenant Luxmoore-Ball and Sergeant P.G. Hill were killed, and seven others wounded. Amazing how

Jerry found them – 3 Company must have shown a light – perhaps a truck switched on its headlamp for a second. These *Nebelwerfer* teams are red-hot, and these German troops are well trained as well as being much experienced in warfare. Another salvo of 'Minnies' fell – but further afield this time. We detest those sinister rocket weapons of his.

We are now still jogging along the road in the captured German Citroen half-track – it has now no reverse gear, so we, at least, must keep on advancing.

1130 hours

I write this crouching in a ditch, Sten cocked, grenades ready, to welcome two sections of Jerry infantry who are said to be advancing up the road towards our positions – report said only two minutes away – and they should be here by now. If they are daft enough to press on they'll be massacred, and I suspect it's a false alarm – though bullets are swishing about overhead now. Don't quite know what's happening.

We are, generally, superbly and abundantly supplied with maps in this campaign, and those of the Caen area are excellent – we were even issued with 'going' maps at 1:25,000 scale showing geological features that were advantageous (or disadvantageous) to an armoured advance – and we were issued with defensive overprint maps, also at 1:25,000 scale, showing enemy strongpoints, gun-pits, trenches, outposts etc, revised to within a couple of days of our attack. I noticed that many of these defence works that looked so formidable in the bright blue printer's ink on these maps, either were not there at all or were less formidable when we came to them on the ground. But as an Ordnance Surveyor I cannot help a sneaking pride in the RE's achievements in cartography for this campaign. But this *Bocage* country is a surveyor's nightmare. It is country that can be surveyed accurately only by conventional ground survey methods, and then only laboriously and with much difficulty.

The *Bocage* is wholly unsuited for aerial survey and this, I assume, is how the maps we are using now were made. And even RE survey (the best, I believe, in the world) can do no more than produce a 1:50,000 sketch-map of the *Bocage* by air survey. And these maps are not so much inaccurate in survey as in representation of detail, and in this they can be dead treacherous. Most roads are shown in red dotted (pecked) lines – their quality graded by width but, obviously this interpretation from air photographs is a bit by guesswork – and what is shown as a road may prove to be an impassable farm track, and vice versa, and it is only too easy to mistake one's route and, unless a compass is used, find oneself wandering about behind the enemy lines. But, even at best, a modern battle situation map is an untidy affair.

At 'O' group we carefully draw our advance routes or centre lines (C/Ls) in coloured chinagraph pencil on the talc-covered map, and mark up our objective for the day, and our proposed harbour areas for the night. And all looks very tidy, well-planned, organized and shipshape, and would no doubt, all work out as planned, but for one thing – the enemy. It is he who messes up our colourful, and quite pretty, situation maps. From intelligence reports we mark up known enemy dispositions in tidy blue circles, or ovals, with the units' designation written inside. We mark up our own and neighbouring units in red. And all seems set (on our maps) for a tidy, pitched battle in Blenheim or Waterloo style, and the battle begins, but not tidily, as at Waterloo. Reports come in of enemy contacts from our own divisions and recce units. Some enemy dug-in tanks here – A/Tk guns these – and identifications are often surprising – elements of one division seem mixed with others in battle groups of varying strength. I mark these dispositions in blue chinagraph on the Battalion situation maps, and very soon it becomes a jumble of little circles, or conventional signs for guns, mortars etc, and it looks as if our own troops are in for a bloody battle, and then, miraculously, quarter of an hour later, this apparently formidable opposition has been by-passed or overcome, and the victor is a mile or so on and virtually swanning his way forward.

On the other hand, a unit consistently reporting no contact or opposition, suddenly finds itself involved in a desperate, all-out battle against a force no one knew was there, and again the identifications will be of units belonging to a division we believed to be on someone else's front – but mixed with other units of a division we expect to find on our own front – and at the end of the day our situation map looks a bedraggled and sorry affair, a mass of blue chinagraph symbols and apparently inextricably mixed enemy units spread in a rather ragged line of varying depth across the map and intersecting our proud and prettily coloured centre lines – and we never seem to achieve our planned intentions. Only the arrival of the daily Brigade Intelligence summary enables us to tidy up, and simplify, our enemy identifications and dispositions, and only another 'O' group enables us to erase our ambitious centre lines and redraw them for the next attack. It is a relief to turn to the sit map we maintain of the Russian front where the map scale is so small that an advance of 30 miles hardly shows and one can indulge in broad, sweeping strokes to show 'the picture'.

<u>1500 hours</u>

We are still held up, and none of our objectives has been reached today. The sun is very hot and the metal of the half-track is almost too hot to touch. There is one distinctive and, I believe, large-calibre and long-range gun firing at us – we hear the report of its discharge and seem to wait ages for the shell to arrive. Innumerable fags are smoked to allay the awful boredom and fretful nervousness of hanging about on a road with no cover to hand, other than a roadside bank or ditch, while Jerry shells and mortars such an obvious target. Not that his fire is heavy, or even consistent (except for the one big gun) and he has some miles of troop and vehicle-jammed road to pick on. But it's still very trying to the nervous system, and there are times when one is tempted to scream abuse at the bloody fools (whoever they may be) who are causing the hold-up; because, for some strange reason, one feels safer on the move. An illusion I am sure. And I suspect that we are not even under direct observation and that Jerry may be shelling us 'from the map'. Observed fire would be more accurate and deadly than this, I think. But he may be able to see the great clouds of dust our columns make when on the move, and I suppose we are actually safer at standstill.

[Note added later: at times like this, when we were in convoy, and I had no trench or privacy, I would jot these notes and sketches down on message pads, or on odd bits of paper, and not in my diary notebook – and then in extremely brief and very abbreviated form, so that few men could have understood my notes, and I doubt if a German Intelligence officer could have done so either. The men of the 'I' sec knew, I think, that I kept these notes and that I was not the prolific letter writer I pretended to be. I often wrote them when others seized the opportunity of a halt, or a break, to doze or sleep, and I think I got much less sleep than my fellows, for this reason. I preferred to write – or draw.]

3 August 1944 – 1300 hours

Moved to here. Considerable shelling and mortaring going on – the road rather blocked up. We dug in – the soil here is rock hard. Had to send two of the section on M/Cs to Brigade HQ with returns of enemy casualties and, though Brigade HQ is back, and not forward, from here, they must use the roads and these are deadly dangerous. It's a horrible job detailing two men, or choosing rather, because every man in the section is quite willing to go. And I listen to every burst of shelling and mortaring, believing it to be falling on exactly that piece of road the DRs have reached.

The German opposition is stiffening on our front. I share a trench with 10 Morgan, a very definite advantage in this land of iron-hard soil; for these Welshmen from the mining valleys seem to have an almost nostalgic liking for digging, particularly here where the pickaxe is in use as much as the spade and, of course, in sharing a trench, the labour of digging it is halved.

The Battalion, like other battalions out here, leaves its trail through Normandy of tiny whitewashed wooden crosses and miniature cemeteries. And, so far as I know, I have personally lettered all these crosses and drawn upon each one a small coloured leek; and, though the Battalion has not yet been engaged in any particularly desperate fights, I still seem to have lettered a considerable number of these crosses since we first went into the line a month ago.

There was much small-arms fire this morning, and bullets are whistling about here now. Unlike mortars, bullets give no warning of their approach, but we have grown so used to bullets, either when working in the rifle butts – or on assault courses – or on the firing points, that we take little notice of them, until someone is hit, and that is rare in Battalion HQ. But only war can accustom the soldier to close bombardment by high explosives – thunder-flashes and other fireworks make an anaemic substitute and familiarity with the fearful, razor-jagged shrapnel of HE missiles breeds anything but contempt or indifference in me. But the French people here, seeing nothing of the battle in this thick country and seemingly unaware of the sinister difference in the sound of outgoing and incoming metal, go about their business nonchalantly enough on the farm and in the orchards. But they, men and women, show much pity towards our wounded brought by Bren-carriers or field ambulances from the battle and carried into the farm here, where our RAP is sited.

1520 hours

Can hear the Guards' Churchills going in now. These Churchills have a more pronounced squeak and clank than other tanks.

The coloured, life-sized effigies of Christ crucified in the wayside shrines amid the trees are startlingly lifelike. Jerry shells the roads every time he spots a dust-cloud, and here in the *Bocage* only roads can be used – there is no cross-country course for vehicles, and precious little for pedestrians.

The enemy seems to be trying to camouflage his Mark IV tanks to look

GERMAN "MARK IV" TANK KNOCKED OUT.

like Panthers and Tigers – though I think it is the sheets of metal he uses to protect tracks and sprockets etc against our PIAT bombs that confuses our people into mistaking Mk IV for heavier tanks, and it is the section's job to identify and list all KO'd enemy AFVs and supply their registration numbers to Brigade HQ, as well as to count accurately the enemy dead on our front, so that our army can avoid overestimating enemy losses as happened in Libya when several units would claim the same tanks as their own victims, and Eighth Army, believing the German armour to be only half its actual strength, dangerously underestimated its enemy. By recording registration numbers, no AFV can be counted more than once. Our PIATs seem to be working very well against German armour. One takes the work of the REs for granted, though it is no joke building bridges under fire.

2130 hours

This country is pleasant, and so close that it hides much of the horror of war and hides from us too the company and battalion battles that are fought quite near us – and this Caumont offensive is less a battle than a multitude of miniature battles fought by more or less isolated battalions and companies – and the *Bocage* favours the defence every time.

No recent news about the Yanks; it seems that Vire is **not** ours. The 1st Bill Browns have been mortared non-stop for thirty hours. And the officer reporting this remarked, in a typical Guards' style understatement, that the Grenadiers were 'not too happy about it'. They are in a dangerously exposed position. The din all about us hectic as the battle hots up – can hear our Vickers machine guns joining in now.

4 August 1944 – Command Post – 1515 hours

Meanwhile the Battalion advance continued – but now against no opposition, and we are now beyond our last set objective. Last night it seemed that we were up against toughish opposition – this morning – nothing! Though Jerry shells are still falling around here now; but the road, which last night was a deathtrap, is now comparatively safe. There's the 'whoosh' of his long-range gun again.

S is said to have shot off his own foot – that game's not worth it; and he's not the first in the Battalion to attempt to get out of it by a self-inflicted wound; and on the night when we were waiting formed up at Bayeux to go next morning into the Cagny attack, an officer came over and told the IO that one of our men (I couldn't catch his name) had just shot off his own foot with a Sten gun. The IO received the news in silence, and I am quite certain that his thoughts were exactly mine as he considered the matter. There is fleeting regard for the courage of a man who can deliberately shoot off his own foot; there is intense envy of this man who has now escaped, not only death, or possibly worse mutilation, but who is now relieved of the awful pre-battle anxiety that still afflicts the rest of us. Whatever else happens to him, he is sure eventually to see his home and family again – for men are no longer executed in our Army for self-inflicted wounds, as they were in the last war. He has escaped; but if we all did this there would be no Battalion, no fighting Army, left. And envy sharpens the rage one feels against this man who has pulled a fast one over the rest of us who must go on, and my anger coincided with Captain Robertson's who remarked, after the long pause, 'The sh*t – the rotten sh*t!' I find that men are reasonably tolerant towards those who show most fear – provided these men stick it. They will at least retain some self-respect at last. But the man who wounds himself can have no self-respect to start with. It is for this, I think, that he is held in contempt by his fellows.

Our rifle companies have been pretty badly shaken up, and have been under almost constant mortar and shellfire for long periods of time. Our losses are not grievous, but they are mounting now. We are expecting more prisoners in, and now they, even the Germans, expressively go through the motions of tearing off their badges and insignia and throwing them away and shouting 'Germany (or Hitler) kaput!' But not the SS – they remove their detested insignia as a precaution, but they do not shout 'finish'.

5 August 1944

We came under command of 44 Brigade of 15th (S) Division – the Cheux fellows, and the Battalion, or rather Prince of Wales and 2 Company, attacked the village of Montchamp. Until then our advance had met no opposition. But glum news came back to Battalion HQ as the evening wore on. It was an anxious time. PoW Company and 2 Company went in, found the village deserted and pushed on to the far end of it when suddenly they bumped into a counter-attack by a battle group of 9 SS Panzer Div, and this force included five Panther tanks, and in seconds Montchamp became an inferno of close combat and blazing houses. All our supporting weapons, tanks and anti-tank guns etc were jammed along the narrow road leading to the village and the two unsupported companies had to rely on their PIATs but, though the PIAT has proved satisfactory so far, and a Panther can be destroyed by this infantry weapon, the tank must be hit in a vulnerable spot, it must be in just the right position, and even then a degree of luck is needed. On this occasion everything was against the PIAT and the bombs just bounced off the armour of the massive Panthers who thus had things all their own way. The Germans isolated our two companies by laying down a heavy screen of shell and mortar fire through which only tanks could move and expect to survive. But our Bren-carriers (which were clear of the congested roads) went through this fire barrier to bring our wounded out of the blazing village. The carriers had no hope of engaging the Panthers, but, as at Arras in 1940 when Dicky Furness[1] died with them – over and over again, our Carrier Platoon behaves heroically in battle.

Command post went in with the two companies and got badly mauled by grenades and bullets, and Colonel Heber-Percy controlled the fight from his scout car until he was hit and badly wounded in the left shoulder, but he held on until the crisis was past, and was at last evacuated to hospital. But before he went he said that the Battalion had done marvellously, and that, from Heber-Percy, is high praise – he will be a great loss to the Battalion; and so we have now virtually lost four commanding officers in five or six weeks. Maurice Turnbull commanding 2 Company was killed and Sir Richard Powell of PoW Company missing, and almost certainly dead.

This is the grimmest fight we've had so far in this campaign, and casualties in the two rifle companies have been heavy – they have taken a severe knock, and those survivors I have seen have in their eye that faraway, punch-drunk look I first saw in the eyes of the stragglers of 15 (S) Div in the sunken road at Cheux after they had been overrun by Jerry flame-throwers and tanks, and there seems a strangely dignified humility, however temporary, in men who have just survived the horror and shock of a bad drubbing in close combat. This soon goes in most men, but immediately after the action one seems to be talking to a man who is not really here at all. It is a look I have also seen in the eyes of some German prisoners who have taken as much, or more, than they can really stand. And, talking to our survivors from Montchamp, I felt rather ashamed of the relative comfort and security of Battalion HQ in these *Bocage* battles. In such close country we remain concealed, and safe, from enemy attentions. 9 SS Panzer and 125 Panzer Grenadier Regiment still against us.

This slaughter in such beautiful, undulating and serene-looking countryside seems more hideous than on the open plains around Caen where one can actually see the panoramic mess of war and there, except on roads, one is never certain when one is under enemy observation, and Deg and Dai (51 Davies) following up the advance prior to Montchamp, reached the top of a hill on their motor-cycle – found all very quiet and peaceful, the view attractive – and so decided, while awaiting the next bound forward, leisurely to attend to the call of nature during which they discussed the beauty of the surrounding countryside. In fact they were in full view of Jerry's artillery OPs, and only seconds after they remounted the M/C and rode off down into the valley, a shower of shells fell upon the ridge and, had they lingered longer, Degville and Davies must both have been torn apart by this fire. A daft thing, especially for members of an 'I' Section to do.

---

1. Lieutenant the Hon C. Furness was awarded the VC posthumously.

But, though Battalion HQ gets it cushy now, we have lost a number of our own fellows in Montchamp – signallers and stretcher-bearers etc of HQ Company.

Today is sunny and fine again. Our guns are at it now, and there's some small-arms fire going somewhere near here. I nearly shot off my own foot last night. 10 Morgan and I were sitting on the earth parapet of our trench and cleaning our weapons, and I cleaned my Sten with the magazine still inserted as this (though illegal) makes the weapon easier to grip. Having cleaned it I automatically went through the motions of rifle-cleaning, cocked the mechanism, pointed the gun to earth and squeezed the trigger and I was badly shaken by my carelessness as the bullets splayed all round the toe of my boot, and 10 Morgan, sitting alongside me, seemed to jump a foot into the air as bullets ploughed into the earth within 2 feet of his backside. Fortunately the RSM's attention was diverted at that moment by the arrival of another batch of prisoners being doubled in at the gate leading to our orchard. Snowy was pretty savage (as he always is when the Battalion takes casualties) and he doubled this bunch up to the 'I' Sec in very quick time.

An almost continuous roar and clatter of tanks passing now. Who would have believed, had I actually shot up my own foot last night, that it was accidental? Makes one wonder if some such cases aren't accidental after all. The Sten is a cheap, but dangerous weapon. Strange that I should have written on this subject only a short while before the incident last night.

This morning I lettered one of our wooden crosses for the grave of a captured SS Panzer grenadier, who died on his way back to the ADS – also one of O'Neill of our Anti-tank Platoon. Poor old Paddy – he was a nice fellow too – funny, a Mick in the Welsh Guards. White butterflies are flying around my trench. It was a butterfly, I think, that caused the death of the German soldier in 'All Quiet on the Western Front'. Sweet nature and war don't really mix.

There's a ghastly bend just up the road from here that is now called 'Dead-Horse Corner' where lie a (or lay) a mass of dead enemy artillery horses caught there and slain by our guns or planes. The corner stank to high heaven so that the horses had to be buried on account of it.

Roberts has just handed me the remains of a bottle of English beer. I closed my eyes, put the bottle to my lips and drank the lovely stuff, and I could see for a few seconds the sunlit common and pubs and church at Chislehurst – and Stella too. I'm an idiot! Felt apprehensive last night; not, for once, on my own account, but for the Battalion. So many of our fine fellows being killed or wounded. Tanks are still moving up. Everyone praises the Royal Army Medical Corps drivers – say they're heroes.

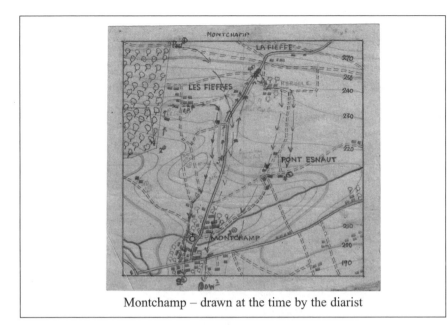

Montchamp – drawn at the time by the diarist

6 August 1944 – Orchard

GERMAN " PANTHER " TANK.

Now, after the battle, a more coherent picture of the Montchamp scrap emerges. The 19 SS Panzer Grenadier Regiment sent into the village about 100 infantrymen supported by four Panthers, and one Mk IV tank, plus, it is said two Tigers (but I doubt the Tigers – there is no evidence of their yard-wide tracks in Montchamp, and I am sure that some men in our rifle companies mistake the 49-ton – though massive – Panther for the 60-ton

111

Tiger). Our two companies, in spite of their losses in previous operations, probably outnumbered the Jerry infantry by forty or fifty men – I don't know exactly. The German infantry kept well by their tanks and did not come forward of their protection and the tank men, fluffing that we had no heavier supporting weapons than PIATs, adopted very bold tactics – they turned massed MG fire along the roots of all hedges where our men had, or may have, taken cover, and they used their 75mm guns against even isolated, or solitary targets, and it is said that Sir Richard Powell and his servant, having fired a PIAT bomb at a Panther, and seen the bomb bounce off the tank, were instantly fired at by the Panther's 75mm gun at very close range, and both men must have been instantly killed though, curiously, the officer's body has not been found in Montchamp.

BRITISH "PROJECTOR INFANTRY ANTI-TANK" (PIAT).

Our companies, caught on the hop in the stream of cannon and MG crossfire from the tanks, and dismayed by the failure of their PIATs to put a single tank out of action, were hopelessly pinned to the ground. A man in civilian clothing, wearing a white shirt and the blue working jean slacks of a French peasant (and presumably a Panzer grenadier in disguise) appeared at a cottage window and sniped at, and winged our CO and seconds later the sniper disappeared, killed by a stream of Sten bullets and by a PIAT bomb that blew him, and the window, to smithereens. The enemy tank commanders came in with open turrets and at least the PIATs disposed of these foolhardy, or brave, warriors, and some of our fellows managed to lob grenades into open turrets, which must have killed their crews but does not seem to have knocked out the tanks which were either driven, or towed, out of the village when the SS retired for no enemy tank remained in Montchamp.

Today a 3 Company man was brought into the RAP after being missing for thirty-six hours; he was discovered, wounded and conscious, but very delirious, in a very wet ditch. 3 Company was not involved in the Montchamp do, but this man had obviously been involved with German tanks, and he kept crying out over and over again – until he was jabbed and his wounds dressed, 'Tigers! – Tigers! – Tigers!' Poor devil. I wondered what fantastic nightmare was scourging his slap-happy wits. Before they withdrew the Germans heavily mined and booby-trapped the village – they have a craze for laying mines in old tank tracks in the ground.

Tales of SS fanaticism are confirmed by our fellows in Montchamp – 19 SS, sensing their advantage, came on with their tanks, shouting, screaming and actually singing patriotic songs, and this weird, macabre behaviour is confirmed by too many of our fellows for it to be exaggeration, though some guardsmen are convinced that these particular SS men were very drunk also. But their tactics were too shrewd for this, I think. Jerry captured one of our 2nd Battalion 3-tonner cooker trucks and later drove this vehicle down the road towards our own companies who, deceived, allowed it to approach near enough for the SS men in it to open fire on our fellows. The truck was swiftly shot up and set afire and its occupants killed, but one man, the driver, or cab passenger, with blood pouring from his mouth, broke out hideously into a patriotic German song as he tried to get out of the blazing vehicle, but he collapsed with his stomach resting on the cab door, his head and trunk hanging down outside the truck, and he alternately sang and screamed with pain as the flames devoured his lower regions, and he died. Small wonder that troops who will fight as fanatically as this provide such stubborn defence to our advance through the *Bocage*.

Nevertheless our fellows were not all that impressed by the infantry who took quite a pasting when they actually came to grips with our companies – it was our powerlessness against the tanks, and the poor performance of the PIATs that shook our men, and some of them are rather bitter that the troop of supporting 2nd Battalion Coldstream tanks did not manage to get into Montchamp, and some believe that the troop commander, hearing that there were Tiger tanks in Montchamp, deliberately hung back, knowing that, even with one of his tanks a 17-pounder, he still had little or no chance against these German monsters. But I find it hard to believe that any Guards' officer would deliberately hold back, and certainly, had they not been involved in the same jammed-up road, our own Carden-Lloyds and A/Tk guns would have been pushed through into Montchamp and through the curtain of fire that cut off PoW and 2 Companies. Our carriers, because they were clear of the jammed road, went in without hesitation to support our companies and evacuate the wounded.

These men of PoW Company still have that odd, humble, yet dignified look in their eyes, and they tell of horrible happenings quietly, convincingly, and without the bombast of men who seek to impress others who were not there. What they say now is obviously the truth as they saw it – they have no need to exaggerate. In fact they seem almost unaware of the person to whom they are talking. All the men say that it was wrong of us to get over-confident, because we have overrun objectives without meeting much resistance, to advance against an objective without adequate recce and before our supporting weapons were able to debouch from the narrow *Bocage* roads. We have been taught a lesson – we knew SS Panzer Troops were on our front, but this sudden confrontation with 9th SS took us by surprise and at great disadvantage.

1330 hours

Now on the move again – up towards the guns once more, and this orchard, so noisy in the battle when we came to it, is now so calm and peaceful under the hot August sun. Horses graze, cockerels crow, and not a shell or mortar has fallen in the orchard since we moved in here, though the road has been under fire, and so have acres behind us and on our flank, and this is the peculiarity of battle in the *Bocage* – whole areas, excepting the roads, remain unscathed by war – only here and there, and generally in villages like Montchamp do small but ferocious and very destructive combats between opposing battle groups occur, and then, as the supporting artillery and mortar fire comes down, a village, or a ridge is wrecked by the sordid devastation of close combat, and I am glad that the civvies in this farm have got away with it. We move now.

1400 hours

Halted again – beyond 'Dead Horse Corner', which still reeks horribly though many horses were burned or buried. Our rifle companies had more or less a rest last night, i.e. the Battalion remained in position, but the battle drifted beyond us. Some 9th SS prisoners through our hands last night. Among them an Alsatian and a Hungarian. Former said that he was forced to join the SS compulsorily, and under threat of death – and the Hungarian said he wanted to join us and to fight against Jerry because he had been duped into joining by tales of privilege and higher pay etc. He added that the Hungarians now fighting in SS units are only waiting their chance to desert. He is obviously a mercenary and his is not a moral conversion. He also said that many even of 9th SS were non-Germans, but this, in view of the fight this division and 10th SS Panzer are putting up, I find hard to believe.

The charm of these valleys and heavily wooded hills is appealing and very English – but it's very sticky country to fight in (see plate nos. 19, 20, 21, 'Scenes at Montchamp'). We pass two dead Jerries lying plumb across a side road, and we halted near another dead Jerry kneeling in a ditch and bent forward as if just exhausted – this in Montchamp – made a quick

1. Charles Murrell, April 1940.

2. On board *Scythia*, en route to Gibraltar, September 1939. Left to right: Wilcox, 22 Harris, Cureton, 25 Williams, Murrell.

3. Intelligence Section – 1st Battalion Welsh Guards, 1942. Left to right, back row: Pullen, 25 Williams, Degville, Stacey, Murrell. Front row: Blanchette, Sgt. Burgess, Captain Miller, Sgt. Wilcox, Carey.

4. Dawn breaking over Dunkirk beaches during withdrawal, end of May 1940.

5. Dunkirk, 1940.

6. Camouflaged American LST no. 541 lying off Tilbury – loaded with Divisional tanks and vehicle.

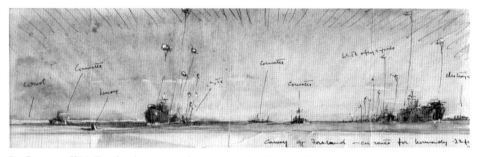

7. Convoy off N. Foreland, en route for Normandy, 22 June 1944.

8. Typhoons attacking 12th SS tanks and shells falling behind hangars on Carpiquet Aerodrome, from OP at 2030 hours 6 July 1944 – Caen in background.

9. 5th Guards Armoured Brigade moving up to attack south of Caen, morning of 18 July 1944. Men of 1st Battalion washing prior to follow-up by 32nd Infantry Brigade.

10. 1st Battalion Welsh Guards attacking Cagny, afternoon of 18 July 1944.

11. Cagny, 20 July 1944.

12. RSM 'Snowy' Baker, Cagny, July 1944.

13. Captain Andrew Graham, December 1944.

14. After the rain at Cagny only carriers and jeeps would be used to remove the wounded – jeeps were adapted to carry stretchers.

15. Night raid, Colombelles, 25 July 1944.

16. Rest area, Colombelles, 27 July 1944.

17. Norman farmhouse, Sallen – Battalion harbour area before *Bocage* battle, 1 August 1944.

18. Untitled and unfinished – Le Haut Perrier, 13 August 1944.

Scenes at Montchamp, 6–7 August 1944.

19. **Above:** 'Written off' 9th SS.
20. **Left:** Prisoner of 9th SS Panzer Division.
21. **Below:** Some graves of PoW Company.

22. & 23. The road to Brussels, 3 September 1944.

24. Impression of Antwerp Cathedral, 30 October 1944.

25. Convent at Sittard from school attic, 19 November 1944 (unfinished on account of enemy shelling).

26. Nijmegen Bridge or Grenadier Bridge, 3 November 1944.

27. Intelligence Section in hen coop, Venraij Sector, Holland, 5 November 1944.

28. Operations room, prior to 'Veritable', Vught, Holland, 8 February 1945.

29. Winter in Holland, January 1945. Cromwell tanks of 2nd Battalion, Welsh Guards.

30. The church of Hoegaarden, 29 January 1945.

31. Churchill tank of Independent Tank Brigade, Hassum Station, Germany, 27 February 1945.

32. 5th Guards Armoured Brigade moving up to concentration area via Hassum Station, Germany, February 1945.

33. Sherman and flail tanks moving through morning mist towards Goch, early morning of 28 February 1945.

34. Shell-torn cemetery at Siebengewald, Holland, 4 March 1945.

35. **Left:** In the Rhineland Battle, near Kevelar, Germany, 5 March 1945. German mill and Divisional Advanced Dressing Station.

36. **Below:** Churchill tank with spigot mortar passing a 2nd Battalion Cromwell – Wetten, Germany, 6 March 1945.

sketch of him in his camouflaged smock. Gruesome, I suppose, but an odd way to die. Montchamp a pretty awful mess.

7 August 1944 – 0620 hours

Stand-down has just been ordered – it is almost light – a bird chirping in the apple tree above my trench – a cockerel crows. Somewhere the click of a pickaxe as somebody improves his slit trench – our 25-pounder guns fire single ranging shots – a misty-blue morning. We are now dug in with the rifle companies on the high ground they gained on Saturday evening and we look down on the village of Montchamp – a name our Battalion will remember for a long time yet.

Prince of Wales Company sergeants now going round rousing their men again – those who got down to kip again after stand-down. Talked with men of PoW Company last night and one officer says that Jerry's tank/infantry co-operation is better than ours, i.e. their pattern in *Bocage* country is that Panthers, intending to occupy an adjacent meadow, move up to the surrounding hedge and push through it – their 75mm gun shells each corner and the centre of the opposite hedge while the tanks' MGs open fire all along the roots of surrounding hedges, firing about a foot above ground level, thus effectively pinning down any troops using the hedges and ditches as cover – it was death for any man to look up – then the tanks crash into the field and up to the opposite hedge – firing all the time – their infantry following close behind the tanks – not our idea of tanks drawing the enemy fire to enable our infantry to infiltrate round the hedges bordering the meadow. The same officer said that men have definitely lost confidence in the PIAT – the hull of one Panther was hit dead square – as were the tracks of another – both with no result, and this at ranges from 30 to 50 yards. He added that German infantry were easy meat away from the protection of their tanks – and their tactics were not very subtle.

It is difficult to assess who was to blame for the Montchamp fiasco – it seems to have been PoW Company's fault for marching forward and outstripping their supporting tanks, carriers and A/Tk guns still jammed tight on the narrow road and, because they were short of ammo, our supporting artillery could fire for only three minutes and so our two companies were left unsupported and in the open against the well co-ordinated SS counter-attack which included the infantry, five tanks, armoured half-tracks and ample artillery and mortar fire.

As regards the action itself, our companies took them up more than we knew at the time – and we took more prisoners than they and these prisoners confirm that the SS losses were heavy and it is believed that Jerry not only removed his wounded men and tanks, but also many of his dead as well. And the SS seem, like the Guards, to look after their own, whether dead or alive. All was very confusing, and none ashamed to say how, when the tanks ran amok among them they, in various ways, got out once the order to do so was received in dribs and drabs – near anarchy this to guardsmen accustomed to moving always in disciplined cohesion, and all speak highly of Gerry Fowke who took over when the CO was hit, and who got the survivors out. A quiet, likeable officer, Gerry was always a favourite subaltern on Bank picquet in peacetime. Even so, our fellows withdrew by sections under NCOs or senior soldiers, but platoon and company cohesion was impossible once the tanks got loose.

Our fellows speak highly of the guts of these SS men – of their screaming, shouting and singing fanaticism – of a tank commander sitting on the lip of the turret, firing, cowboy-style, with his automatic Luger at any hostile target he saw and he seemed to know many of the supporting infantry by name: 'Panzer Grenadier so-and-so, do this, or do that!' and he ably directed the fight until ten bullets and a PIAT bomb ripped him to pieces. Men speak of the ruthlessness of house-to-house fighting – of a sergeant bursting into a room, SS men raised their hands in surrender, and how the sergeant cut them all down with automatic fire – of how on such an occasion a man, keyed to a very high pitch of fear and excitement and with finger on trigger, does not stop to think once he sees an enemy uniform, but automatically squeezes his trigger before he himself gets it – the niceties of Geneva convention rules are hard to observe by men keyed to such a high degree of tension.

Major Miller is up to his neck in guts, but this is the second time he has gone forward of his objective and suffered heavy casualties as a result. Courage, without a sound co-ordinated plan, is useless in modern warfare.

Summaries have noted that SS troops, though reputedly sadistic, and even lethal, vandals towards civilians and property, are militarily very correct in their dealings with enemy soldiers – at least towards those enemy troops they respect. And the behaviour of the SS in Montchamp towards our wounded seems to confirm this – they treated our men's wounds and left food and water for two days with them – they even said that they would not take our wounded back with them when they withdrew, because of the difficulty of getting wounded men back to their ADS – adding that our wounded would be more comfortable and stand more chance of survival if left there until our troops re-took the village. Our CO also sat on the roof of his scout car directing 2 Company and PoW Company – he's a maniac too, and he too potted at everything hostile with his revolver. Lucky he wasn't killed.

The general was here yesterday, and he is extremely pleased with the Battalion. The Micks too put up a good show at Maisoncelles. The general added that the 'big picture' is terrific and, if our situation map is accurate, then Jerry really is in a bad way.

8 August 1944 – 1515 hours

Moved to here and we dug in again – this time in softer earth in the ground of a delightfully fascinating château built with a curved facade and with beautiful grey slate roofs and we are dug-in amid huge, lofty oak trees and near a tree avenue that leads up to the superb house.

Degville was made up to lance corporal yesterday – had to don his best BD and march in dead reg to CO's. Brian made up too – am glad – they're good blokes.

We have just had a lecture from our new CO (the unbearable Major Gresham). He spoke of the men's criticism of 2nd Coldstream tanks not supporting our companies at Montchamp – saying the fault lay entirely with our own Battalion. Here I agree – but one wonders if there may not be some truth about the Coldies tanks holding back? The Major threatened punishment to any man caught criticizing the Coldstream officer I/C the tank troop.

The new CO added that the Montchamp operation was a great success, and so it was, until we went on beyond our final objective and got a bloody nose in the village itself.

French horses and carts go up and down this road now – yet only a few days ago it was unhealthy for even a tank to do so. Tactical unit signs blossom at gates as a road becomes safe, or safer, and one of the most ominous sights in the *Bocage* is a dead quiet and apparently peaceful stretch of open road, with no sign of life or movement – of tactical signs – or of war about it. But even when a road is under intense enemy fire, some intrepid sappers plant mine-warning signs on the verges, and erect other warning signs near the tops of hills. 'Slow – one (or five) mph. dust brings shells – you have been warned.' These signs also put the breeze up the wayfarer, but they do reassure him that, however dangerous the road, British troops have already passed this way. But the peaceful, tree-avenued lane, deathly quiet except for the cooing of wood pigeons and the humming of insects, is far more frightening – it is the unknown, intensely sinister and menacing in its rustic and summery charm. It is the parlour into which the spider invites the fly – and one is aware of the nerve-racking strain such places must impose upon the men of the Household Cavalry whose job it is to push their armoured cars down these tree tunnels and menacing avenues on reconnaissance, or on patrol.

Fresh rations today – OK too. The section clubbed round today to collect some fags and rations for some importunate and wretched refugees. The refugees here have hung some tiny baby washing on a line strung between trees. Our section is gradually acquiring more German than British kit, equipment and weapons. Very restful here, but I fear the bull may start at any moment – drill parades, inspections and so on – especially with Gresham as CO. IO getting into a rage because his servant, 51 Davies, was out on duty with the section last night and Rob needed something done for his own comfort. These officers behave like stupid and spoilt children at times. To hell with an officer's servant job – particularly when the RSM asks one of them 'Have you dug your master's trench yet?'

One will live in one's own junk-hole for a fortnight – yet on coming to a new area where there are already trenches dug, one does not fancy them, and generally we dig our own new ones if the situation is not too unsafe. Haven't worked this out yet – think it may have something to do with a superstitious fear or revulsion that the previous tenant is deceased – and there is almost a phobia against occupying German trenches – for in these the peculiar German smell lingers for a long time after they have been evacuated.

I hurriedly lettered more white crosses before we left yesterday, and each one had its leek. I don't like doing this job – though I do it ungrudgingly, however pushed I may be at the time. The Adjutant will not come near me when I am lettering a cross and I think some other fellows regard my task with the same slight repugnance with which civvies regard an undertaker or a funeral monumental mason. But the RSM's attitude in this is robust enough. He sees to it that every grave is as posh as time and circumstances will allow and the Padre's sorrow, and the sincere care with which he buried our dead, is comforting to those still alive. Not only does he and the RSM ensure that everybody buried has the man's identity disc with it, but they also put one of our round, grey tobacco tins into the mound of each grave; inside is a description of the dead man – number, rank, name – just in case my lettering (in Indian ink on the whitewashed wooden cross) should fade before the IWGC can transfer the body to one of their fine cemeteries.

I took particular care over poor old Sheppard's cross – a quiet, reliable, and very lovable fellow whose wife and kids must have adored him. Exactly what the RSM feels about all this, I am not sure, and it doesn't really matter, because, in his gusty, boyish way he does his damnedest to make every grave as posh as the next. He is very angry when we get a pasting and lose a number of dead, and when this happens he gets us up to get an extra heave-on our prisoners when they are brought into Battalion HQ. How much sorrow, if any, he feels for the individual dead, I don't know. War makes one a bit callous in this respect as, I suppose, in even the finest of hospitals, doctors and nurses must acquire a degree of callousness towards death where it occurs so often – otherwise, I imagine, they could not carry on. And the soldier in war is only too well aware that he may be the next 'for it' as I wonder, with macabre curiosity, who will letter a cross for me if I snuff it out here. The Padre placed a sprig of phlox on Sheppard's and on others' graves, and where our miniature cemeteries are near civvies, the graves are massed with flowers by the French.

All German prisoners seem to carry on them some liquorice-like, black, yeasty bread and many have cider in their water bottles and crushed fags and packets of baccy – and most of them carry a number of snapshots on them – obviously wartime snaps – and there seems to be no shortage of films in Germany as there is in England. Always there is the rather tattered wallet – generally a broken piece of mirror – they are more vain I think than our fellows – bunches of letters – pocket knives, and among these SS plenty of contraceptives. Some religious and pornographic literature, and obscene photographs – though not all SS prisoners carry the latter.

8

The *Bocage*: Le Bas Perrier and Chenedolle 10 August–17 August 1944

The final action of the 1st Battalion, now under the command of Lieutenant Colonel Gresham, in Normandy was to be near Le Bas Perrier, an action in which the whole of 32 Guards Brigade and some of the armour of the Division were involved. The 1st Battalion took over positions around Le Bas Perrier from the 1st Battalion Herefordshire Regiment in the early hours of 10 August. It was an uncomfortable position with Le Haut Perrier in front of them, Houssemagne on their left flank and the long ridge north of Houssemagne which lay well behind them and which was in enemy hands. They received orders to attack Le Haut Perrier and Chenedolle on the morning of the 11th and then to push south to cut the Vire-Vassy road.

The action was difficult, though successful, and by 16 August they had crossed the Vire-Vassy road and occupied positions based on Boulay aux Chats. The fighting in Normandy for the 1WG was now over.

10 August 1944 – Le Bas Perrier

Another glorious day – hot and sunny. We moved off at midnight. We crawled along the road in our vehicles showing dimmed convoy lights – white tracer shells went up from the front line. A large fire blazed on our right – I believe from Vire – and some glowing lights added to the menace that troops who approach the front line by night will always know – brilliant flashes from the mouths of our artillery as we pass through our gun lines – and the crump-crump of enemy shells landing. By day one can travel at only one mph on these roads – the enemy see the dust – and he shells TFO.

Our fellows who took over from 11th Armoured say that the men they relieved, the Herefords, were like men sick – and some of them even left behind their packs and equipment in their haste to get away from the dreadful ridge. They had been there only twenty-four hours, but it was a very trying ordeal, and some of 11 Armoured Div anti-tank gunners had been there longer and were even more slap-happy – the gunners generally get less rest than the infantry – and that's precious little. It seems a hellish sort of position all round. One of our own 17-pounder A/Tk guns is waiting to get a Panther which only shows its nose to shoot and then withdraws behind cover. Two of our Bren-carriers hit and are now blazing relics. The enemy SS are very close, and it is fatal for our fellows to get out of their slit trenches in daylight.

We captured a German engineer, acting as infantryman, this morning. An encouraging sign that the SS on our front are very short of riflemen. It is 9th SS who still face our Battalion. Jerry's shelling a lot, but nothing has fallen here yet – touch wood! Brought our order-of-battle maps up to date. German 'Moaning Minnies' are fearsome things – and the Russians' more melodramatic, but very fitting, name for them obviously has appeal. One of our fellows was brought into the RAP, wounded and delirious, and over and over again he kept repeating: 'Sobbing Sisters – the Sobbing Sisters!' The order, system and administration of this campaign are in startling contrast to that of 1940. These SS units facing us must be very tired by now. Someone is cheerily shouting 'Tea up! Come an' get it!'

War reminds me of a film I saw: 'Night Must Fall'. I dread the night in war – it seems much more terrifying than day, though, for once, our rifle companies must welcome night now, for they cannot stir from their trenches by day. It's a grim position on the Bas Perrier ridge – the Herefords did not exaggerate. Guess I'm gifted, or cursed, with too vivid an imagination – for this, I think, is what makes cowards of men. Let's go and get some tea, 'Char for Charlie' – good stuff tea – better than beer sometimes. CQMS seems peevish these days. Officers from the recce party guide us into our new positions by such signposts as 'past KO'd Mk IV smelling of BO (body odour)' – 'past burnt-out Boche half-track' – 'powerful smell of dead cow' – 'two graves alongside road' – 'smashed crucifix' etc, etc.

11 August – Le Bas Perrier – 0645 hours

The husky click of mortars being fired and bursts of heavy and light MG fire and artillery fire – the barrage opened up at first light, and for a while we were shelled by our own 5.5 medium guns – gunners say that the barrels are worn too much, and this causes inaccuracies in range. Can hear MG 42s in action – so Jerry's still around and fighting back, and German counter-barrage and defensive fire task shells are dropping around the Battalion now. But it's a lovely morning and birds are singing. The 'Pah-pah-brrr' of,

I believe, a *Spandau*. Muffled crumps over the ridge – they're searching for our mortars, I think.

0810 hours

Much small-arms activity still – but receding – so looks like some success. A lot of enemy artillery and 'Minnie' fire over on the ridge, the sun is rising, and through the high hedges and dust, he is radiating golden beams – rather like the Japanese flag.

My four motor-cyclists went off at 1615 hours – hope OK. One can hear the unmistakable sound of Churchills in action. Chenedolle (already christened 'China Doll') is the village in dispute beyond the Le Bas Perrier ridge. Laugharne has gone off in search of milk.

1150 hours

More Jerry mortaring and arty fire – some quite near. Don't know what is their target – unless it's the road. Coldstream Guards are attacking now. 08 Williams has been killed. Poor old Bill – one of the best.

1630 hours

The battle is still on. Sixty-three men have already passed through the Battalion RAP – I don't know how many of the Battalion have been killed – and now the RAP, sited in a small quarry near here, has been hit by a salvo of shells; it was chock full of casualties and the carnage is appalling. The MO and his Medical Sergeant (Dobbs) wounded too badly to carry on. Grove, whose kidneys were hanging out of his body from a previous wound was (perhaps mercifully) torn apart by the shells and instantly killed, but many others, who may have lived, were also killed in the RAP. Our MO was a good fellow. Hope he's not too badly hurt.

As proof of the quality of our SS opponents, we have, so far, had only four prisoners through our hands – indeed, there is a nasty rumour afoot that neither side intends taking live prisoners.

Five Panthers have been knocked out in our area – one by a 3 Company PIAT. Good show – after the poor performance – or bad luck – of the PIATs at Montchamp – 3 Company report that they have killed many Germans. The prisoners were of 9th SS. Had to send two more 'I' fellows up that deadly road to CP. I hate this. It seems that every time my motor-cyclists set off a deadly burst of hate descends upon exactly that part of the road where I estimate them to be. The grand weather continues, but everywhere is a fog of fine dust.

I estimate that it takes Jerry about a minute and a half to range on to the crossroads. At least it takes them one and a half minutes to observe the disturbed dust and then fire. But by that time our people have usually gone – if not in a column. Deg and Trevor are back here and lie here kipping –

out to the wide with tiredness. They're good fellows – may they be looked after. The IO insists I remain with the maps at Battalion HQ and not act as a DR. Only when the Section mans an OP do I join them now.

Everyone asks for news – there are plenty of rumours, but it is not an 'I' sergeant's job to spread these. Strangely, authentic Army news is always, for us, behind the BBC news bulletins. Considerable flak flying about last night. These losses of ours depress me.

<u>1907 hours</u>

We have lost touch with CP – always an ominous sign – though the shelling seems to have died down a little. Wish to Christ Brian and Dai would turn up – they out counting German dead and captured equipment. Mr Koppel, looking at the situation map, said 'It looks more healthy now – the front.' The RSM replied, 'It does in the papers, Sir.' And that about sums it up for us – there's nothing very healthy about Chenedolle and the Bas Perrier ridge just now. These SS facing us are fighting like demons. They're shelling the road again – Damn!

<u>2005 hours</u>

Stand-to. I have a ghastly headache, but all our fellows, bar Trevor, are back now. Everyone here in Battalion HQ looks glum – it's been a sad day for the Battalion and the Brigade too. Watched Typhoons and bombers strafing Jerry tanks le Busq way. Encouraging sight. Here's Trevor – thank heaven!

<u>12 August 1944 – Le Bas Perrier – 1900 hours</u>

RAF bombed our lines – urgent calls for ground identifications strips and celanese triangles – and yesterday we were shelled by our own guns – almost the last straw this for the stricken rifle companies.

Have just finished lettering six more crosses. I went over to our little local 'cemetery'. Each company has it own miniature cemetery – ours consists at present of seven graves – mostly wounded men killed when the RAP was hit – the side of each grave is carefully turfed – all are in line, as if on parade – all are neat and spruce and tidy.

Tony had joined me at the graves, and we stood admiring Snowy's handiwork and wondering just what the huge RSM really thought about it all – he who had, at some time or other, bullied and nagged and bagged these dead men who were now permanently AWOL from his jurisdiction. And we both felt that the RSM's obviously sincere sympathy was slightly tinged with the annoyance that an over-possessive parent might feel towards one who had taken away one of his children – annoyance that these men were no longer under his orders and control – annoyance that soldiers not of the Brigade of Guards, and therefore soldiers of a lesser breed, should – or could – kill a British guardsman of his, the RSM's Battalion.

But there was no malice in our whimsical conjectures. Snowy is good out here. The evening sun on the white crosses and the trim graves under a leafy hedge in a Normandy meadow gave an impression of peace and quiet, and inevitably I thought of Rupert Brooke's verse, 'If I should die, think only this of me.'

We left the graves and walked back to the bivouac where somebody was whistling 'The Merry Widow'. A strange coincidence – though I wondered if there was not perhaps some association of ideas here – it could be, though the whistler sounded cheerful enough – and life goes on.

My nerves seem badly strained. I think that yesterday's casualties and worry about the Section the main cause. Hope I'm not 'cracking up'. Strange if so because where this *Bocage* fighting has been pretty lethal for the Battalion as a whole, it has been dead cushy for me personally compared with Cheux and Cagny. With the Battalion taking a bit of a knock one feels out of it – not part of one's unit – back here. Strange that my morale should droop because I did not participate closely in something I really desperately wished to avoid. I got something of the same feeling, only to a lesser degree, when I managed to dodge some particularly hard and unpleasant stunt back in England. A sense of guilt – almost of worthlessness.

Brian 'won' 4,000 francs from prisoners – he shared this between the Section – good of him.

13 August 1944 – Le Bas Perrier

Another smashing day of sun and heat. All very quiet on our front, and the enemy had withdrawn and contact with him lost altogether, though his guns are still lobbing shells onto the roads near here. So two Acorn [note added later: 'ACORN' – Wireless code name for Intelligence Units] personnel were ordered to report to CP this morning at first light and were instructed to go forward of the Battalion and establish an OP watching the Vire-Vassy road and as much of our front as the close nature of the *Bocage* would allow.

Brian Hoare and Herb Stacey went forward in the misty first light, but could see nothing from the high ground beyond Le Haut Perrier, and so they went forward until they could observe the road, and that, because of the mist, was almost on the road itself! And a mile and a half forward of our leading rifle company. And here, when the mist cleared a little, they found themselves plumb on top of a German standing patrol. They had taken with them a signaller and a D5 field telephone, and they reported back what they saw. But with full daylight the strong German patrol became active and so inquisitive, that our OP had at last to get out of it sharp, leaving the D5 behind, but destroying a length of the tell-tale cable leading from it. They certainly had guts to venture so far into this no-man's-land, but I cursed their folly as I and 51 Davies prepared to go up on his M/C to relieve Brian and Herb – for at this time the OP was still in position on, or very near, the Vire-Vassy road, along which German transport and troops still passed.

SIGNALLER USING DS. FIELD TELEPHONE (LINE).

We had had our dinners early to let the two 'I' men in the OP get back for their food; and my personal anxiety about going to man an OP over a mile forward of our rifle companies was not soothed by the RSM who had just returned from CP with hair-raising tales of the dangerous position in which Herb and Brian had established themselves. Obviously the IO, now at CP, approved or he would have ordered them back; and, as I was next 'for it' with the IO's servant Davies, I could not suggest to the IO that the OP should be withdrawn from its present situation, which was virtually within the enemy's line. And I found Snowy's semi-jocular 'Well – best of luck Sgt Murrell, been nice knowing you' not only tactless, but intensely alarming and irritating also, and as Dai and I got astride his bike and prepared to depart I was aware of Battalion HQ's interest in us, as if we were doomed men; and I later discovered that this audacious OP was the talk of the whole Battalion – which was not in action at the time, and so had little else to think about.

The powerful bike crept at two mph over the crests of hills and past the laconic 'Dust Brings Shells' warning boards, and on past the grimmer signs of ditched British vehicles wrecked and burnt by German shells, and much smashed German equipment lay ditched also. Even at this speed the dust is awful – one gets black from it. So down into a scenically attractive, but foully odorous, valley, passing on our right the village of Presles – the place Jerry's been pasting so liberally. Towards us came another M/C carrying Brian and Stacey and we were surprised and very relieved to see them. Not only had they gone forward to the Vire-Vassy Road, but a Signals truck, laying cable, had followed them down the road through Chenedolle, and had actually remained in their OP for some hours reporting what they saw, and had evacuated it only a short time before we met them on the road, and that was when they realized that they were in the area held by Jerry's standing patrol.

Unknown to themselves (until they reported back to CP) they had established the OP inside one of our artillery defensive fire task zones, and when they reported the presence of the Germans, down came our own artillery right on top of the OP – an unnerving experience, but they escaped back through this fire, which pinned Jerry down and, had it not been for our own DF barrage, Brian reckoned the Jerry patrol must have overrun the OP and that he and Stacey must have been killed or captured. They went off back to Battalion HQ and their dinner, and 51 and I continued our slow and unnerving ride to CP through the malodorous but relatively attractive countryside. Only as we neared the Haut Perrier ridge, where our rifle companies and CP lay, did the scenery suddenly and violently change.

Here, in a few days of savagely fierce fighting, a sector of the lush, leafy, summer-green *Bocage* has been transformed into a wilderness of utter destruction. Here the hedges have almost disappeared where tanks and guns and carriers charged through them – the whole area is criss-crossed by hundreds of tank tracks – great trees have been felled and withered and burnt by shellfire, and the place is pockmarked by shell craters – and still smouldering, or burning, British and German tanks litter the zone, as do the grey-black helmets of the enemy, each with its SS flash in black on a silver shield. Thick layers of whitish-grey dust have now settled over this awful spot, so that there is no colour left at all – all is monochrome – like a scene from hell – as if someone had sliced a portion of the 1916–17 Somme and stuck it, with mischievous and macabre humour, atop a hill in the scenically beautiful *Bocage* country of Normandy. The destruction here is probably no worse than the anarchistic chaos of Colombelles – but there it was general; here it is an inverted oasis of destruction in an area otherwise superficially untouched by war; and this indeed is the pattern of war in the *Bocage*.

It needs very little imagination to appreciate what our companies (and the enemy's companies too) have endured on this, and on the Bas Perrier ridge, or to understand the eagerness of the Herefords to be gone when we came in to relieve them. But all is quiet on the ridge now – three Panthers lie knocked-out within 50 yards or so of CP. The place abounds in hideous sights and evil smells. Tank men seem to die more horribly than most others. (We've just been machine-gunned and bombed on this ridge by planes we believe to have been Thunderbolts – Snowy rushed around spreading celanese ground recognition panels and strips. Perhaps Jerry is using captured planes against us? The planes had Allied markings. They caught us on the hop – the bastards! No AA fire went up at them until it was too late – everyone reached for their guns and cover – don't know how many – if any – of our fellows hit, but they have set one of our ammunition lorries on fire – always an alarming occurrence, if one is anywhere near to it.)

When Dai and I arrived at CP we learned – to my relief – that the OP idea had been called off. This being so I had a bit of a toot to the IO that the OP had been so far forward – but Rob was as astonished as everyone else when Brian opened up communication with CP, via his D5, and gave his position. Their orders had been to establish the OP just the other side of the Haut Perrier ridge whence they could observe the Vire-Vassy road – they had carried out their instructions to the letter so far as the road went. Rob was obviously pleased with his two men. In lieu of a new OP, the IO told us to go into Chenedolle, occupied by our troops yesterday (5th Coldstream) but from which they later withdrew, and the village is now well into 'no-man's-land'. We were to investigate and confirm a Panther tank that 3 Company claimed to have destroyed just beyond the village, some 1,000 yards beyond where our rifle companies now lay. The place has a pretty name, but today it is no pretty sight. Not a cottage, not a shed, is intact. The village was deathly quiet. The only living things we saw were a dying cow, two nervous-looking chickens and a tame rabbit in a cage. We released the rabbit, but would not shoot the cow for fear of attracting attention to ourselves; though, except for dead Germans, the place seemed to be deserted.

But we still face 9th SS and, though Brian had recently returned through the village, we could not know that a German patrol, or even a larger combat force, was not intent upon re-occupying Chenedolle – the lesson of Montchamp was too recent for complacency. The sinister silence and the possibility that Jerry had returned in the night to mine and booby-trap the village, added to the horror of the devastation wrought by artillery, mortars and close-quarter, house-to-house fighting and tank combat. This local destruction seems even more sordid than the awful, large-scale destruction wreaked by our heavy bombers at Caen, and we walked warily, our Stens loaded and cocked and at the ready to fire. Dai seemed calm enough and I suppose I did too, though I felt as nervous as hell. A Jerry sniper or many snipers, might have been in any of those ruined houses. We found no Panthers in the village, but followed a Panther's tracks, tracing them through the foul-smelling orchards and so on to the road running through Chenedolle – but no Panther.

We went on, through the village, and three-quarters of a mile beyond it, to investigate what Davies thought was a Panther's 75mm gun sticking out of a thicket hedge. We first studied this through our binoculars and I noticed, as I had noticed at Cheux, that this localized and magnified view of apparently deserted and hostile territory seems to make it more menacingly quiet, more dangerous and sinister, than when viewed with the naked eye. I was certain that the object of our curiosity was only a felled sapling – but Dai swore it was a 75mm gun, and so I, being a sergeant, and so obliged to show no trace of the windiness I felt, gave in to the guardsman, and together we went to investigate. It was, indeed, a fallen sapling, a silver birch. We searched all round the village and the adjacent orchards – but we entered no buildings – these might well be deathtraps. Still no Panther, and no sign of a living human being. Obviously the tank had been towed away during the night.

Honour satisfied, we decided to return to CP via the Chenedolle-Haut Perrier road – we had originally approached the village by a cross-country route – and now we made our way along a very narrow lane, completely covered overhead by leafy trees. At any other time I might have revelled in the play of sunlight through this lacy roof of green leaves, and in the moving, dappled sun shadows at my feet – but not this morning. The lane joined the road at a sharp angle and, as we neared the road we stopped dead still to see, on the road itself, the top of a scout car, stationary. But we relaxed as we saw that its occupant, who carefully studied through glasses the road ahead, was British. 'Imagine,' said Dai, 'if we were Jerries, we could easily creep up and lob a grenade into it – CHRIST – LOOK!' He broke off to point to the end of our leafy lane where another scout car, covering the leading car, was posted, and I found myself gaping at the two grim-set faces of the car's occupants watching us intently, and, for the first time, I found myself staring into the muzzle of a Bren gun trained upon me with dead-in-earnest intent – the man's hostile eyes and the finger, squeezed tight on the trigger, brooked no delay on our part in calling out identifying ourselves before this second car fixed our duff. But they fluffed in time.

A SCOUT CAR

They were a recce troop of the Household Cavalry, cautiously feeling their way forward to contact Jerry once more. They had been told that there were no British troops forward of the ridge, nearly a mile back, where our rifle companies lay, and they added that Dai and I were lucky to be alive; in the indistinct broken shadows of the lane we were not easy to identify – Davies still wore his DR's steel helmet – like a Jerry's – and it was only the shape of my ordinary British helmet that gave us the benefit of the doubt. But for that, we were assured, we would have 'had it' and no messing! Gave the HC Recce Commander our information, and location of German standing patrol as it was known to us three hours before, and we left them to their recce and walked on up the road to Le Haut Perrier, feeling much happier to know that some scout and armoured cars of the Household Cavalry now lay between us and the enemy. But we'd not gone far when a hefty stonk of shells or mortars made us dive into the roadside ditch, but the stuff fell behind us, on Chenedolle I think, perhaps Jerry had fluffed to the HCR patrol.

Much smashed Jerry equipment strewed the road area as we neared Le Haut Perrier, and the German dead, rotting quickly in the hot August sunshine looked, and smelt, pretty hideous. Particularly nauseating were three dead Germans lying in a group at the entrance to a narrow, sunken, tree-covered lane where it joined the Vire road. This lane, with its high, steep banks, formed a deep and natural trench, and, as far as the eye could see along it, it was full of Nazi dead – mostly, I think, engineers of 9th SS who had been used as infantry in the battle. It looked as though our artillery and mortars had slain many of these men. Masses of equipment littered the lane, and I restrained Dai from tinkering with the German equivalent of one of our number 19 sets – just in case – though it did not look as if Jerry had had time to set booby traps. SS helmets lay everywhere in the area, and I picked up one of them, intending to keep it as a souvenir of what may well have been our last battle in Normandy – unless, of course, Jerry does another 'Montchamp' on Chenedolle and the Haut Perrier ridge.

Certainly the three dead Jerries at the entrance to the lane had been killed all at the same time, either by mortar fire, or shot from close quarters – they had collapsed together in one ghastly, nightmarish group. One man lay, and the other two half-knelt together in the centre of the narrow lane. They must have been dead for some days and the heat of the August sun had already decomposed parts of them. I have read of rotten death in the stories of men who fought in the last war, and I have seen some of it myself – here in Normandy (see plate no. 18). But no pen can adequately describe the full repellent horror and shame of the real thing. A man freshly mangled by a shell or mortar bomb is comparatively wholesome to see. A gifted artist, wearing a gas mask to endure the awful stench, should paint these horrors. The man who lay on the ground wore no helmet – it had rolled away. What skin was left of his face had turned black – but most of the facial skin had gone – was going, even as we watched – it was being eaten by dozens, and hundreds, of long, fat, white maggots that wriggled quickly to and fro in a disgusting, writhing bunch in and out of the socket of the eye they had already devoured and over the man's already-bared cheekbone, and I hated those thriving white maggots more than anything else about this nightmare group. This man's body was not bloated – the other two were. The centre figure, kneeling, and fixed by rigor mortis in a bent forward position, I shall never forget. He was not yet eaten – at least his face wasn't – and it is his face I'll not forget. It was yellow-grey, powdered in thick white dust – extremely broad and Mongolian in character, and it wore an almost idiotic leer. The teeth, yellow-grey and with clots of blood adhering to them, were bared, and flies busied themselves about the thick, obscene lips that framed the foul and dusty teeth. Stupid staring, blue-looking eyes, half-covered by swollen lids and shaded by white, dust-coated eyelashes, leered up at us as if we, and not he, were the joke. His SS helmet lay askew atop the thick, matted yellow hair that resembled an artificial wig under its coating of dust. His was the face of a stage made-up monster.

These three men, with the dust clinging thickly to the stubble of their chins and cheeks were horribly fascinating to see. But, as I stood watching I barely breathed, and had to move away to take a deep breath, for I would not do so in the unspeakable odour surrounding those three monsters. I suppose it is morbid to write this. But no photographer, or painter or writer could really pass on to posterity this particular aspect of the evil and horror of war. These things should be 'Tussaued' in wax and set in glass cases in a war museum and the evil stench of them compounded into a gas that could be released by the viewer at the press of a button so that posterity may know something of the sordid degradation that war inflicts upon human life. But even then, unless the tortuous writhing of the revolting white parasites could be exactly simulated, the full horrific impact of the thing would be lost. And anyway, in the name of common decency, such an obscenity would never be exhibited in public – and perhaps shouldn't be. This horrifying decomposition of the body under a hot sun is only a very temporary state – but death itself is permanent. To the war widow or bereaved mother the sordid shame of exhibited putrefaction, and the nobility of a British war cemetery and the Whitehall Cenotaph, would present an insoluble equation.

Dead horses and cows and chickens and pigs, and the dampy smell of charred timber and scorched masonry added greater pungency to the reek of Chenedolle and the Perrier ridge. Feeling disgusted to be a man at all, I turned away with Dai, and we reported back to CP. I had thrown away the SS man's helmet rather than face jeers and cracks about Red Indians and scalps – but the area around CP is well strewn with 9th SS helmets.

At CP we found our Pioneer Sergeant, 'Pop' Hedditch, proudly showing the IO his trace of the booby traps he and his men had sown in Chenedolle that morning – and 'Pop' seemed a bit annoyed when I told the IO that we had apparently crossed over a booby trap set in the village street without getting blown up on it. We had not been told of the Pioneers' activities in

Chenedolle, as the Household Cavalry had not been told about Dai and I being forward to the Battalion. Feeling rather like James who was never told anything, I moaned to the IO about it. But he too had known nothing about the Pioneer patrol's work in advance.

Dai remarked that nowhere in our travels had we seen a dead civilian – or a live one. They, at least, must have got away in time, though what their thoughts will be when they return to their farms and homes, I'd rather not imagine. But Chenedolle may not be finished with the war yet. I believed that Jerry was pulling out to escape the trap at Falaise, but my complacency has been badly shaken to see that our tanks are being dug in here, and even the Household Cavalry are digging their armoured cars and themselves, in defensive positions. Obviously some big shot somewhere believes that Jerry will counter-attack the Perrier ridge. Certainly there seems to be more shelling around Chenedolle than before. Ignorance is bliss indeed – Dai and I obviously lived in a bit of a fool's paradise as we meandered around Chenedolle – and Brian and Herb can deem themselves lucky to be alive at all. Had to do patrol reports (patreps) on our return to Battalion HQ, and to send in casualty returns. Have had enough excitement for one day.

Back at Battalion HQ I lettered two more crosses for two of our dead. Two young officers – reinforcements whom I did not know, arrived at Battalion HQ and sat talking to me as I worked and while they awaited transport to take them up to join their companies. They seemed only young boys to me. I felt rather sorry for them – there were no officers around Battalion HQ at the time who could talk with them, and put them at their ease and so they sat with me under an apple tree, and I wondered what they were thinking, these two young subalterns – strangers to the Battalion who had arrived to find sergeants busily preparing two white crosses to surmount two new graves. But the breeding of Harrow, or Rugby, or of whatever public school they came from, prevailed, and, though their eyes wandered towards the crosses I lettered, they maintained the usual flow of flippant conversation that all Guards' officers adopt and they gave no sign at all of what they might be thinking.

But war inevitably imposes some familiarity between officers and men – even in the Guards – and these subalterns who join us now are war intakes – all have been through the Guards Depot, and served as rankers. They know our patter and our way of life. Some come from less grand public schools than did our peacetime officers, and sometimes stoicism and reserve give way almost to confidences, as when a newly-joined subaltern recently told his platoon sergeant, half in jest and half-bitterly, that he was sure that his father would be more proud of him if he died winning a medal for valour than if he returned alive, but without one. Some of the men brought here for burial looked bad where shrapnel had carved them up, but at least it is a fresh badness, and not the putrefying obscenity of

Chenedolle. The Padre and the RSM do all they can to see that our fellows are quickly and decently buried. The Germans, retiring, have not the same opportunity, though we are convinced that, whenever it is possible, the SS remove not only their wounded, but some of their dead also.

They brought up some beer this evening. Too dark now to write any more – though stand-to is still on.

14 August 1944

Listened to, and watched, the IO briefing NCOs for night patrol. Their faces calm enough. 'Intense patrol activity' as reported on BBC news sounds dull enough, and the listener grumpily switches off – 'nothing happening' – or waits for something big and exciting to be announced – but for the youthful sergeant and his four men, prowling by night through the stinking, booby-trapped, mine-infested ruins of Chenedolle, it is very different. Men know a queasiness in their guts before an attack – but at least they go into it together; but patrol work is a lonely and deadly job. I should hate it. In fact a Jerry patrol was waiting for our Chenedolle patrol and our fellows were cut up – a horrible job.

Another very fine day of sun and clear skies, though some early mist. According to the IO, the Thunderbolt planes that have been catching us on the hop and giving us a dog's life are planes captured, and used, by Jerry – but they have retained the Allied markings. Rightly or wrongly we are all suspicious of the skill of American fliers, and particularly of their navigation – but in this case we have obviously been 'doing the Yanks wrong'. The HCR Recce patrol reported that Chenedolle was very heavily mortared soon after Davies and I left the village. Luck plays a large part in war.

Back to Brigade HQ – Montchamp, our first really serious battle, looked a nasty mess. Had another moan to IO about 'I' Section OPs going so far forward to our own lines. There are only six of us, and we can't afford unnecessary losses, and there is no really good first line Intelligence personnel to replace any such loss. Brian and Herb were not only heavily shelled by our own guns, but were most severely machine-gunned by Jerry troops also. It's amazing they got back alive. Had chance to examine 'Pop' Hedditch's mine and booby-trap trace more carefully today and, if his plan is correct, then Dai and I are lucky to have got away with it also. We were wary enough of such traps – but didn't at the time know that there were 'friendly' traps also in Chenedolle. 'Pop' is a good fellow and would wish us no harm, but I suspect that he still feels a bit sore that Dai and I are still alive, and in one piece.

Intelligence work too can be lonely, and deadly, at times though normally we get it cushy by comparison with the rifleman's lot in war.

Strangely enough though, it is when the Battalion is actually in action that I get most leisure time to write – even then people will drop in to the 'I' trench to see the situation maps – but I sometimes get hours alone when I write this stuff under the guise of letters home, or on army message pads. I write too much, as all I write, and draw, has to be carried in the pocket of my canvas trousers, and it's pretty bulky already, however small and however abbreviated I make these notes, and the number of drawings is mounting considerably too. But now, with the Battalion more or less out of action, people wander about more looking for entertainment – and with the strategic situation so fluid and exciting now, the 'I' trench gets a constant stream of visitors, and I have to write this in my 'diary' notebook in my own trench.

The Battalion has lost ninety-six known dead, mostly around Montchamp and here, and I estimate other casualties at about 250, but I think the rest of 32 Guards Brigade have suffered more heavy casualties than we have. I don't know the Division's tank losses, but it is our four infantry battalions who have really copped it in the *Bocage*.

Everyone is now after the Luger pistols carried by German officers since news has gone round that pistol-crazy Yanks will pay ten pounds, in English notes, for one of them.

8.45 pm

They found a 9th SS Panzer man in a house at Chenedolle. He is badly burned – has been there for three days and nights and was, in fact, there yesterday when Dai and I were prowling around the place. He has been evacuated to our ADS. He was too delirious to talk but this is proof that 9th SS tanks were in Chenedolle, and that at least one came to grief and 3 Company's claim seems substantiated. The CO and the RSM say that interrogators of German prisoners at Divisional HQ report 9th SS captives saying that 9th SS refer to the GAD as 'Churchill's Butchers'. If true, this is rather quaint, coming from 9th SS. Hardly a compliment, but, coming from them, I suppose it could be taken as such. Our artillery has moved up, and is much nearer our lines today. Hope this doesn't mean a lot of counter-battery fire falling on us. There has lately been quite a spot of German gunfire around here – but no mortars I think. Still, it's quite a comeback to get stonked again.

By trial and error quite a tolerable species of latrine has now been devised by our 's**t-house wallahs' – our 'sanitary engineers' – using two-pack ration boxes and so, now that all is more or less peaceful again, we can once more enjoy a leisurely brood in the sun though the crudely cut 'seats' of these thunder-boxes cut into one's flesh a bit.

17 August 1944

We are now on the Perrier ridge with CP and the rifle companies. Moved here at 1600 hours yesterday. This is a foul place – every building in the hamlet is shattered or burnt – our people are clearing the mess now – but dead cows and dead Germans still abound here. Writers refer to the sickly-sweet smell of death – but here, mixed with the acrid smell of charred timbers and masonry and scorched metal, I find the smell sour and nauseating and not unlike that of sweaty and long unwashed socks and feet.

Forty yards from me lies a Panther tank – a half-burnt corpse occupies the driving seat – the ground is pitted with shell and mortar holes. Every tree near here is splintered and a thick coating of light grey-brown dust covers everything. Live and dud shells and mortar bombs, SS helmets, German and British equipment lie everywhere. I put an SS helmet into our truck as a souvenir. Here and there larger craters denote where aerial bombs have fallen – slit trenches galore – theirs and ours. Jerry's are generally shallower than ours. I suppose because, generally, guardsmen are taller, but the Germans half-cover their trenches with much greater protection.

Great piles of logs and faggots are used here and some trenches, where the mattresses were burst open, look to be covered in dusty snow and, incredibly, one trench is half-covered by the now rotting corpse of a cow! What kind of man could voluntarily live and sleep under a rotting carcass for cover? After nearly ten years in the Army, and six weeks fighting out here, I am not squeamish; but I find eating food in places like this, and at Colombelles, a bit unappetizing – and I don't think I could eat much in a trench covered by a festering, maggoty and reeking dead cow. *Chacun à son goût*, I suppose. And in the static, trench-bound war of 1914–18 front-line soldiers must have lived (some perhaps for years) in much more horrible conditions than these. There's no doubt about war – it strips life pretty bare at times – as indeed (in its way) does the Guards Depot, though the Depot, with its meticulous precision in all things – its fastidious cleanliness – its absolute law and order, is the very antithesis of the filth and anarchy and decay of war. Yet at Caterham too life is stripped bare – unless Caterham has changed very much since 1933.

Had three sergeants and a CSM as prisoners here yesterday – all from 3rd/5th Parachute Division. Full-blown Nazis these – though militarily very correct. Sergeant S, acquisitive as ever, is a great robber of German corpses – including, Tony tells me, the three horrors who lay in a group of sheer putrefaction, and who so shook Dai and me as we stared at them. S is a bit of a ghoul – the only man of Corporal Woods' squad whom I disliked at the Depot. It is the job of 'I' Section men to search enemy dead – for information – though loot, of course, is taken and kept also. But for neither intelligence, nor loot, would I handle those three dead monsters.

Two British airmen have just turned up here – they had to bale out on D-Day, and they were hidden by the French, until the people fled from their homes, as war approached them ten days ago but the airmen stayed put –

hid from Jerry, and kept the eye down when our advance brought the battle to their doorstep; beyond that, they knew nothing of what had happened during the past fortnight but, observing that the 'tumult and the shouting' had died away, and being hungry, they emerged from their hidey-hole and went out, looking for eggs. They heard British voices and discovered our Pioneer Platoon also looking for eggs.

Can't forget the degrading sights inside some of these cottages – burnt beams, tile-less roofs, shell-holes through the walls, correspondence and trinkets torn from cupboards and drawers and scattered everywhere. Clothing and children's toys strewn all over the floors – every drawer and recess has been thoroughly ransacked by, I like to think, German troops – but little remains that has not been stolen or despoiled or killed. A few hutch rabbits have survived, and these run about the abandoned gardens, eating at will, and yesterday I opened the door of an outhouse to release a starving goat and her kid to graze on what grass is left here. Now several women have returned to their homes here, and their sorrow is sad to see. I feel oddly guilty near these women. I feel as if we are a crowd of kids playing some destructive kind of game. Nonsense really, I suppose. We don't want to be here, and it's no game. But I feel that this is how a peasant woman, standing amid the vandalism and wreckage of her home, must reason. A Jerry plane was dropping flares and bombs somewhere behind us last night.

To Brigade HQ – this seems a very serene place, though it's had its fair share of hostile attention, and handsome Lord Rosse, the Brigade IO always looks as calm and neat and clean as he would back in England, and his pleasant, cool manner more than matches his immaculate appearance.

We are due to go into six days' Army reserve if the situation permits. Personally, I cannot see why our armour, once it was squeezed out of the *Bocage* battle, was not switched back into the Caen sector – maybe not enough room for manoeuvre there for us – or maybe the Division has been too much cut about to be of much use until it has been reinforced. Anyway, the Division, and especially the infantry battalions, badly need a decent break. Alright for me to talk! That gap must be absolute hell for the Germans involved.

The *Bocage*: Rully (Rest Area) 18 August–28 August 1944

18 August – Rully

A good day – some cloud. We moved here last night – all grateful to leave that stinking ridge. Poor old 'Corporal Lace' was Officer I/C cow party. His job – to list and then bury all the dead cows within a mile radius of Le Bas Perrier – at least we don't actually bury them now by hand. A bulldozer is borrowed from the 79th Armoured Division – a specialized Division called 'The Zoo' because of its collection of special equipment – these are known as 'The Funnies', e.g. it has Buffaloes, Crocodiles, Kangaroos and flail tanks – all known as AVREs[1] though there is nothing very funny about the performance and role of some of these 'Funnies'. But this place is unspoilt (or undamaged) by war, though the civvies have departed and Jerry was here until very recently, and the smell of him is everywhere.

Germans have lived in, and looted, this farmhouse where Battalion HQ lies now, and the dining-room table is littered with empty German fag packets. The RSM has had the farmhouse doors nailed up until civvies return, and it's close arrest for any man caught inside the farmhouse. At the T-junction on the Vire-Vassy road, below Chenedolle, we passed the smashed crucifix of a wayside shrine and I stared to see what looked like a completely naked German corpse lying in the ditch below a hedge. It was a coloured image of Christ, and the effect of the paint used on the body was exactly the smooth, matt, greasepaint-like texture and tone of dead humans – the hair of this image was an auburn colour. This crucifix could have been destroyed by shellfire, but the next shrine along the road appeared to have been destroyed out of sheer vandalism by the SS.

---

1. Buffaloes – Amphibious Armoured Vehicles; Crocodiles – Churchill tank flame-throwers with fuel trailer; Kangaroos – Infantry (personnel) Carriers; flail tanks – chains attached to a revolving drum mounted on a tank used for mine-clearing; AVREs – Armoured Vehicles Royal Engineers.

The Sigs Officer says that the Normans agree that the conduct of German occupation troops was satisfactory, but that the SS were a crowd of vandals. The Falaise gap is now closed. No official estimate yet of the numbers trapped – maybe 20,000 or 30,000 – but one thing is certain: German Seventh Army, if not destroyed, is in a state of complete confusion. There is depressing news of the bombing of Canadians and Poles by heavy bombers of RAF and Yank Air Force. Great pity – we expected so much of the Polish Armed Division, and now it has been badly cut about by its own side! The outer trap now looks like closing on the Germans. It seems that Paris may be bypassed by the advancing Yanks since we would have to feed the city if we liberated it now.

<u>20 August 1944</u>

A grand day – though some 50 per cent cloud – the situation map looks confusing. German units in the bag are losing all cohesion and (as current jargon has it) 'cannibalization of units is rife'. The RAF claims to have destroyed 300 enemy tanks in the past forty-eight hours – no doubt many of these are SP guns – even so such losses are significant – much armour obviously still remains trapped. A NAAFI canteen van turned up here today – carried blended chocolate, biscuits, etc, and, for once, guardsmen are flush with money – not from pay, but from cash looted from German prisoners and dead and, but for some rationing, men could have bought up a great deal more. Fags and chocolate and particularly soap are more valuable than cash when illicit trading is done with the French for eggs and chickens etc. Some men believe that these goodies will, if and when the opportunity occurs, also buy the carnal favours of pretty *mademoiselles*; but those of us who were in France, in 1939–40 think differently. The licentiousness of the Rue Pigalle and Folies Bergères does not seem to extend beyond Paris, and French girls, if not more moral, certainly seem more cautious than their British counterparts.

The news summary suggests that there is a serious rift between the SS and the *Wehrmacht*, and this, I think, is significant. Only thus can the war end quickly. Here, if anywhere, can the German nation turn on the Nazis and the SS. The summary says that the best hospitals are reserved for the SS and preferential treatment is given to Nazi warriors. And prisoners claim that the SS push them into battle with revolvers.

The Battalion has been re-organized – our 2 Rifle Company disbanded because of our losses and X Company Scots Guards (transferred from the Micks) takes its place. Tough luck for these Jocks leaving the Micks, but this Company has a fine reputation. Some first line reinforcements have also arrived and Snowy soon got the Pioneer Platoon on making a height standard so that no short-arses of 3 Company should sneak into 4

Company, and no man of 4 Company maximum height should get into the Jam Boys.[1]

I am in-waiting tomorrow – and there's to be a Battalion drill parade – Roll on Death! It's an awful job to scrounge a drop of Bluebell with which to clean one's brasses – the stuff's rarer than gold out here.

<u>22 August 1944</u>

I view the Division's resumption of an operational role with mixed feelings. Cowardly and lethargic Murrell wants to remain here lapping it up in safety, but amateur reporter Murrell itches to be away reporting history as it is made. A bit futile really, because this war is already being reported by professionals as no war has ever been reported before. This stuff, written by a ranker during the Crimean war, might be of some value – just my luck to have my war when the whole Army is educated, and can read and write, and when journalists galore are in the offing. Though, I suppose, there has never before been a war when a man in an infantry battalion, even if he could write, would have found himself in my position, with relative privacy and time and opportunity and with readily available material to hand, to write all this rubbish. But it's not going to be so easy for me when winter comes and the days shorten. But I think the war in the west will be over before this happens. In fact some men and some officers here seem to think that unless GAD gets cracking soon, we shall fight no more battles – but merely be used to mop up the German remnants and occupy their country. I would like to know the organization of Patton's armoured divisions; these are stated, in the *Guardian*, to be the most mobile armoured force that modern science can produce. Is it, I wonder, my ideal of an all-tracked, or half-tracked, all-armed division?

<u>28 August 1944</u>

Sir R. Powell has now turned up here – he looked very grey and ill. He had temporarily lost his memory. A Panther's 75mm gun, fired at point-blank range, killed his servant, who lay alongside him, and knocked the officer unconscious at Montchamp. The 9th SS carried him off – but he escaped – reached Paris, and rejoined the Battalion when he could.

Don't feel a bit like leaving these peaceful surroundings – why doesn't Jerry grow wise to himself and fluff? A drill parade this morning – the usual bore. There's a cricket going like billy-o on my right. This is probably our last night in Normandy – roll on!

---

1. Prince of Wales Company.

PART THREE

BRUSSELS TO THE RHINELAND,
2 September 1944
–26 March 1945

10

The Liberation of Brussels
2 September–5 September 1944

On 2 September the Guards Armoured Division was reorganized into four Regimental battle groups – Grenadier, Coldstream, Irish and Welsh – each consisting of a battalion of tanks and a battalion of infantry. They were to be allocated to 5 or 32 Guards Brigade as required, though in the immediate future and generally the Welsh Guards went with 32 Guards Brigade. The 1st and 2nd Battalions formed the Welsh Guards group. A few days previously, 2 Company of 1WG was disbanded because of losses and X Company Scots Guards took its place.

The Second British Army with XXX Corps (which included GAD) as its spearhead advanced at great speed through L'Aigle, Beauvais, Villers Cottenue, Villers Bretonneux and across the Seine at Vernon – always to ecstatic welcomes. On 1 September the 1st Battalion reached Arras and they entered, to a tremendous reception, the town they had been the last to leave in 1940. They came across the FFI (French Forces of the Interior or Maquis), 'these gentlemen, looking like brigands…the FFI not a sham – they're really mopping up well'.

2 September 1944 – Douai – 1750 hours

Reveille was at 9.00 am. Rained during night and Trevor and I into truck to kip – sun in morning but rain later and rain is teeming down now – impossible to dry out blankets – now at Quincy-Douai. Battalion came same route from Arras that it followed in 1940 – some men even in the same billets here – our trucks formed up in the stubble. French flags all over town – flowers – rosettes – all sorts of things showered on us – the tanks with green laced wire-netting camouflages round their turrets and with flung flowers covering them look like mobile gardens.

My boil is troublesome – makes one feel lousy. Our fags are going fast – it's a dead loss to stop in a village or a town. The girls look well-dressed and their wide, light skirts fluttering in the breeze awoke a general response from men having had little or no contact with civilians for the past three months or so. Sometimes a kiddie would ask *Nicht cigaretten?* forgetting himself, so guess they stung the Boche for fags as well.

People round here seem hungry and one is ashamed to take one's food and eat it before them. After reveille the people of Arras came out to inspect our harbour area – old men, kids and young girls, asking for fags, sardines, chocolate, biscuits and what-not. Adams was doing a rear on an improvised thunder-box within a very low camouflage net enclosure, when two young beauties passed and wished him *bon jour* – the screens consisting only of the low camouflage net, Adams was somewhat abashed.

Many of the Battalion 'zig-zag' last evening – people went mad when they realized we were here in 1940 and those of PoW Company, who were at St Nicholas then were recognized by the town folk. Could see Vimy Ridge and memorial and the town hall in the sunshine. So much has happened since I last gazed on that scene.

Rain just teeming down at present. Rain spoils everything. Passed a 12th SS Panzer Division half-track burnt out last night. Some of the dead horses here have been used by the French for meat and L said a butcher's shop he passed smelt not unlike Chenedolle some mornings after the battle.

A dead German, his boots and socks stripped off him, lay at a crossroads at Douai. Around him was a crowd of French men, women and children, cheering us like mad as we passed. For some odd reason I thought of the German's mother. How cheap life really is and how silly the things we worry about in life! Even home and family – even death itself. How insignificant one, a hundred or a thousand deaths, compared with the chaos that is in our world today! Somehow these cheering French people standing over, and utterly ignoring, the corpse of this dead German or Austrian, or Polish, Russian, Dutch or even Alsatian conscript, seemed to point out the insignificance of the individual – he lay there, in a gutter, undignified, no doubt the object of coarse jests as his boots and sweaty socks were removed and the rubbish in his pockets ransacked. Later his remains will lie in a military cemetery – his name chiselled on a war memorial's stone – 'He gave his life' – but how ignobly – and that bundle of soiled canvas cloth could have been, can still be – me.

***

After Douai 32 Guards Brigade, led by the Welsh Guards, raced 5 Guards Brigade to Brussels at top speed. They went through Leuze (having bypassed Tournai), Enghien and Hal. The 'race' took place on two centre lines, the Welsh Group on the left and the Grenadier Group on the right. The Welsh Group won and the Welsh Guards entered Brussels on 3 September to an ecstatic reception.

<u>3 September 1944 – Belgium</u>

Five years ago today war was declared and I sailed for Gibraltar. We crossed the Belgian border just now. All French bunting was removed by order from vehicles and tanks and guns before the march commenced. This is a race with 5 Guards Armoured Brigade to Brussels. At 'O' group last night the usual lengthy, tedious 'Intentions and Methods' etc of the operation order were missing – the intention being simply to race 5 Brigade to Brussels by last light today.

Startled by this daring and rather optimistic intention, I glanced at the faces of the officers and warrant officers present – the hurricane lamps and torches that illuminated the outhouse gave enough light to show that they too were startled by the unusual pithy and racy order – then they slowly grinned their appreciation – centre lines and bounds were recorded and the 'O' group broke up very good-humouredly. Ninety miles in a day – I was sceptical – the order said little enemy opposition expected, but there must be many Germans milling about between here and Brussels. Airborne divisions are to be dropped [note added later: no airborne units were used in the event]. People bombarding trucks with pears and plums and cake – more flags here than ever.

Yanks got onto our centre line before us – they just can't wait – they are laying cable and going back for supplies – our people seem to be herding them off our C/L. Apparently they banged in yesterday and got a bloody nose from Jerry last evening.

2-INCH MORTAR USED BY INFANTRY.

At Douai last night two young girls from a nearby house came over to welcome the section in our bivouac and gave us cognac – both were in mourning – it seemed that they could not do enough for us – yet we learned from them that their father had been killed during a British air-raid on the town a few weeks previous. These people are realistic in their views – they bore us no ill will, accepting the sacrifices that liberation entails – even so, as I sipped their cognac, I was not at ease with them, though I admired their own frankness and courage and tried to believe that we bore no responsibility for their misfortune and almost succeeded. Only Caen leaves a haunting sense almost of shame and the memory of the dazed and shaken people of that district gazing upon the savage wreckage of house or cottage cannot easily be forgotten.

Armée Blanche imprest cars careering through the town like Wild West shows – blokes in them brandishing revolvers in the air – the Cross of Lorraine painted in red on the cars and trucks. German resistance ahead overcome – some wounded and prisoners and a couple of dead alongside road.

Very few vehicles have dropped out and this march quite historic and well done – God knows how they'll manage for supplies though.

1750 hours

Battalion HQ 'battle' – shots were suddenly fired and tracer bullets flew over truck and we lined ditches alongside road. Some German firing from field on our right – spotted one man and we opened up – Captain Holland had a pot with rifle – thought he'd got him – decided not so called up a 2-inch mortar – but rifle companies out. Enemy appears to have been this one man on our flank – he must have been scared stiff – though several came in to surrender.

This excitement over, I watched our tanks and armoured cars firing at a mass of German supply vehicles (stationary) on a lateral road. I watched them catch fire and blaze – it seemed unfair, but my mind went back to an almost identical scene when in 1940 I lay in a ditch and watched German planes firing a stationary convoy of RASC vehicles. The armour has done well – all along the road lie wrecked German vehicles, half-tracks and guns – a good bag – most of them blazing furiously. The civvies stuck around greeting us until our 'battle' began. Shots flying all around now – though we now on the move – passed a press car – its occupant busily photographing another mass of blazing vehicles and equipment – a few dead Jerries lying around and some prisoners – about eighty prisoners, burning trucks.

2045 hours

Now entering Brussels – it's terrific too! We are first in and are being mobbed – the column can only crawl – wines, liqueurs and fruits galore – had to get out of truck with Trevor to relieve ourselves – a crowd followed us up side street – managed to shake them off and began to attend to pressing need when a group of young men and girls bore down upon us – seized our arms even before we had finished, kissed us, patted our backs, and told us that the building opposite was a hospital full of German wounded and they insisted, and quite in earnest, that we wasted no time in entering the hospital and killing every German in the place – *tous* – *tous* – we had to struggle to get back to the truck – beer – liqueurs – kisses – it is dark now – I am a little drunk – what a night – still waiting to crawl on. God knows what is happening – one doesn't care. A great fire raging nearby – Palais de Justice?

4 September 1944 – Boulevard de Waterloo, Brussels

Should have described the news red hot last night but was too tired. We were ordered to dig in alongside the pavement of Boulevard de Waterloo. I quite expected an air-raid, and bombs amid those cheering crowds would have been terrible – the shops and cafés were lit up and unscreened long after dark – a huge bonfire raged for hours where they had piled up and set light to the barricades. The Palais de Justice, set alight by SS and Gestapo to burn their documents, burned all night and blazed up furiously at intervals and lighted up the whole centre of the town. The roads through Brussels really were paved with flowers and tanks and trucks were smothered in bouquets and flags. Never, in my life, can I hope to see so many sincerely happy faces – the people delirious with joy and the column took hours to get through them – white-helmeted gendarmes blowing shriek whistles – ambulance and tram car and fire-engine bells – machine-gun and rifle fire from Rexist headquarters on our left where we watched *Armée Blanche* digging out Belgian traitors. They just dig them out of buildings, line them up in the street and shoot them – all the passions were abroad in Brussels last night – they still are today.

Enormous crowds round each truck – wines, liqueurs, beer – whole bottles of rare wines were given us and we must have kissed half the women of Brussels. Unfortunately, as they spotted us in the trucks, they pulled our heads down and all grabbed hold of the plastered boil on the back of my neck – so the kisses I received were mixed joy and pain involving a sort of masochism. Girls climbed into jeeps, trucks or tanks – even into the CO's car and could not be removed. They stood on running boards and kiddies sat on the wings of cars. But I think most touching of all were the old folk – particularly elderly women. They came up – clasped one's hand in theirs and said 'Zank you Tommy – zank you for coming – zank you.' Everyone's gratitude was self-evident. No one could fail to be moved by this great, spontaneous, tumultuous welcome. *Vive les Anglais.*

Brussels has not seen such a night since 1918 or perhaps, though emotions then were mixed, for excitement, that of 18 June 1815. All here want to see German Youth utterly exterminated. A woman, well-dressed, her age guessed about 55 to 60 limped up to us – she was crying, and quietly and gravely she shook our hands and, turning to me, thanked me. She had harboured two British prisoners and had suffered two years' imprisonment for it during which time, and to urge her to betray others, they had broken her thigh five times. She was so quiet, told her story in good English and so simply and, in her quiet way showed such gratitude, that I forgot for a moment the excitement going on all around and felt humble that she should have selected me to thank as representative of the British Army – I told her that we had to thank her and her kind. She shook hands again and limped away.

All notions of air-raid precautions had been forgotten – lights on – cafés open – the curfew finished – all night long they thronged the streets – expansive gestures with finger across throat *Hitler kaput*. As the liquor flowed so the welcome grew in intensity – the people sang 'Tipperary' and 'Siegfried Line' – a beautiful young girl spoke to us in school English – she too had harboured an airman – imprisoned for six months – she asked me to kiss her – as I did she closed her eyes – seemed half in a dream and it occurred to me that many of the women of Brussels would give themselves, and as I have heard, many did, to their liberators for that night – by this I do not mean the harpies but decent young women – the whole teeming crowd was in that mood – to give something, anything, to the men of the Guards Armoured Division – and I begin to appreciate how much they loathe the Germans and how they value their freedom.

Soon the squabbles and jealousies, self-interest, exploitation, political hatreds will reassert themselves but last night I saw something I might never see again – mass joy, sincerity, gratitude and true generosity – I saw a thousand faces and not an ugly or deformed face among them – yet there were ugly and deformed faces among them as there are in any thousand faces – there must have been – what a thing physical expression must be. A tank tore through the cleared road – its headlights blazing full and some machine-gun fire sounded. I remember the words spoken by the young girl I kissed – she gave me a bottle of cognac and when I offered to pay it was then she asked me to kiss her and said *Pour le vainceur tous est libre Monsieur*. And those words summed up the emotion of the whole of Brussels last night. A great full moon rose behind the buildings, to light the streets thronged with happy Belgians.

Belgium has a soul today such as she had not in 1815 – two long periods of German occupation have forged her into a nation. Long avenue of trees – the truck looks like a fruit stall – no cooked meal last night – Company Commander said he thought we had probably had enough food given us, but I felt hungry for more substantial food.

We kipped on the pavements and I fell asleep watching the shoes of men, women and children passing or stopping to watch us – there were no screens and we had to use a large open air-raid trench – damned awkward. Reveille at 0700 hours – the Palais continued to burn throughout the night – people didn't mind and they cheered heartily each time the wind caught it and it grew in intensity – intermittent firing continued throughout the

" CROMWELL " ADVANCING AT SPEED.

night – no sniping here in this street so far and none expected. All asking for souvenirs – all thank us heartily for liberating them.

Chalked all over tanks and trucks were the names of the places we'd come through and the times we passed through – we had to remove these today – whether owing to regimental discipline or because they expect battle soon and don't want us looking like a circus or because of security I cannot say. Belgians say Germans looted them TFO during the four years – corn etc taken to Germany. Our Battalion and 2WG Armoured lined up along boulevard here. People came to watch us rise, work, shave and breakfast and almost as we attended to calls of nature – though we looked an oddly-dressed band of victors in our denims. People are thronging the streets now and are almost as vivacious and excited as last night.

German planes flew over the city early – a lot of cloud – AA let rip at them – wonder if a recce for their bombers? Our 2nd Battalion did good work yesterday and caught German motorized convoys many times – three shells and three lorries in flames – one car loaded with money – glass watches etc. What a terrific night! One I shall never forget – nor will Brussels. All people of Brussels say that. Now people are examining our battle scars on the trucks – shattered windscreens etc. Makes one feel quite heroic and no need to tell them that we were in slit trenches alongside trucks when the damage was caused. Don't know where we go from here.

Had a good kip and feel much refreshed. Sheer excitement kept truck and tank drivers at it yesterday. Douai – Brussels – a lengthy hop and quite an achievement. Only wish war were ended – but behind all this surely lie more battles again and that is a sobering reflection. Nevertheless, whatever happens to me now I've witnessed the liberation of a European capital – it's a grand sight and sensation. A pity that those who fought and died in Normandy to gain a mile or so of ground at great cost could not have witnessed the lightning advances of the past few days and the Division fulfilling its preconceived role – the Cromwell tanks are ideal for this kind of job. We beat 5 Armoured Brigade to it.

1315 hours – Boulevard de Waterloo

Move soon – the tanks are off already – revving and roaring through the streets – pontoons going up towards Holland or Germany. The battle of Germany looms close. Would have liked to 'visit' Holland. Roll on! No fags – all given to French and Belgians – we all in same boat – great hospitality – some tales of systematic German looting – all proud to tell of their hidden radio receivers. It is fête day today. At Dunkirk we experienced the humiliation of defeat – here today we have, literally and actually, tasted the fruits of victory. Hope I may yet know the joys of total victory. Passed a dead Jerry or collaborator hanging by his neck from a roof in the area occupied by Irish Guards – had been strung up by Belgians. We are now in Forêt de Soignes – many shots from its depths and I guess it's pretty full of Huns. Here it was, on this road, that Wellington's troops were to pass to Waterloo, and his wounded to return to Brussels on that eventful night of 18 June 1815.

Don't know where we go from here but just in front is a signpost, its arms saying significantly, 'Aachen, Dusseldorf'. German army signs of a standard type and all painted in yellow and black. The white stars on tanks and trucks make people believe we're Yanks. More flowers this morning – *Vive le Tommy* – 'I bloody well hope so,' answered a voice from the vehicle ahead. They shout 'OK?' again thinking we are Yanks.

Fine sunny morning now and much warmer. We ashamed of our public ablutions – our towels dirty etc, and one is particularly conscious of the scum round top of biscuit tin, its water used several times, when elegantly dressed and perfumed women or girls are among the audience. During a temporary halt on the way here a woman came up to truck and lifted up her child to be kissed and pleaded with me for soap – a tiny piece, any size. I was using some perfumed stuff – dug it out – half-used – and gave it to her – she rubbed it over her hands and face and smelt it and gave it to the child to smell and they thanked me as though I'd given them a diamond.

There are no doubting Thomases among us now concerning the rottenness of the German new order. The greatest cynics among us are impressed by this touching demonstration by the people of this liberated capital city. On our trucks they chalk *Merci aux nos liberatans*. Light-cream painted trams and trailers packed to overflowing with cheering folk – their bells incessantly ringing and the fainter toot of French motor horns – pink and yellow-tipped matches.

11

Beeringen, Helchteren and Hechtel 6 September– 16 September 1944

After a small action at Wavre on 5 September and tougher fighting beyond the Albert Canal at Beeringen and Helchteren, the 1st Battalion encountered some particularly stubborn resistance at Hechtel. They first attacked Hechtel on 7 September and after being repulsed they attacked again on subsequent days and finally captured it on 12 September, having killed, wounded or taken prisoner over 800 of the enemy.

6 September 1944 – Between Pael and Beeringen – 1700 hours

Now here at Albert Canal. PoW Company are across – seized the bridge – some mortar or gunfire and shots from all sides – 120 prisoners so far. Thirty prisoners including six SS brought in to Battalion HQ last night – all pretty browned off – lined them up and searched them – scruffy as usual and made strange contrast with our officers sitting well-groomed and drinking at the garden tables and chatting to well-dressed women. Herded them in to TCL and with them into Brussels where we took them to *École Militaire* where Belgians in National uniform took them over.

1 was feeling mellow when a call came from the Padre to assist in burying some of 4 Company dead, killed at Wavre – collected our picks and shovels and dug. Hurricane lamps were used to assist as it was then quite dark – the graves finished, the dead carried from the Bren-carriers. I felt rather ashamed of the fact that I was helping bury men who had been fighting while I had been drinking – a dark-haired youth was lowered into our grave – his face, but not his name, was familiar to me. The hurricane lamp showed his features grey and his black hair matted – even at that time I automatically noted that the hair needed the usual close regimental crop – a streak of clotted blood trickled from his mouth – possibly the alcohol had sharpened my observing faculties for the scene is most vivid now and

I shall, I think, remember it often – the black pit of the grave – the grey of the man's face – its rather sharp features – and the contrasting colours of the masses of flowers already brought by Belgian civilians – lying at the edge of the grave in the lamplight – the Padre's sorrowful face, and the RSM eagerly exhorting us to make the graves as posh as possible will remain a most vivid memory with me. The graves were filled in and smothered with flowers.

Bridging equipment is going up now and now the tanks are following. We were all given a cigar from Churchill this morning. Odd the Russians not helping the Poles in Warsaw? Wonder if they do intend attacking Germany?

Had cognac last night – pre-war stuff. Belgian national colours as per REMEs. Five wounded from X Company Scots Guards – small-arms fire very close to – wonder what sort of defence we'll find at Jerry frontier? We're quite close to it now. Slag heap over trees – believe used as OP. Kiddies wandering about here – dangerous. Speech here is Flemish and I noticed that civilian hostility towards prisoners nothing like so evident as in Brussels. Beyond – more firing – officers wearing Luger pistols. A yellow smoke candle prudently lighted as planes flew over and trucks and tanks have yellow or cerise celanese stripes over them – nobody fancies being 'typhooned'.

German convoy slit trenches dug all along road Flers-Brussell with wooden stakes at each one to guide drivers to them when attacked by British planes – all deep and regularly spaced – posts are painted white and have straw tied to them. Was sorry to leave the last place – the Cliquot Rouge – civvies drinking at tables as we lined up and searched prisoners – we pushed them around and bullied them more than usual for the benefit of the attractive women and sleek men at the tables drinking with our officers. The fag famine continues.

7 September 1944 – Beeringen

A most unpleasant day so far and looks like becoming worse. The Albert Canal bridged OK over temporary wooden bridge seized by PoW Company and we are now here. Were due to move off at midnight – rain lashing down all night and an October/November-like gale blowing now. Moved about 500 yards by first light and were stuck on the road in our 'soft' vehicles before mortar and shellfire commenced. With the grey, chilly dawn the Germans opened up on us and we took to the ditches – the Dutch Brigade came up. Stuff started bursting uncomfortably close – 02 Sergeant Roberts and Corporal Jones left the ditch alongside me to cross the road but were hit before they reached the other side – both badly wounded. 02 yelling for a tourniquet – calls for stretcher-bearers – Jerry dropping HE and smoke –

mainly from mortars – the first bombardment died away – our gunners having apparently wiped out Jerry's OPs.

Cooks started preparing breakfast on road when bombardment

STRETCHER-BEARERS.

recommenced heavier than ever and I thought a hit certain – then that 02 was hit. Eventually O/C coolly directed trucks – turned these and we hared back here – still the wrong side of Albert Canal. Breakfasts, and now 1520 hours waiting to move over – with German guns or mortars still shelling the road. Some twenty prisoners through this morning. In the midst of all this finally my boil burst – thank heaven.

At first the tanks went into action covered with flowers and nosegays – now they are grimly grey again – stripped of all garnishing. I feel that this stubborn German defence caught us on the hop – he's started shelling and mortaring again – don't feel a bit happy about all this – as someone said, 'After the Lord Mayor's show comes the dung cart.'

Sun now out temporarily though gusty – we dug slit trenches and I thought then, 'I'll never moan if Stella asks me to dig the garden.' This morning I really was, and am now, apprehensive – more stuff dropping around now – a mass of GAD tanks has gone through and our left C/L should be shifting him by now – but he's still over there – we all had a drop of our cognac just now. Personally I could do with a wallop.

No civvies in the offing today – all well down their cellars. More shells – we dug deeply here – sandy and easy digging – more shells – wrap up! Something mighty close just then.

All the POWs say that SS are driving them to fight by pointing loaded firearms at their backs. Why don't the bloody fools do something about it while they still have weapons? I can see a windmill from here – apart from this, the desolate landscape bears little resemblance to the be-tulipped and luscious impressions of Holland one derives from picture books – the most prominent feature here being a grey slag heap constantly plastered by our gunners and harbouring, I suppose, German OPs. This, I suppose, is the

1944 version of the Battle of the Albert Canal? Have heard no small-arms fire for some time, but our own guns have just opened up closer and I jumped – my nerves all to blazes these days. Roll on!

8 September 1944 – Helchteren – 2400 hours

Scrap at Beeringen died down and we crossed at about 8.30 pm last night. There's some shelling there still – Meese has been killed along with others when a PoW TCL took a shell to itself. It rained during the night – the gale wind of yesterday (Typhoons have just come over, we shaking a bit in case they make a mistake). Some bullets flying overhead at odd moments. The Battalion is now attacking Hechtel together with 2nd Armoured Battalion. Our SPs opened up just behind us, shattered windows in a nearby house and made me jump. Some German shells have fallen and small-arms fire is coming from close behind us.

A glorious morning – sun – clear sky and air like wine. Clouded over and grew cold later and Typhoons circled overhead – took some time to find their targets and went in with that hideous whoosh-whoosh of their rockets horrible to hear from here and hideous to be under. This is an odd, sometimes nerve-racking type of warfare – a bridgehead is formed against opposition and before opposition is crushed our tanks are 10 miles on – the soft vehicles having a very thin time of it behind. Yesterday was a good one for the tanks. Estimated 400 Germans killed and over 1,000 prisoners taken by the Division. We and the Micks had at least 500 prisoners between us.

A Dutch SS man brought in this morning – made him dig our slit trenches for us – as we did yesterday. All prisoners terribly anxious to confirm that they are not of the SS. As soon as someone asks 'Are these SS?' they cry *Nicht SS* and point to their *Wehrmacht* badges on their breasts. I cannot understand why the *Wehrmacht* does not turn on the SS while there is still time. It's the only way that Germany can end the war for herself.

9 September 1944 – Helchteren

2nd Battalion officers said tanks badly in need of maintenance – we've advanced over 400 miles now since leaving Normandy just over a week ago. Many fires were burning all around us – the Germans seemed to be firing on us from all quarters – most confusing – locals scared – me too!

Intelligence truck a great problem now with three aboard. Off again now. Roads deadly with so many 88s about and no flank protection – feel very apprehensive. News not so good – shall be glad to see the end of this op and a few more troops on flanks. German prisoners seem pretty badly shaken up too – reviled Hitler and all his works – not so the SS and paratroops; we are fighting these gentry now in Hechtel – but the Flak people not so zealous. Germans evidently intend holding this area –

Hechtel an important road centre – their opposition is fairly tough. Truck disorganized again – blokes leave kit and all has to be packed again.

About 8.00 pm

Standing to in wood. I for a hellish ride to Brigade this afternoon with prisoners and in a captured German truck (3-tonner). I was bobbing in case our own tanks let loose at the German vehicle – some miles back at Helchteren all the personnel of an artillery battery were lining the roadside ditches – their arms and vehicles had evidently been left in a hurry – they were not parked well into right-hand side of road and we could not pass until we got hold of an officer who rather shamefacedly ordered some of his gunners out to clear the road – just off the road and around the houses and positions we occupied two days ago, men were stalking and hunting the German snipers whose bullets were passing across the road. So on, and not sorry either, some of our 'A' echelon trucks under RQMS Jenkins were following, but turned and went in another direction – couldn't make out who was who, or what was happening – fortunately it was all small-arms stuff, but I was relieved when we were clear of the battle area – our truck, newly painted in unmistakable German camouflage was liable to be shot up by both sides – the railway halt at Helchteren appeared to be hottest spot. Between Hechtel and Helchteren the country is flat and wooded in Aldershot-Pirbright style – a long track on which we were bogged and had to push truck – 2 miles between guards and next unit RA and all the way along the track one imagined that every slag heap, pit-head and church tower held a horrible Hun observer. A blasted heath indeed!

A strange battle, with Micks 10 miles ahead storming the Escaut and the Germans fighting just over the Albert Canal and sorting out echelons of supply vehicles! Our companies have taken and held the village and are now relieved. Back further the 11th Armoured Division were coming up to clear up the C/L and situation around Helchteren – a cheering sign and Corporal Carey and Brigade HQ says that 50 Div are across the Albert Canal – but I have seen no sign of their kit as yet. This type of warfare is deadly on the nerves and the blasted rain adds to one's sorrows – looking for 'A' echelon near Brigade – delivered captured truck and equipment to Brigade HQ – even Brigade HQ seeing to its own defence here. Hope to God I can read this in a year's time and know all was well.

Major Lister badly hit and is lying out on the road near Hechtel. He's considered dead by now – a lion-hearted man – it seems he just walked off down the road to die – always said he wanted to see what was on 'the other side' – a great loss to the Battalion – I wonder if such a suicide is morally or theologically wrong? No one can get near to him to get his body – the German parachutists in Hechtel have the road so thoroughly covered. This German counter-attack is not kidding I think – some shelling near. It rains now – burst of MG fire fairly close – our own guns going now – Jerry shells falling – unpleasant, unsettled sort of feeling. Frankly I hope he doesn't reach here – am preparing to burn these diaries and thinking much of Stella.

10 September 1944 – A wood near Hechtel – 1000 hours

The Divisional Commander is very pleased with the bridgehead – but it was touch and go yesterday – and a company lost a 6-pounder A/Tk gun. We are up against no mean foe – the 2/3 Parachute Regiments and no longer against the 719th Infantry Division. No incidents during the night – all well dug-in and double sentries posted on this post – the whole camp alert and ready for instant action – during night some tanks came into harbour area – some careless torch-flashing and rather dangerous.

More stuff across the canal now. I think 11th Armoured Division and particularly the GAD are praised a lot for the work of the past ten days – the GAD a spearhead with a capital S at present – in fact we are more like the whole spear at the moment – our mortars and artillery now putting down a considerable volume of fire on Hechtel – the flash from the muzzles of the mortars. How nice to be in Civvy Street upon such a day! No more news of Major Lister – the sharp 'phew' of our shells overhead. Wonder if this is another counter-attack? We've the Escaut to cross yet.

11 September 1944 – A wood near Hechtel

Shifted this morning to clearing in copse and not far from village – terrific din going on – close by a Vickers MG post in the sand dunes – eight of them just here in fact all pumping .303 into village as fast as they can – in fact every weapon available to our battle group is in use – SPs and 17-pounders firing HE – mortars – artillery and tanks going full blast at the village which the German paratroopers are holding so fanatically. Hechtel is an important crossroad on our C/L. The Micks and Grenadiers gained a great coup last night by capturing a bridge intact over the Escaut Canal – HCR there too. The Corps Commander, General Horrocks, delighted – he apparently cursed the village of Hechtel though – supplies cannot reach Escaut by road until Hechtel is cleared. Our fellows just couldn't get it – they have it now I believe and my section has gone in to count up German dead and identify destroyed and captured equipment. Stood to last night but no incidents – six prisoners were brought in at 11.00 pm – an awkward hour to receive prisoners – could not dispose of them – shoved them under tarpaulins – pay books showed four of them aged between 17 and 19 years. Little did they know that, if their compatriots attacked and got in among us they were for the knives' carving, Captain Robertson having given us the grim order to shoot all six as every one of us would be needed in event of an attack at night.

<u>1830 hours</u>

A large bunch of prisoners brought in breathless, having been doubled in by Stacey on a motor-bike. One man, accused of pitching civvies out of a shelter in the village and burning the house – also accused of having thrown an old man onto burning debris. He was stood apart, facing a tree, hands on head. Around him stood men, women and children from the village accusing him – spitting at him and trying to reach him. The remaining prisoners were lined up, searched, identified and doubled back to brigade cage for interrogation and internment. RSM very annoyed over accused paratrooper whose sangfroid in face of the hostile crowd of civilians and seeming contempt for the Sten gun pressed against his back was irritating. 'I'll show you, you bastard,' and the RSM ordered us to fetch a spade: 'We'll make him dig a hole to bury the empty ration tins.' Snowy thrust the spade at him and pointed towards the cooker. I didn't like the proceedings, for I knew the man would think just what the RSM wanted him to think, but, fascinated, I could not remove my eyes from the man's face as I watched, for the first time in my life, the reactions of a man who believed himself to be already condemned to death. The simple act of handing him a spade dispelled all the contemptuous calm on the German's face. He howled, pleaded, grovelled and then resisted. The angry RSM, huge and powerful, seized him by the collar and proceeded to drag him towards the cooker – an unpleasant sight. The Second-in-Command saw what was happening, stopped it, and even in front of us, rebuked the RSM. We were ordered to wheel the prisoner off under close escort to Brigade. I don't think the village will fall tonight.

Heard 6 o'clock news announcing seizure of bridgehead over Escaut Canal. Sounds fine to hear the suave voice announce this, and so easy, but it doesn't look so bright for the handful of Irish and Grenadier Guards and Household Cavalry, isolated, with Germans in front, on both flanks and in rear, who are holding that bridgehead tonight. Must admit that the German defence of Hechtel is pretty admirable – they are using bazookas there now. All German prisoners talking of a new secret weapon to be launched in three days' time. [Note added later: the V2.] It doesn't do to scoff, but this might be only a morale booster. Resigned to scrapping away through Germany now – be a longish job – roll on! Day has kept fine.

<u>12 September 1944 – Sand dunes near Hechtel – 1050 hours</u>

Another cold but smashing morning – kipped in sandy slit – no incidents beyond normal harassing fire during night – the village is now afire and it is pitiful to see the distress of the refugees from the village. Seems to have been a truce last evening to evacuate civilians since neither side fired during their slow, sorrowful procession from the village to within our lines.

Apparently the priest begged our local commanders not to destroy the village by bombardment as there were really very few Germans in it. However, we were ordered to be under cover in our slit trenches at 0815 hours this morning as precaution against half-hour's concentrated bombardment of Hechtel by SP guns, tank guns, mortars, MGs and every weapon that could pour steel and lead into this village.

During this bombardment an aged, red-eyed woman, half-hysterical and in tears sat near me, comforted by her weary, red-eyed daughter – it was her husband that had been shut in the burning house by the paratrooper. She was too tired, or indifferent in her grief, to move back with the rest of the refugees and she just sat there, rocking to and fro in her daughter's arms while all around every available weapon opened up and overhead the rushing whine and startling explosions of the Long Tom's[1] shells added to the furious, maddening din – it is all terribly tragic – war's a swine. Sand dunes here as at Dunkirk. The companies are fighting their way into the village now and clearing same – these paratroopers of the Hermann Goering Training Unit are of good quality and are fighting tenaciously.

<u>1445 hours</u>

Battle of Hechtel has now ended. The companies have cleared the village. 3 Company alone has taken 342 prisoners! Must be well over 400 all told – fifty surrendered when grenades were flung into the crypt of the church – the tanks fired four HE shells into it as well, and out they came. The sun is warm now – the chug-chugging of battery-chargers. We are moving up to the new bridgehead across Escaut. Seems rather more cohesion about our front now. The section followed up into village – I in front of truck – many dead – mostly with blue-black faces. I counted these – took some pay books – identified and checked knocked-out enemy tanks, guns, SPs etc. Several Welsh guardsmen lay dead in their slit trenches – savage, close combat – the village in ruins – a messy business – some 150 German dead.

During final attack on Hechtel a young girl, and not unattractive despite her recently cropped hair, came up to Captain Graham, the Signals officer, who was talking to me – she spoke in French and was moaning because the villagers had cut off all her hair. The SO, bland, polite, but unsympathetic asked, in his good French, what he could do about it. She said she kept a shop in Hechtel, had sold stuff to, but had not mucked in with Jerry and she was angry because British troops had stood by and watched while the villagers cropped her hair and had not prevented it – so advised her to leave district for a while. We now off.

Watched more natives come from village – even after their ordeal they smiled and waved to us. All over now bar the shouting. Total enemy

---

1. American 155mm (6-inch) howitzer.

casualties dead, wounded and prisoners over 850! The priest made quite an understatement – no wonder the village held for so long!

**

From 13 to 16 September the 1st Battalion was in a 'rest' area having moved up to the Escaut Canal where the Irish Guards group had bypassed Hechtel and captured the bridge over the canal intact. This opened the way for operation 'Market Garden'.

15 September 1944 – About midnight

Have just finished marking up maps for next operation. This next one looks like being a sticky operation. I thought Jerry was fighting here for more than just canal lines. Some fifteen Hechtel Huns brought in tonight – chased in rather – unkempt-looking shower. Guess we'd be too in their shoes – one prisoner almost fainting from exhaustion. *Armée Blanche* brought them in to us – lined them up and in a twinkling had relieved them of watches, valuables, etc. CO made them return them. One youth of *Armée Blanche* spat hatred at them for fully five minutes. His two brothers had been killed by Germans at Hechtel – never have I witnessed such venom and utter hatred as on that youth's face as he cursed in Flemish or German, the breathless, nervous, dishevelled Germans. A large crowd of civilians gathered round as we inspected their pay books and papers, all obviously happy to see Germans humiliated. They just loathe the Boche around here.

16 September 1944 – 1500 hours

Came back in a TCL. Swanks[1] for breakfast – and bacon – bacon is dead loss. Men wandering around looking for their group of eight and particularly for the man with the tin. This individual can sometimes be traced by his constant yell, 'Anybody got a jack-knife?' The tins squirt long jets of scalding fat when pierced for opening – gold-coloured tins.

Spent the morning lettering crosses for some of our dead – some twenty-seven dead of our Battalion at Hechtel. Took special pains over Major Lister's cross – not because he was an officer but because I admired and revered the great-hearted man who died at Hechtel, and many simple folk in London's East End will mourn him. In 1940 he told his batman he'd not see the war through. Church said, and I've thought too, that he knew he was going to die during the war. Some men say that he was two-faced. He had his faults – pretending to abhor bull and spit and polish yet plastering it on at the same time – but he was a great leader – the greatest-hearted man I've known and Colonel Heber-Percy is another. Major Lister died, as I am sure he wished to die, in battle – and in close combat at that. So many are

---

1. Sausages.

killed by mortars or shells – his was a bullet and it must have slain him instantly – Church was there when he was found. He was not popular with his fellow officers. Captain Henderson, another decent officer, was killed in Hechtel too. He was wounded in the base of the spine at Wavre – but would not go back.

The sergeants' mess open tonight – think I'll go and get happy. We lost some good fellows at Hechtel – about twenty-seven dead. There is a platoon of Welsh guardsmen now in X Company Scots Guards – how odd – what a mix up!

$\overline{1\,2}$

'Market Garden' and the 'Island' 17 September– 6 October 1944

To get from the Escaut Canal to Arnhem on the Rhine, some 50 miles away, involved crossing three major and five smaller rivers and canals. That part of the operation to capture as many bridges intact over these waterways was codenamed 'Market' and was to be carried out by British and American Airborne Forces. This was to include the vital bridges at Grave on the Maas, Nijmegen on the Waal and Arnhem on the Rhine. The other half of the operation, codenamed 'Garden', was for XXX Corps, spearheaded by GAD, to relieve each crossing in succession through St Oedenrode, Veghel, Uden, Grave, Nijmegen and onto Arnhem. When the Welsh Guards reached Nijmegen on 19 September, the American Airborne Forces and Grenadiers had captured the bridges intact. After a small flank action near Valkenswaard on the way, the Welsh Guards were involved in fighting near Lent and at Bemmel and Aam where they pushed the line to its most forward position.

The country between the Waal and the Rhine was known as the 'Island' and there they remained until 6 October. The 1st Battalion Welsh Guards were shifted about in order to strengthen parts of the line and to be on hand should the enemy attack.

The failure to reach Arnhem, heavy though intermittent rain, the unavailability of their excellent 'compo' packs and the flat and monotonous landscape all made for a depressing period. There was also the usual shelling and mortaring and heavy *Luftwaffe* activity as the enemy made a concentrated attack on Nijmegen and the bridgehead though casualties were not heavy. The highly regarded Lieutenant Colonel Heber-Percy returned to take command of the Battalion, having recovered from his wounds.

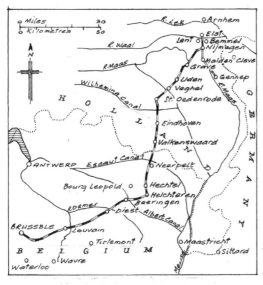

FROM BRUSSELS TO THE RHINELAND

17 September 1944 – 1400 hours

Well – here we go once again – into Holland we hope – at one point shall be less than 3 miles from German frontier – roll on. A Corps of Signals johnny singing a song about the Zuider Zee and Amsterdam – I wonder? Day is fairly fine – some high cloud but no rain – yet! Received defensive overprints – many yellow celanese strips on vehicles today – there are Typhoons about and one takes no chances where Tiffies are concerned. One troop of RA firing smoke burst. All folks here dressed in their Sunday best – they gape at us as we feed – annoying.

18 September 1944 – 0830 hours

A cold, grey morning – we moved off about 0715 hours – now held up – not even across Escaut canal yet. Can hear Big Ben booming on the radio set. Long rolls of greasy paper on breakfast bacon – all colours of signal cable – everyone to lats – awoke in night to shelling – probably a German SP close up to bridge – night has its terrors – the 'whoosh' of gun-firing, and the crack of explosions close by.

1145 hours

Now in Holland – the petite, dainty French and Belgian girls change to husky, healthy, hefty wenches. Road north of canal littered with debris – British and German dead mingled, witnesses of savage fight – the Micks have had to break out of their bridgehead. At one point on the road lay nine knocked out Irish Guards' Sherman tanks – almost nose to tail – victims of an ambush by 88s or bazookas that must have allowed advanced troops through to have caught these nine tanks in such close order of column. We are halted again. Shots coming from woods on right of road – not so healthy! Orange frocks on girls and orange armbands on men.

GERMAN "PANZERFAUST," COMMONLY CALLED A "BAZOOKA."

1335 hours

Still stationary – we are double-banked along road – hold-up on our C/L and Division held up too – but contact with 'feathered friends' (code name for airborne troops) established. 'Sugar-sugar' tanks (i.e. SS tanks) reported at Helmond. Odd this 'baby talk' code for R/T, particularly when a sugar-sugar tank is mentioned – for German tanks alone are bad news – when they are manned by SS troops it means grim fighting for our people. Doesn't look as though we'll get far today.

1630 hours

Still here on the road. REs coming up to bridge a canal. Not too pleasant this loitering – particularly as one watches the sun grow redder and dip lower. It will be dark within three hours – time is so vital. Hope 5 Armoured Brigade can get through to paratroopers. They too are being harassed by German tanks. Very little air activity yet it has been a good day for it. One is extremely conscious of one's exposed right flank – shall be glad to see the Zuider Zee.

1825 hours

The sun now setting – we're poking our noses into it with a vengeance this time. It's this absurd race with 5 Armoured Brigade bizz. A dead loss leaving the Division C/L – I'm not at all happy about things. On R/T we refer to our 2nd Tank Battalion as 'big brother' and they refer to us as 'little brother'. I hate the nights. I suppose I'm a coward? Still – the others don't like them either. Valkenswaard knocked about a bit through fighting – and their reception of us quite warm considering. Roll on. I find myself full of all sorts of misgivings over this bizz. Ours not to reason why I guess.

19 September 1944 – 0750 hours

Several planes flying low overhead last night caused some anxiety and some furious digging in the soft, black, thin, sandy soil. Suspect now that they were British – a low ground mist at sunset predicted a finer day – and, indeed, this morning is excellent – a heavy mist first thing low down on ground. The tops of trees, turrets of tanks and guns looked most impressive – bluey-grey silhouettes seeming to rest upon cloud – slit trenches everywhere – now the sun is up and the mist is clearing – drove through narrow woodland track with our Sten guns ready at alert – the dark yellow of tank-crews fires in the mist.

0935 hours

Glorious now – the trees shimmering in the breeze and sunshine – one's courage soars upon such a morning. Passed a dead German soldier in ditch in wood. One kipping, or might have been dead, alongside road yesterday. Our guns firing now. The Household Cavalry reported to have reached the Maas River – well done! Hope the tanks can get through too. One smokes too much – spout of smoke and flame flares upward from rear of Cromwell tanks as they rev up. Nostalgic smell of sun on dew-drenched silver birches – this area is much like Petts Wood at home.

An English-speaking Dutch girl reported sixty Jerries with *Spandau* and A/Tk weapons in a house half a kilometre from here. We promptly set her upon the pillion of a DR's motor-cycle and she was whisked down to CO's tank amid roars of approval from guardsmen who appreciated the splendid quantity of limb she showed – limb that ended, as one would expect in Holland, in a most substantial and unglamorous pair of blue drawers – had it been in France or Belgium – well!

At halts out come the petrol fires – a blackened biscuit tin full of sand or earth soaked in petrol – the 'whoosh' as they catch fire alarming – char up! Adjutant listened to R/T report of recce reaching Maas/Waal canal – 'what NAAFI issue of Mars Bars?'

We are now in Eindhoven – people in funny hats and gay clothes – predominantly orange in colour – reception very cordial but more reserved than in France or Belgium and they even wear their gay clothes and funny hats seriously. Debonair gendarmes in smart black uniforms – the women dowdy after France and Belgium. Now up with US paratroopers in their swashbuckling attire. Many Dutch speak English – they produce bullet-shattered windows and windscreens. The imperturbable Captain Graham murmuring 'Oh dear – oh dear' as the crowds pressed their noses against the windows of the 'Queen Mary' to gaze with awe upon his great orange moustaches – 'I shall never go to the zoo again.' Eton remains Eton though the world's turned upside down. The civvies and particularly kids asking for

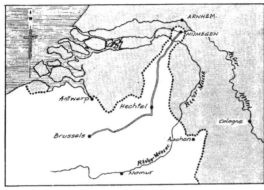

THE ADVANCE TOWARDS ARNHEM.

food. *Zigarettes*? 'Good luck,' they say here.

1525 hours

Halted again. Report that the bridge at St Oedenrode under heavy mortar fire – all folks indoors and the Yankee paratroops at alert and down their foxholes – we fairly tore through – missed the mortars and no incidents with us. Troop-carrying planes going over now – one on fire – has just dropped – huge pall of smoke – hit by flak.

1715 hours

Now closing up – the sun shining on shiny steel tracks of line of our tanks moving north-east. Spires and a dome of town ahead. Paratroops dropped on left of bridge the Germans were mortaring as we passed. Day still glorious – into harbour now I think – roll on.

20 September 1944 – Grave – 0735 hours

I kipped in room of a house last night – the first time for about three months. I was ordered to contact the American paratroops commander on a bridge. All in darkness – our vehicles double and treble-banked along road – some confusion and some shooting from across Canal? We head-to-tail and beautiful targets – some vehicles showing lights – a fire burning on our right towards Germany. USA paratroopers with large American flags sewn on their upper arms.

Our cooker located in grounds of an asylum – these houses neat and tidy with well-trimmed hedges and lawns – more like England. Have scarcely seen an old building yet in Holland – yet there is something traditionally Dutch even in their modern architecture. Looks like being a hard fight for the town in Nijmegen – shall be glad when we've passed it. Pontoons were going up last night and some this morning.

Moved round here to asylum. Watched two or three *Fokker-Waffes* reconnoitering our area. They flew low through the rain-clouds (though it has kept fine so far).

Security is now awful. Map references relating to dispositions given in clear over radio and maps with localities marked, left carelessly by officers – we are too confident. The 9th SS Panzer Division reported reforming. We might cop it one day. 11th Armoured Division, supposed to be our flank protection, has only two Battalions over the Escaut Canal – writer in rear! And XII Corps, on our other flank still far back. In fact our 'front' is exactly the width of the main road – no flank protection at all! The attack on the convoy at Eindhoven an example of the vulnerability of our exposed flanks and rear.

We're marching in single file – right across the enemy's front. He, by his dispositions, expecting us to wheel right into Germany. It's obvious that some of our infantry will have to face east along axis of advance and hold that flank, though XXX Corps apparently has all available transport – so how are infantry divisions to reach area in time? No trains. All out attack on Nijmegen going in now by Grenadier Guards – more paratroops dropped. We are holding the town – a bunch of mortar bombs or 88s on columns wouldn't at all surprise me. If we can cross at Nijmegen and at Arnhem, the Rhine is turned. Surely Jerry will fight madly for it? But can he afford to move stuff from Yank front? The more we extend his front the weaker he becomes. Supplies by air fell mostly in the Maas – bad luck – some thirty prisoners today.

2200 hours

Now bedding down in boiler room of asylum – minus a bit of coke and sulphur but dry and it has electric light! This afternoon saw fleets of Dakotas (?) dropping supplies between here and Nijmegen – mostly on orange parachutes – though some white – the second wave dropped white – the third and fourth waves orange and green parachutes – a fascinating sight – impressive display of air power. Good news tonight from Nijmegen – Bill Browns now on both sides of Rhine obstacle – so guess the bridge there OK and captured intact – if so we shall be away tomorrow – no communication from Arnhem – hope all OK there yet.

At stand-to there was some fooling with Dutch nurses – CO peeved – then a blitz on officers and so on downwards. Woman with three kids here – her husband taken off by Germans for sheltering British troops. Civvies coming in all day to report Germans at so-and-so – many of them talk English and they seem highly intelligent and much less excitable than the French and Belgians and their information very sound. Two Dutchmen came in with information regarding two British pilots they had found dead and burnt – the CO rather offhand with them – they wanted to make coffins for the two pilots – could not seem to do enough for the English.

21 September 1944 – On hill surrounding asylum – 0730 hours

Writing this, I can see the huge length of Grave Bridge in the morning mist – our tanks are going over it – a continual roar of armour moving up to the bridge. Houses below me.

0930 hours

We are now leaving here – this place gives one an impression of security being surrounded by high buildings and hills and walls – almost a medieval effect in fact.

22 September 1944

We were halted a long time in Nijmegen yesterday – crowds of civvies out on an inspection tour – rather a smart-looking town. Much air activity and many German planes machine-gunning our column – all very confused – our Bren-carriers had a go at them – yet I suspect some of the planes fired at were British – crowds disappeared.

Eventually we moved at about 6.30 pm. I travelling now in the office-body. We were formed up in columns of eight vehicles before a sort of roundabout that was being badly pasted by German shells and mortars and our trucks took the bridge at full speed – in the shelling zone many houses were burning fiercely – our trucks missed the shells. So on over the enormous bridge – its southern end wreathed in smoke and flame and its whole tremendous length littered with scattered kit, papers and letters and debris and many dead Germans.

Arrived at northern side of bridge where it was comparatively calm and peaceful; we found large wooden packing cases full of German army food – polony – sausage meat – bully etc. Don't fancy it at all. There were signs of heavy fighting all along the road from Grave to Nijmegen and particularly over this side of the bridge, though it seems reasonably quiet this side at present. Darkness fell and the glow of fires from Nijmegen, and I presume, Arnhem were accentuated.

Shattered houses and the inevitable dead cows – row of pylons, their wires shelled and trailing drearily – roads and what looks like an electrified railway running along a high embankment to our right – overhead cables – no sign here of the Holland of our nursery books – no tulips or bonneted maids – rather dreary country in fact and the boggy ground keeps our tanks to the rather conspicuous roads. I dug in with Dusty Smith amid cabbages. Some shelling going on and our own mediums, now this side of the bridge, are shelling too. The sight of these two massive bridges, captured intact, gives one a feeling of achievement.

Horrible night came on and our companies took up their positions – and the gunfire continued. A dead American, covered by a canvas sheet, lay alongside our slit trench and was removed by his comrades for burial this morning.

Food was cooked – dead loss sorting out six men to a tin of duff in the darkness – only the flashes from the guns gave sufficient light to ensure that one was getting one's due share and that it was being placed in the mess tin and not on a cabbage. We are among orchards here again. Apples synonymous with shellfire.

This CO is a thorough dead loss – seems always bad-tempered and a most selfish bloke. He chewed up Ianto Evans for not saluting him in the gloom of stand-to – in fact it was still quite dark at the time. An attack going on in Arnhem today.

The people here are very scared, and no wonder! German 88s are the trouble – our tanks are easy meat on the highly conspicuous roads and they're shelling us with HE from them as well. Hope they reach the paratroops today – they're having a hot time at Arnhem. Roll on! The rear link is out of order. The corps on our right and left has not made much progress and there are German pockets all the way back for miles on either side of our centre line. 43 Division passed through us today – time they brought up some infantry divisions. Our infantry brigade is much overworked – we have only four battalions of infantry – enough to support armour, but not sufficient to man extended bridgeheads.

There are reports of supplies and reinforcements for Arnhem now being dropped in the German lines – don't know how true. A rush for Yank sleeping bags that have been dropped by parachute and not picked up. They say that *Luftwaffe* caught our bombers and Dakotas over Arnhem with no fighter support – again don't know how true. Rumours are that 2nd Scots Guards are to take over our Battalion's place in Division owing to our heavy losses and that the Division, once we reach the Zuider Zee, is to police this area – wishful thinking! I think though that there is a possibility of first rumour considering our lack of reinforcements.

<u>2245 hours</u>

Am on guard. Night is here again – there is a whole ring of fires on our right, front and rear. Our mortars are firing and there is some Jerry stuff in reply – some heavy stuff falling again on the other side of the bridge. One feels terribly alone at night in war. Disturbing news has reached us of the cutting of our C/L and vital supply line as far back as Uden. The Bill Browns have been sent back to deal with this (our guns are going like mad from the bridgehead – the melancholy whine of many shells overhead).

To resume – it seems that Guards armoured infantry is much overworked even now – 43 Div is making very slow progress – XII Corps might help us out at Uden; but VIII Corps still too far back to clear that flank – this Division has about shot its bolt – the Grenadiers have gone back to Uden – the Coldstream to help the American Airborne east of Nijmegen, leaving only the Welsh and Irish Group to hold bridgehead with help of 43 Div.

This is a crazy battle – we are pushed 60 miles forward with 10,000 Jerries on our left flank, and some 45,000 (admittedly some under military age) on our right. This marching across an enemy front must be unorthodox – if it comes off then it will be a great triumph – if not, then we'll be in a grave position. We're still some 5 miles from paratroops at Arnhem – so near and yet so far and they're desperately short of ammunition and supplies. This is, indeed, a battle of bridges, fought, almost exclusively, along a single road, and will, however it goes, cause comment and discussion in military circles for years to come. The fact that our Division was chosen to lead it is a compliment, but that's not much of a consolation if we're slumped around here with Jerries eating our rations and smoking our fags. Jerry would clearly like to win back Nijmegen and this bridge we're holding across his precious Rhine. I anticipated something of this sort happening. Am writing this by torchlight and down a slit trench and under a blanket.

A letter from Dearest – all well, but she's feeling the pinch for money. Must try to ask CQMS to allow her more. There go our guns again, that whine of mortars too. Arnhem is the target I guess, let's hope our flanks are cleared soon, we shall have to wheel right soon to protect our C/L – a crazy battle indeed. I can hear a plane now. A little rain today – but generally fine and there have been high vapour trails in sky, though not a lot of air activity. Roll on.

Many DUKWs[1] going up along road and railway – particularly before dark. A solitary jeep, ominously still, on railway track after shelling. The horizon now lights up, glows and dies. Growls in distance – thunder or German guns? Another growl – thunder I think – wrap up if it rains! Latest rumour – Yanks, with eight divisions, making sea-borne landings north of Arnhem – sensible at least. Another growl. Won't be much fun in slit trenches in thunderstorm – has been pretty hot today. Roll on.

23 September 1944 – Lent – 1730 hours

Only two hours' kip – so rather tired. The night kept fine but after stand-down over came low grey clouds and heavy rain – our concentration of gunfire during the night very heavy and almost incessant. Had breakfast in the downpour – a very miserable meal – one's fags too soaked to smoke. The dead cattle are humming quite a bit and some dead Germans lying around don't smell too pleasant either. The weather cleared and we are now here on the other side of the railway and amid villas much like those of a London suburb.

24 September 1944 – Lent

This is a most disturbing spot. Shells are straddling the village now. Three batches of Hun planes, ME 109s, made life hectic – it's all so sudden. Was

---

1. Duplex Drive Amphibious Truck.

strolling across to Intelligence truck – the racket started – I thought it was our own artillery – then Bofors and small-arms fire opened up – I dived for cover into the barn – a terrific racket overhead and bombs fell – one of which made the timbers of the roof of the barn quiver and the floor to quake. Can hear the guns now – they fire – the whine to howl – then the crash as they land – we are now U/C 5 Guards Armoured Brigade. The stuff is now falling on our right and left.

It has now commenced to rain again. Was rather jumpy last night. Managed to get prisoners over bridge and back to Brigade last night. Some smashing pears and apples here in this barn and more of those great corn stalks. It looks like developing into a major battle here. Roll on.

The strength of our Battalion is very weak now – there might be something in this rumour of a changeover with 2SG.

<u>1430 hours</u>

German shells still dropping short and overhead – one cannot feel too complacent about life. I lettered two more crosses. There doesn't seem to be much faith placed in 43 or even in 50 Division – the latter division is, anyway, through its immense losses, only a shadow of its original great self.

Rained again about midday, and looks like more rain coming. Shrapnel from German shells last night were hitting this outhouse – lucky I was near a slit trench as they came over – most unpleasant sensation to hear things dropping continually nearer each time – seems all eternity – one's slit trench seems a mile wide and absurdly shallow.

American paratroops are in the village. There is a subtle difference between bombing and shelling – bombing seems temporary and all of us joke immediately after a bombing incident. But we don't joke over the ever-prevalent threat of shelling. Nijmegen Bridge hit today by bombs – it is still in use though. Annoyance when one is asked for a light by a man who takes one's fag and keeps talking, or takes one's fag possessively to light his own.

<u>25 September 1944 – Lent</u>

Still much air activity – the last barrage made a determined attempt to destroy the bridge. One plane hit by AA fire – a single parachutist now floating to earth from it. It seems there's a change of plan – into Germany from here? All of us very sorry for the Parachute Brigade at Arnhem – tough luck. Am bored stiff – roll on!

<u>26 September 1944 – Elst</u>

On German rations yesterday and today – don't fancy their meats, but good, real butter and excellent ersatz honey – lousy and very limited biscuits. Felt terribly bored having nothing apart from maintaining situation maps to do. A relief to read H.G. Wells *The Dream*. Have eaten too many pears. We moved here (to Elst) at 1.30 pm. To a jam factory at first where much looting on part of higher-ups – the excuse being that, as we are only some 5 miles from Arnhem and at the extreme tip of Second Army's salient, the factory will be shelled and mortared and possibly retaken by Germans, and no civvies seem to be here in charge. Moved from jam factory into a barn – dug in and stood to.

27 September 1944 – 0545 hours

We have just stood down – slept well in the straw in the barn – Am Beek. Some blokes will smoke when lying on straw – dangerous. Our heavies have just opened up. Much dead cattle lying around here. Fineish morning. Think of lots of things first thing in the morning – of this war – its duration and its futility – of bacon and eggs – of Stella and a home fire. I suppose it will end one day? Things seem to be slowing up just now and Russia, knocking out German satellite countries, gets no nearer to Berlin. Another day of boredom and, I suppose, of alarms. Roll on! Another boil on my neck – Damn.

Pitied a terrified little girl of under 10 years who crouched by our truck and went hysterical – she had come to trade eggs and fruit for cigarettes and was caught as German planes came over and our AA guns opened up all around. We tried to calm her as she crouched and sobbed and screamed against the wheel of our truck in the orchard – roll on!

About 1530 hours

Cigarettes came through today – have been smoking German cigars and French fags – ghastly! We couldn't still be cut off as some supplies have got through. We expected to move again today – but not yet.

Feel my job here's a flop at times. Adjutant rather peevish today. Thinking today how things have changed from the slit trenches at Cheux and Cagny – where we all hurried for food – two men at a time – and ate it in our slit trenches and some officers sent their servants for it – to the mobile 'officers' mess' of today with a sideboard and with pictures on its walls. A TCL is used exclusively for carrying officers' kit and a 15-cwt to carry the liquor. The Company Commander uses a 15-cwt exclusively as a bedroom. Things might revert to Cagny days yet. Let's hope not. This, we hope, is only a 'build-up' period.

Just had tea – a large slice of good cheese (square), butter, lots of jam and one tiny piece of black German bread to put it all on. No biscuits or bread is our chief moan – it was pouring with rain and I thought of our companies out there – they're having a rough time. A Brigade order warning us against looting Jerry prisoners – particularly of watches and rings – apparently Jerry just moans his head off when questioned and won't spill any beans for purging.

Clogs worn universally here. Rumoured that there's a cinema show at Arnhem. Men here are huddled round the wet hedges and over petrol fires – winter seems not far away. A lot of aerial activity in the low, stormy clouds just now – that ghastly belch of rockets and some close MG fire.

02 Sergeant Roberts died of his wounds two days after I saw him hit on the road at Beeringen – he had a broken arm in a sling when he was hit and could, had he not insisted on staying here, have been back in England. A man who was disliked and feared back in England – a man who knocked men down in pubs and savagely kicked their faces as they lay on the ground – out here, as a stretcher-bearer and later as a medical sergeant, he has gained a reputation as a hero – his tenderness and care in dealing with wounded – his insistence upon risking his life amid bullets and shells to carry wounded men from where they lay to safety was the talk of the Battalion. Corporal Jones, the Police Corporal who was with him on that road when he was hit has also died from his wounds.

Renewal of order to carry weapons everywhere – proper order – we were beginning to get slack, but why not keep it up?

Winter is near – today's weather the first real sign of it – cheerless and grey – we seem bogged down for ever in this flat, dreary countryside – one wishes heartily for peace. Our airborne troops have been withdrawn to this side of the Neder Rijn – slight setback – so ends the battle for Arnhem and its vital bridge. Only 50 per cent of us had to stand to at first light this morning. Some of Intelligence Section scrounged bread from somewhere – nearly all gone now. The misery of living in soaking wet clothes. The rain drips maddeningly onto, and down, one's neck. Some shells falling quite close this afternoon – slit trenches bogged – more rain – roll on!

28 September 1944 – Elst

Still here. BBC news reports confirmed that what is left of 1st Airborne Division has been withdrawn from Arnhem – it is, indeed, a setback and they suffered very heavy losses – a terrible pity we could not reach them in time. A gunner officer supporting Airborne at Arnhem told me he thought more could have been done – he said that each time the centre line was cut our line-of-command people on the spot just withdrew and sat back until Montgomery came up in a temper and sorted things out – he said that, as a result of the Germans cutting us off he had to limit his guns to very few shells per day and added that, with some fourteen divisions of Second Army behind us, it was fantastic that half of Guards Armoured Division had to be sent back from the Nijmegen battle to assist the American 82nd Airborne SE of Nijmegen and to clear the centre line 30 miles back.

The 43rd Infantry Division did get through to Arnhem and so did some of the armoured cars of Household Cavalry, but our wrecked and burnt-out tanks on the main roads and those bogged down in the black earth tracks along which they tried to reach Arnhem bear witness that our armour could do no more. We never learn our own losses but, from what I have seen, they have been heavy – the Micks, particularly, have suffered heavy tank and infantry losses. Apparently, even while the Division was holding the Escaut bridgehead the Germans issued an order which was subsequently captured by us – it was issued prior to their savage all-out counter-attack against our bridgehead over the Escaut Canal some twelve days ago – in it was stated that the GAD had been in action continuously for fifteen days, had been spearheading the British advance, had suffered severe casualties and was likely to be extremely tired and demoralized and that the projected counter-attack on our bridgehead would fling these demoralized troops back over the Escaut Canal!

They obviously exaggerated our losses, but it must have surprised them to find the same division fighting its way out of the Escaut bridgehead some two days later and advancing nearly 60 miles until today we are within 5 miles of Arnhem. Certain now that we must face a winter campaign in Holland or Germany. It was a case of so near and yet so far.

29 September 1944

The bridge has been blown either by a submarine or by men swimming to bridge – apparently the railway bridge is destroyed and the road bridge hit by a bomb – much depression and gloom. Showed guns and a NAAFI van arrived later so bridge must still be usable, how odd to think of the NAAFI running the gauntlet of shelling and bombing over Nijmegen Bridge to bring us teas and wads! Very welcome too! The birds singing among these lofty trees are grand to hear. We move again tomorrow – to a defensive position – maybe Hitler's big counter-attack is on its way? So far the day has kept from rain.

1 October 1944 – 0700 hours

A most terrific stonking in progress. Jerry is counter-attacking along entire Nijmegen bridgehead perimeter. Stuff has been coming over all night and particularly since 5.30 am. Ted Edwards overheard the conversations to the adjutant on R/T. Apparently we, in reserve, take no action – yet! Our own guns are going hell for leather. Slept OK but rain came in just by my head – dead loss – raining hard now – a pity since our aircraft can take no part in the battle – main attack will come from SE I suppose. Our people seem confident they can hold him – let's hope so – the loss of Nijmegen would be a serious blow – some aircraft up now and Jerry shells falling pretty close. Looks like counter-battery work at present.

2200 hours

Hell to pay still – our guns have been going non-stop for three hours now

– incessant smoking and the violent bombardment have given me a wicked headache. Some Jerry stuff dropping nearish again now. Adjutant says the position has become stabilized. The 7th Green Howards have held their ground – they have had a rough time – so have the Micks. *Spandau* fire still nearish. Bah-pah-brrrrrh! A glorious full moon and low racing clouds – a great, black cloud – like a gorilla, or maybe an eagle obscuring the moon – an odd sight. The full moon shining over the square meadow of this area looks much as a painting of the Dutch school – or is it my imagination?

GERMAN INFANTRY WITH "*SPANDAU*" MACHINE GUN, "*SCHMEISER*" LIGHT AUTOMATIC AND HAND GRENADES.

A brilliant glare from Elst where the jam factory and town are on fire. Refugee Dutch civvies and girls mucking in with blokes – our guns sound nearer, as though they have moved forward towards us. One feels resigned to all this – one almost despairs at times of seeing the war out. Roll on! The smell of luscious green grass and trees by night is delightful. Too good a night for war. Fascinating reflections of the flames at Elst upon the low cloud – and the lazily soaring red blobs of our AA against this exciting night sky most interesting. Though there has been very little Jerry air activity today.

<u>3 October 1944 – 1200 hours</u>

The Brigade IO arrived by jeep, had been caught and straddled by enemy bombing. Tremendous roars of laughter from his fellow officers on their learning of his narrow escape and experiences in a wet ditch and much pulling of his leg.

The scene unpleasantly reminiscent of one from last war – motor convoys – subdued lights from regimental signs of units bordering the road – the faintly illuminated red cross signs of an advanced dressing station (ADS) – signallers trailing wire from a carrier – a full moon – silver now – threw dark and confusing tree shadows across the road – a low and heavy mist clung to the earth – three or four fires on our right (started by recent bombing) blazed angrily. Ack-ack rose above the great bridge to our rear at Nijmegen – we passed lines of black and silent trucks, and guns in fields. The blast and yellow-white flickering flame as our guns, growing nearer, opened up and some Sherman tanks of Irish Guards – black and monstrous in the moonlight – their 17-pounder guns seeming doubly long, loomed and lurched towards us, and the little jeep was edged almost into the ditch to let them pass. So on through our own artillery and forward to Battalion HQ. The sentry from the new batch of reinforcements challenged us and the journey was over.

Felt annoyed over newspaper column re 7th Armoured Division – says GAD OK but suffering heavy casualties owing to tank crews jumping up to salute and banging their heads on turrets. 7 Armoured Div and other desert units have not been so hot over here (always excepting the 50th Division). Even the Germans refer to 7th Armoured as the 'Normandy mice' and they gained a bad reputation in Normandy. The 51st Highland Division not too spectacular either for all the boosting they get from the press. The casualties among 50th Tank Transporter Division tell their own story – they have more than maintained their desert fame. Certainly 7 Armoured Div cannot hold a candle to 11 Armoured Div and it has been the 11th and Guards Armoured that have done most of the tank work over here, and done it well. As tank men, 6 Guards Tank Independent Brigade will take some beating – much of their reputation must go to Duggie Greenacre (their Brigadier).

Today I lettered a cross for Guardsman Harvey of 3 Company. Took greater pains than usual over this, since his father, who is a sergeant in our 2nd Battalion is on his way over to see the grave where his son is buried – this one is not quite as all other graves are – the mourners will see these, not as Sergeant Harvey will his son's, as a rough white cross – but as neat and chiselled stones, so I did my best.

A dismal day still – rain and a cold wind. I writing this in cab of office-body truck.

4 October 1944 – 1500 hours

Deg and Brian in slit with me this morning – all laughing like hell as shells fell. They were big babies too! Cordite must recall for me, if I live through all this and get back to Civvy Street, the unpleasantness of the constant shell threat. The uncertainty of never knowing when the howl warning (if lucky) sends one flat and pumps the heart – each shell seeming nearer than the last – the cheapness of life and limb – one's sense of impotence and physical frailty against the threshing, jagged steel and one's vulnerability to the awful razor-sharp steel fragments that are shot, white-hot and at terrifying speed in all directions and at all angles. I'll try to remember all this if ever I become bored by peacetime routine.

5 October 1944

Fair amount artillery activity – mainly guns – though occasionally a Jerry shell whined or crashed near enough to cause us to glance round at ditch and once or twice we took cover in the barn. Sometimes the low whirr of our own shells going over made us duck until we heard report of guns as well. We are unanimous that the shell that gets you is practically soundless (though I heard that 88 at Cheux) – one that 'rushes' will have you unless you're down – one that 'whistles' may unluckily get you at 100 yards or so – one that 'whines' merely needs half an ear a-cock. Those that 'sigh' are harmless to those that hear them sighing. Much the same applies to bombs as well – save for those A/P (anti-personnel bombs) devils. One wonders, as the old gang goes one way and other new faces appear, how much longer one will be lucky? Ten little niggers sort of idea. One nevertheless feels a keen twinge of envy for those with a Blighty, but not permanent wounds. They've had a dabble – they can say that.

Someone said as we listened to *Spandau* and Bren fire mixing it that it sounded like a gigantic cat purring – very apt too! Section was sent to search (i.e. loot) some railway trucks here at Elst and Burt of PoW got stuff from shattered shop – black treacle etc.

Man and wife, owners of house in which Battalion HQ is installed have evacuated, but appear each day to get food etc from kitchen – seem a nice young couple – they have guts to make the journey I think. I happened to be near window in kitchen lettering the Jock's cross when they arrived – as the woman looked at it she wept a little. They've built yet another little Jock-and-Taff cemetery alongside the hedgerow. That would be a strange experience for a suburban family in, say, Chislehurst, to leave home and returning, finding a small cemetery in their back garden. The bodies will, of course, be exhumed and re-buried by the War Graves Commission. Some more good chaps gone.

Coming back from CP, I watched in clear blue sky dozens of vapour-trails and saw squadrons of great bombers overhead – there was nothing sinister in that sight – they looked like delicate moths – frail – sort of boneless – effect of the sun I suppose – only their droning was menacing.

Meanwhile the American push at Aachen has petered out – we are at a dead end here – though why we don't wheel right and cross the Neder Rijn between Arnhem and Nijmegen I don't know. We'd be across the whole Rhine then. Roll on!

13

Winter in Holland and Belgium 7 October 1944– 31 January 1945

The Guards Armoured Division was relieved on 6 October and the two Welsh Guards Battalions returned to the Malden area, close to Nijmegen, where they stayed for nearly a month and where they were refreshed. They were in counter-attack reserve and their duties were light. They had been in almost continuous action for over a month and needed reinforcing and refitting and 4 Company was reformed after their losses at Helchteren and Hechtel. There were forty-eight-hour leaves in Brussels and Antwerp.

On 4 November they relieved another battalion at Veulen, a small isolated hamlet 20 miles south of Nijmegen. They were there a week and the weather was appalling. Movement in the deep mud was almost impossible. With that and heavy shelling and mortaring their situation was extremely uncomfortable.

They, in turn, were relieved on 11 November and moved to the Sittard sector, 40 miles south of Veulen. Sittard is a small town less than 3 miles from the German border and the Welsh Guards held the front at the German villages of Millen and Tuddern just over the border. It was a fairly quiet area of the front and generally uneventful. They remained in the area for over a month and on 17 December they came out to 'rest' in Belgium.

7 October 1944 – 1800 hours

Moved here yesterday morning – can still hear our guns on flanks – but nice and peaceful – though some bombs awoke me once or twice after night fell. Crossing Nijmegen Bridge usual touch of adventure since bridge and town are still under fire from medium and long-range guns. Several landed before our truck crossed the pontoon bridge and some fell after – the road bridge works well in sunshine – its great blue arch – a historic bridge now – or will be. All round the bridge – on both sides of river is desolation –

smashed and burnt-out houses – the town is gradually being reduced to ruins – a great shame. There's something a little uncanny about Nijmegen.

9 October 1944 – 1920 hours

Reveille 0800 hours – went to Divisional Club at Grave on back of Brian's M/C. OK but too crowded at nights. Cinema show for rest. Masses of traffic on road. Emblems of almost all 2nd Army units – mainly light and medium AA going up over Grave Bridge towards Nijmegen.

A church service at 1430 hours. Padre Payne is leaving us and a damned shame too! He's not made me one whit holier – nor has he tried – but he's taught me how fine human nature can be. We all like him – only now that he's leaving us do we realize how much we're going to miss him. I hope I meet him again. His farewell speech was sincere – though his emotion, or rather, the effort to control his emotion, was too great to allow him fully to express in words what we knew he meant. He was talking to a few of us not so long ago and told us sorrowfully that this Regiment was one of the worst in the Army for blasphemy and foul language – yet no man deliberately swore or blasphemed knowing him to be near – he was broad-minded, his sense of duty great – he was an example to all. He did not care for war and its perils, yet he often went places to the dead where shelling was persistent. His job entailed some most unpleasant tasks – some of the bodies he's had to identify and search and bury have been revolting sights. He's a great little man – Welsh all the way through and the best that Wales can breed – and that is saying much. I hope I can shake his hand before he goes. As Colonel Heber-Percy said, 'We all congratulate Padre Payne upon his promotion – we all wish he hadn't got it!' His last service in the little Dutch barn I'll not forget. I remember thinking, as our Padre departed, of Shakespeare's *Henry V* and of the King's assessment of Fluellen's qualities: 'There is much care and valour in this Welshman.'

15 October 1944

These American paratroopers often come across to us to swap fur-lined jackets or to offer ten pounds in English money for Luger pistols – they are pistol crazy, and when they have acquired a pistol they make shoulder holsters, just like film gangsters – in fact Americans seem to try to 'live' film lives. Another Yank bowled up after two sections of paratroopers had passed through our lines. Asked which section was a man short – when told said 'Guess that must be my crowd – I only got two clips of cartridges – we're going to do an attack – guess that's enough though.' A rather slap-happy crowd – but they seem good enough troops and I rather like their casual regard for the business. [Note added later: these were in fact fine and well-trained soldiers of the famous US 82nd Airborne Division.] Also tale of doggo firing – 13 Jones suspected.

30 October 1944 – Antwerp (on a forty-eight-hour leave)

Now sitting in a café in the square and facing Antwerp Cathedral. It's a dream in grey stone and blue slate and marred (temporarily) only by some scaffolding, high up on right side. Tried to enter cathedral, but all doors firmly shut. The Gothic in architecture appeals to me immensely – waiter here tried to rook me out of my change – this after giving him an English fag and a generous tip – bells of cathedral chiming now. Have at last found a reasonable beer – lager, but at fourteen francs per glass. Last night paid forty-five francs (4/6d) for glass of cognac. Club here damned good – a bed-bunk – food off a plate and a lavatory with chain! Flying bombs falling near here – one fell as I neared cathedral. Windows in and out – much glass on street – air-raid warnings – that sounds odd – fitting boards to windows – all very clear here – some well-dressed women – civvies – seems a paradise to us – but it's this cathedral that has got me! (See plate no. 24, 'Impression of Antwerp Cathedral'.) A Belgian flag flying from its peak – a grey autumnal day – the whole edifice, sky and atmosphere a study in subtle variations of grey – cobbled streets – tram bells.

To cinema last night. In outside still cases saw, in dim lamplight, much leg and limb – seemed just the thing. Turned out to be a Yankee anti-VD show – serves me right.

Woman from Arras – had to ask her to have drink in café – wine at thirty-five francs a glass – hate feeling a sucker – started pawing me – didn't feel like that – not with her anyway. But the sight of respectable and pretty women in the streets makes me pine for Stella. People asking for fags – this is a very fine city – as good as, if not better than, Brussels. 11th Armoured and Guards here – into a great multiple store – super place – plenty of everything. Stella would love some of their articles – but all very dear here – plenty of wonderful pastries – can buy no other food save as a meal.

31 October 1944 – Nijmegen

Now back here – left Antwerp with many regrets but with little money. Out last night. To café near cathedral where had some strong beer. Scarcely a soul there – huge place – rather near flying bomb area got on rather well with a young woman – had a long talk – she at Louvain and spoke of indiscriminate British bombing there – bad show if true – some flying bombs fell near – she terrified, then pointed to waiter and said, 'Him frightened' – rather amusing.

So on to dockside cafés – music from wireless and bands – entered one where British troops and Belgians were doing 'Knees Up Mother Brown' – some big dive – marines, local dead-end kids and young girls 15 to 17 dancing – hard nuts too. To other cafés – this Dockland area must be target for V weapons as they were falling close – usual harlots in most cafés – entered one astonishing joint – behind the bar a bloke (I'm sure male) with his hair done up at back in a bun! At counter sat a beautiful blonde with marcelled hair – also male. Waiter was tall youth in crimson silk blouse and with long hair – almost kissed me as he brought my beer and only my contemptuous scowl prevented his trying. Café comprised all-male cast, and all as queer as coots. There's something disgustingly humiliating in receiving from males these provocative, come-hither, coquettish glances that are so stimulating when they come from a pretty woman. There was, I believe, one woman, of about 40, dancing with a gunner, and she seemed completely nuts and I suspect that two gunners there were queer too.

Drank beer quickly and wandered back towards centre of city and met a Horse Guardsman – with him for drinks and eventually to docks again – entered rather low-down café in which an attractive and not particularly 'tarty' girl caught my eye – she was a seductive type, I rather drunk – went upstairs with her – usual feigned passion and I, through drink and misplaced embarrassment over my rather wild and woolly army underwear, found difficulty in concentrating on the task in hand and actually apologized to the naked girl lying patiently on the bed. Felt somehow that the honour of the British Army was at stake in this. Eventually redeemed the Army's name feeling a fool and a mug as I paid steep price of 200 francs.

Got on very well with my French though most people in Antwerp seem to speak English. This morning was misty and I up, after breakfast, to the Grande Place for one more look at the great cathedral – it towered partly hidden in the mist and looking more dream-like than ever. Yet it does not need mist or twilight to enhance its beauty as do so many London churches (though I realize that in a rare crisp sunlight Wren's churches compete successfully with any). But this cathedral can well stand up to the full glare of day.

<u>3 November 1944 – Nijmegen</u>

Ready to move onto Veulen front. Not so good. Much rushing about as usual. Determined to get the sketch I recceed yesterday – I climbed a tree on high ground whence I could see Nijmegen Bridge (see plate no. 26) and I made my drawing. Damned uncomfortable but I've got it. Also one from river's edge – feel a bit exposed here. From my tree I could see far beyond German lines and presumably they had the wood under observation. A couple of shells landed in water bridge-wards but omitted these from sketch. Also rough sketch of Antwerp Cathedral.

<u>4 November 1944 – near Ijsselstein – 2200 hours</u>

Battalion now in position – dreary bleak countryside – scarcely a house not in ruins – an odd sector – on approaching the usual grey whiff of smoke lingering in the air and the ominous emptiness and dearth of tactical signboards spoke of airburst and the proximity of the enemy. All very quiet. Did not, as usual, pass through our own guns belly-aching – they were, if anything, deadly still. Front is very thinly held in 'pockets' based on hamlet strongpoints some distance apart and RSM says Jerry patrols this area slipping between 'pockets'.

One shell whined overhead and exploded near village and the Adjutant and I had a hectic ride back from command post at Veulen – area is a marsh and two routes to Veulen are under observation for 2 miles or so. Ditched half-track and abandoned it when shelling and mortaring began – couldn't see Lister doing that.

A cold, but sunny, clear day and tonight the stars glow and the Milky Way shows clear – and we could see trails of British bombers as they passed overhead. We dug in – found a trench already dug and moved in. The house here and its belongings in an indescribable mess – everything as per Le Bas Perrier – Jerry began it I should think since those are German helmets, clothing, greatcoats etc here. But British troops have lived here as well – made char. Am sorry to leave Nijmegen. It was CO Micks' choice to take over again there or come here – can't blame him for picking Nijmegen.

5 November 1944 – Veulen – 2130 hours

A gale sweeping across the marshes and rain lashing the window of this little outhouse. After devil of a lot of trouble fixed up blackout, scrounged a stove and have got it glowing red-hot and it's warm in here – the guard is in adjacent hen-coop. Ours lit by hurricane lamp. Tried a sketch of it (see plate no. 27, 'Intelligence Section – Venraij Sector, Holland'). Also made sketch today from half-track of Ijsselstein village under shellfire.

Night is ominous here, guard in trenches no joke. Like Izel in 1939 all over again but with enemy close at hand now. One feels oneself very much observed in this flat, open country.

Three fires glowing on skyline – red streaks from west to east – corn cobs stored in cages off the ground. Looked again through Stella's pictures – roll on! Bed warm I guess. Expect I'll be on guard tomorrow night – this second night. Must be lousy for companies tonight.

7 November 1944 – Veulen

Wind of last evening rose to gale force later and the lashing rain made the guard a most uncomfortable one. One or two more bombs were dropped. Slept warm, at least for the little sleep I had – no incidents but visited five times by officers and WOs. In gale just couldn't hear them approaching. Dawn about 6.45 – grey – wind still high – our 5.5s going in rear – so far very little German shelling today – touch wood. Support Company just down road has laid loads of trip-wires connected to flame and booby-traps. Masses of dead pigs around – owners of farm turned up here today. Porter hurriedly hid a slain young porker in Adjutant's sleeping bag. Watched flying bombs (V1s) going over earlier. Deg says he saw it rise from site.

The warmth and the illusory sense of security of the cook-house (possibly because cooking's the only thing that goes on here as at home). Some casualties in companies yesterday – not many. Ground very muddy – can't see an armoured offensive getting far in this lot – but maybe a slow advance on the Ruhr would pay dividends? IO and others believe that occupation of Ruhr would finish Huns – don't know. Certainly they'd have a mighty chilly winter. Marked up maps today. Feel damned tired. Duty men must get tired and fed up.

Was waiting for transport from Mr Koppel to go and pick up Stacey when over came a salvo of mortars that fell just short of barn on other side of road – about 2-inch calibre. No one took a terrible lot of notice. Brian who saw only the smoke said 'miles away'. Always an optimist, Brian. Then came another dose and the farm opposite caught fire. The thatched roof, obviously selected, set alive by a phosphorous bomb, blazed up in no time – an ambulance arrived. All the Company and much of Rifle Company's transport were sheltered in the farm buildings.

Darkness fell – RSM drove out some 3-tonners including, I believe, one of ammo from burning barn but the dug-in trucks all round the blazing buildings could not be extricated from the muddy quagmire – one or two largish blazing fragments fell near the nine haystacks surrounding our, and the MO's, dug-in trucks – they were stuck and we laboured furiously to free them. The haystacks, thoroughly soaked by rain, didn't, however, catch fire. From the blazing trucks ammunition began exploding, and mortar and grenade fragments flew everywhere and huge masses of sparks soared aloft – the flames crackled savagely – an awful and fascinating sight – the best display was when the flares took fire and we rushed into outhouse to avoid fiery rockets and the blue-white particles that showered upon us. Only two fellows injured – marvellous – but eight trucks burned out. Good shooting on Jerry's part.

Quite expected another burst or two – seemed inevitable as the night grew darker and our bonfire greater. We could not shift our truck by its engine and brute force and awaited the Bren gun-carrier which had towed some of the burning trucks from the blazing buildings – at last it came to us and even then hell of a job to get our 15-cwt out – much digging – swearing – lamp-flashing (not that this mattered). A shorter tow rope – a mighty heave and out she came. Felt horribly exposed and sort of naked working there in glare of flames.

Rather a terrifying thing, fire by night in full view of the opposition. But occasionally the magnificent blending of colours – the cherry-red, the

179

bluey-white and yellow of the flames and blending of pink-brown smoke into streaky blue and purple of storm clouds made a fascinating picture, the sheer beauty of which overcame the fear if not the awe of the occasion. The mortars fell as a 3-tonner entered farm. Possibly from Jerry patrol that had laid up nearby all day? Our trailer is still there – fetch it tomorrow – felt very exposed also when walking up the road. A Jerry patrol would have had a duff target in us.

Now in a large barn some 300 yards away – not much better since we're still under observation and a phosphorous mortar bomb on this lot wouldn't make things too healthy. Another pleasant Dutch home gone west – a bloody shame. It would be Jerry's policy anyway to burn these houses to prevent their use as billets – *c'est la guerre* – and I guess we can expect a repetition of the incident. Roll on Friday night – feel damned tired – today's was, I am sure, well-observed fire – quite unpleasant experience – needs stronger nerves than mine to remain indifferent to constant shell and mortar threat. Ah well! Poor Herb's still out – but guess he's well dug-in at Div HQ. IO said no transport available and reason for temporary shortage not far to seek, and in any case no one can use lights on roads after dark owing to observation by Hun.

A dead loss this flat open country. Have seen countless fires here on continent but first time I've had to hang around one for two or three hours and had time to study fascinating colours and form so close to. A regrettable but wonderful sight.

<u>9 November 1944 – 1000 hours</u>

Sergeant Randall rushed in rousing companies in robust Depot-style – very chilly morning – sun came up but now mixture of snow, ice and rain is falling. A 3 Company carrier taking up the breakfast dixies to the company blew up on a mine. These carrier men run a gauntlet of shells and mortars each run. As meals cannot be cooked in Veulen and by companies (owing to proximity of enemy) it all has to be cooked in rear area and taken in containers along the exposed track to the companies – these tracks Jerry mines during the night and we can see numerous explosions on the two tracks – they're bloody heroes. Unsafe to send soft-skinned vehicles up save by night and tracks too muddy. I bobbing last night on naked candles amid the straw of barn. Chick, fooling, let go a burst of Sten fire near Old Joe's[1] foot. Joe, always inclined to stutter, stood pointing to his foot and, in his indignation, stuttering furiously. Before he could mouth his disapproval, Chick said 'That's only a sighter so stop moaning.' Lucky he wasn't spotted though.

---

1. Joe Darlington.

Looks as though Jerry's got something with this liquid air shell – might get him places – most unpleasant – even a trench at some distance from burst no help as, apparently, explosion somehow absorbs oxygen from air around and the lungs collapse and death follows. IO told me to keep report under my hat so I alone, of rankers, have this inspiring information to brood over. Little news on the front line this morning – two months of fine

" JEEP " PASSING
BOGGED-DOWN " SHERMAN."

weather would be a boon. Lost a half of my mess tin. Trips to Antwerp and Brussels still going. Roll on!

10 November 1944 – Command Post – Veulen

Bags of rum last night – quite soused. To Support Company with Brian and Deg to take maps. Warned for a taping party across country (presumably for relief of companies by another unit) – not on and then warned to take over from IO again at CP. We came up in a jeep – tracks in appalling state and even some carriers are bellied. Jeep made it OK and we were not fired upon and I felt anything but hurt over the enemy's indifference towards the solitary jeep and my own importance. We used the log road and he generally has a smack at passengers on this route.

As I arrived they had just finished burying Powell in the verge of the village road and a burst of mortaring had sent Padre and burial party to cover of nearby barn. Padre had tobacco tin containing Powell's identity disc and papers all ready – he and the party had had near misses and some were wounded. Padre turned to attend them and, after a burst of mortar fire I strolled out, placed the tin decently on the grave and walked back. I did it because I could see they didn't want to, and the Padre himself had been badly shaken up, and because I was the only NCO present and it was little enough. But these fellows have had six days and nights – the four companies ringed round command post, defending, or holding, this village;

they are a concentrated target and six days and nights in such a place under nearly continual bombardment tears the nerves to shreds. I was fresh to, and unmoved, by their experiences and could well afford to be casual in their presence. I ran very little risk but appreciated that they, having been exposed for some time deepening the slit trench grave and burying the body and having got away with it, apart from a couple wounded, had reached the stage where it seemed tempting fate to expose themselves again in that task. This Padre's nothing like the man Padre Payne was.

Companies dug in all around here – CP in cellar entered through low hole in building wall and its entrance protected from shell-splinters by armoured half-track set just clear of it and covering it. The cellar whitewashed, low-ceilinged, 6-volt signal bulbs light it, turning straw on deck into streaks of gold – a carpet of gold in fact. Good food here considering shelling and mortaring and CP, being not under direct observation, cooks own food in outhouse. Considerable mortaring and shelling and one burst right outside door of RAP as 'O' Group was awaiting CO's orders and blew in the fanlight – odd cuts but no one hurt and no one perturbed. Company's lost several men from this shelling however.

These static positions make war seem absurd. Both sides mortar and shell any odd target – a few men – a suspected latrine – a farmhouse of no vital importance is fiercely contested – mines are laid and booby-traps set; each side rivals the other in planned cunning – men die and at the end of the day the line is as before. In a war of attrition it might make some sense, if there is sense in such warfare. German parachutists are opposite us – no gentle babies – but then neither are the men in this mob, particularly under Heber-Percy. A takeover here a most sticky business.

Listened all day to the CO and Battery Commander conducting shoots and organizing patrols. Graham very amusing. A big show on at 2.30 am – a patrol. Linesman's job a deadly one here. Carriers bogged down on track with PoW Company's dinners – hard luck that. Hope we can get all this stuff out. We put a biggish barrage down at 5.15 and Jerry replied fiercely. OP reported a Jerry staff officer's car – many shots at them from 25-pounders and even mediums, but no luck I think. Very peculiar these little Battalion battles every now and then – a Bren behind goes off or one hears a *Spandau* close to. Roll on relief – get browned off sticking around with nowhere to go. Men refer to the 'slit trench quickstep' and the 'Moaning Minnie minuet'. The men who go so calmly on patrols and particularly night patrols, are heroes.

Odd to hear officers gravely discussing best means of dragging back a German corpse for identification. No glamour – no nothing! Indeed, this corpse has been a centre of attraction for some days – Brigade or Division badly want an identification – we know the opposition are parachutists, but not the Battalion they belong to. This corpse (killed on patrol?) lies tantalizingly near both lines. Heber-Percy is determined to have it – the Germans that he shan't. We want it to identify, they to bury and deny information, so there he lies dangerous to reach by either side – the object of a miniature war – covered by guns of both sides and flares as well at night. So strange to hear expensive accents of Harrow or Eton or Winchester gravely discussing plans and methods of acquiring this corpse.

11 November 1944 – Veulen

Twenty-six years ago tonight the last war was over – this one's still on – so what? Kipped among the élite at command post. Captain Graham is (as I heard a Gunner officer say) 'worth his weight in gold' – if not to the actual physical discomfiture of the Hun, at least to the morale of his own side – most amusing chap – rankers say he's living 200 years after his time and, indeed, his graceful manners are more of the eighteenth than the twentieth century, while his enormous, absurdly exaggerated, orange whiskers set in a thick, pink, healthy face and surmounted by bright-blue eyes alight with mischievous and irrepressible humour remind one vaguely of cavaliers or Elizabethan characters straight from Shakespeare's pen.

Takeover by the 3rd Monmouths terrible job in such a zone. Tracks bogged. Only the log road is barely passable but this is being heavily shelled or 'stonked' ('stonk' seems a word here to stay) at times.

Monmouth CO and Company officers etc arrived. Apart from CO and a couple more they are all in CP, ranker-officers. Seems odd to meet a Cockney major or a Welshy captain. Suppose it's a step in right direction – don't know – but I prefer it the old way. They sat on the straw, ranging themselves against the cellar wall – they had a nasty job to do. They stared as a well-modulated voice murmured, 'fifteen men on a dead man's chest' and, stooping to enter the cellar, in came Andy Graham. As he unbent and stood upright I saw he held a great glass jar of rum in his arms. Somehow this seemed to suit him perfectly – he looked fantastically pink and clean in the lamplight – he had, I gathered, been given the job of supervising an extra rum issue. Smiling courteously, his quizzical eyebrows raised, he politely offered rum to all present. The Monmouths stared fascinated, as Andy, in his inimitable way, murmured little jokes that made the whole war a ridiculous nonsense.

Koppel and one or two other officers arrived and I believe the Monmouth officers thought their light-hearted banter was the result of an over-generous rum ration – yet they were quite normal and sober and were quietly doing their jobs as I, who was used to them, knew. But I have no doubt that our officers, keenly aware of the presence of ranker officers (or, as they sometimes unkindly refer to them – 'Charley officers') laid on more heavily than usual that traditional nonchalance that is the hallmark of the Guards officer in grim situations and of which Andy Graham must surely be the 'Beau Ideal'! A form of snobbery perhaps, but also a wonderful triumph of mind over matter and fear, and one that has a beneficial effect upon the morale of those beneath them.

Gus Pennington who was out with a wiring party in no-man's-land was shot in the bottom by the Monmouths after they had relieved our company. O/C Company and Platoon were informed of Gus's party but they seemed rather trigger-happy and opened up as they saw, or heard, their activities – fairly dark night. Two of the stretcher-bearers went out for Gus – too heavy – so four needed. Apparently Gus a flesh-wound – just what he said he always wanted and the right spot – Gus well-padded in that area – a Blighty – and Gus evidently well-pleased and, as he lay on his belly on stretcher, grinning and giving the thumbs-up sign and complimenting Mons on the accuracy of their shooting and fortuitous selection of target. So goes another 'old Sig' and peacetime soldier and a good amusing fellow. I know very few men in Battalion now.

Some shelling and mortaring today – most unpleasant spot this – awful job getting kit away in darkness – and the personnel. Suggestion that some of personnel might travel on a half-track ambulance – vetoed by Heber-Percy and anyway ambulance driver apparently got badly shelled and took half-track back to Battalion HQ. Lost his nerve I suppose. Consequently surplus kit loaded onto jeep in which CO and I were to have ridden. CO said he and one other must walk back with 3 Company, the last to leave, and asked for volunteer. I volunteered and remained in cellar and H-P handed over to CO Monmouths – there were so many defensive fire (DF) tasks from Gunners that this quite a business. Meanwhile got food and rum ration and was embarrassed by too much rum – nearly filled my water bottle. Was a little worried to have the bottle full or almost in presence of CO and big shots but couldn't resist offer.

Each company phoned through to say it was relieved and on its way back and finally 3 Company phoned to say it was on its way at 2200 hours. Colonel Heber-Percy turned to me and said 'Ready, Sergeant Murrell?' We were just climbing out of cellar to join 3 Company when blower went and H-P waited. Evidently Jerry patrol and CO Mons, ordered a DF task shoot. H-P realized that this DF task was temporarily 'out' as we had troops in area ourselves – he went back and took over control of operations – and 3 Company proceeded on its muddy march back to Deurne. This meant the colonel and I were the only two Welsh guardsmen left at Veulen.

To leave such a position as Veulen and march back for 3 miles (in an area covered by German patrols) in the middle of a company of guardsmen is one thing – quite another to do it in the company of one other man – even if he was Heber-Percy, and I clearly saw that as much danger came from the Mons as from Jerry – at least until we were clear of Veulen and its environment – there was the example of Gus Pennington – seemed the

184

occasion for a stimulant and as H-P settled back and I discovered need for call of nature and took opportunity to swig deeply of my bottle.

Back to cellar. H-P chatting with CO Mons – over an hour went by and I out again for another swig. When H-P finally left I was as bold as brass and not caring if whole Hun army lying in ambush along the track. Fortunately H-P knew location and actually challenged one Monmouths' outpost himself – he quiet – an occasional reference to mud or blackness of night – we found and followed the white tape – some shell or mortar bursts behind helped us on our way – a couple of farms blazing and our guns came down on a DF task– otherwise all quiet, and we ran into no Jerry patrols but met several carriers and Carden-Lloyds and guns of Monmouths bogged in the mud en route to the line. An army recovery vehicle was doing its best but there were no officers with them and not much success. Captain Worrall was at end of track having extricated all our transport.

Walking back along route was hard work – knee-deep in mud at times, and once we slipped into a very wet ditch. I made particularly hard work of getting out so that H-P would get himself out first so that I hadn't to go to his assistance; not that I didn't want to, but such assistance meant getting to close-quarters and I was conscious of the fact that my breath must smell very strongly of rum, stronger than the ration would have made it. I don't think he'd have said anything – in the darkness and mud any slight stagger would have passed unnoticed – in fact our journey was one long stagger, but I didn't want him to realize that I was matching his own sangfroid with what was, in fact, a purely artificial one of my own.

Learned later that Mons also killed one of the Royal Norfolk machine-gunners with our Battalion. Now here in a school at Deurne – OK. Wouldn't mind staying here a week. But we're off again at 11.00 tomorrow and back into the line somewhere – dead loss. Mr Bruce wounded again – his second dose this campaign.

It is now 2.00 am – must get to kip – feel tired – drop of tea on our arrival here went down very well. Cooking at CP very good and bags of fresh pork. Dug out clean dry socks – very wet from ditch but rum still warms me. Roll on Civvy Street.

It is five years ago today that we landed at Marseilles – a long time – very, very few of that fine Battalion with us today. We did not think then that this would last five years.

15 November 1944 – Sittard

Set foot in Germany for first time today. Odd experience. At one end of village street one has to ignore German civvies, at other end kids with orange arm-bands clambered on truck when we stopped (for haircut at the *Koppes Café* next door) and one may, if one wishes, pat them on the head. Turned out to be a barber's shop. Cognac and other potent liqueur – all on the house and an excellent haircut bang in front line and we are perfumed like prostitutes.

19 November 1944 – Sittard

Fineish sort of day – was not for church so up to attic to finish off my sketch of convent (see plate no. 25, 'Convent at Sittard, Holland'). Was on last lap when over came a shell – sounded alarmingly close and another crashed through roof of officers' mess 30 yards away. I became acutely aware of the unsoundness of my position – a concrete floor beneath my feet and only tiles between Hun guns and me – collected watercolour box etc and hoofed it to stairs – shells continued to crash nearby and I had a moment of panic as I rushed for stairs and tiles flew off and fragments bounced off concrete floor and shells rushed overhead – the main road badly hit and saw hit on church tower – probably their target – gunners manning OP disappeared from view in double time. Several shells fell on football ground where a match in progress – one fell in gateway where people were rushing out – pretty grim. American and civvies killed and hurt. Captain Robertson saw my sketches today and took them to mess.

20 November 1944

Quiet so far today. Sent for by CO who wanted to keep sketches with Regiment after the war – found it very hard to say 'no' but did so. IO has sent for them again tonight. Didn't care for their being out of my hands with shelling about and so forth. Some bad news from the Companies. CSM Addis went out last night to fix trip flares – one went off – all the men dropped to earth – he stood and was riddled by two magazines of Bren fire from a 3 Company section. Court of inquiry – since they had been warned – but fingers on triggers are prone to jerk when flares go up. Bad luck! A fellow in 3 Company went up on a booby-trap – dead also.

Civvies here anxious to do our washing – we supply soap and they won't accept money – only soap and fags. One can purchase goods in the shops for fags. Even Yankees short of them too – locals will offer twenty francs – five guilden for cig. Fellows playing chess.

3 December 1944 – Sittard

High wind tonight. To Geleen to see a film show. *A Canterbury Tale* at Divisional cinema made me homesick as hell. I enjoyed every second of it – the fine shots of English fields and hedges and the town, the very essence of an English town – summer in wonderful England and Kent. Sgt Blackmore and some others thought it a dead loss – no glamour girls – no excitement. But I lapped it up and came out from the sunny, dreamy cloisters and streets of Canterbury into pelting rain and a wet, dreary black street of a Dutch mining town, the red motor tail-lamps reflecting streaks of molten red light on the black, wet roadway emphasizing the bleakness and dreariness and drabness of the war in Holland. Tea and wad and Doug Marsh to see if he could work the oracle with QM to buy bottle of sergeants' mess whisky. How I pine for England and Kent tonight. Blast the picture!

4 December 1944 – 2000 hours

Very high wind this morning and it howled and whistled and tore the last of the dried red leaves from the trees, a last farewell to the memory of summer. Rain and hail lashed down – cleared later however. The nuns here are kindly women and seem not at all disturbed to have their corridors full of lusty men – and what a mixture – nuns and British guardsmen! They wash our canvas for us and we give them scented soaps from home and what chocolates and sweets we get.

A German patrol last night got through to 3 Company's billet. Two of our men off-duty at the time were cooking chips in the house – the door opened and an impossibly guttural voice said, 'Hands up'. Thinking it a leg-pull and being interested in their gastronomy, one guardsman said, 'Don't f*** about, get your mess tins.' Glanced round and there stood two Jerries who told guardsmen to get their greatcoats. As the two guardsmen went out of the door escorted by three Jerries they turned on the Germans with fists and broke loose – Jerries opened up with automatics – one guardsman got away – the other fell, shot in three places but still living. Alarm raised by fire but Huns got away with it. A pretty good effort and they believed to be SS troops – we shall know tomorrow. They must have come through masses of trip flares and booby-traps and have passed quite near to one of our standing patrols. An incredible performance. One wonders if they'll not stroll into Sittard next!

Definitely must start taking more care of my appearance. Looked myself over in the mirror. Hollow-cheeked, baggy- and dull-eyed – little colour – some blackheads and a shaving rash. In fact I don't look at all fit. Excessive smoking clogs my lungs and has stained my fingers orange, red and brown. Yet I don't feel that I want to feel fitter if it means less smoking. I feel that, if all is well and I come out of this war OK then I'll pull myself together. I just feel unable to do so now – things are too uncertain I suppose. I feel quite depressed at times and find myself paying far too much attention to rumours re our going back. Not a creditable show at all. In fact I think I believe rumours but feel certain something will happen to prevent it. Looks as though we're in for another rather unpleasant battle soon. Roll on.

Odd how the greater the physical comfort and the smaller the danger of a position is, the more morale slumps.

8 December 1944 – Sittard

Off guard at 7.30 am. 11.00 pm – 4.00 am seemed deadly long. No incidents but some flares dropped somewhere. A man under arrest. Wind now howling round attic roof. Stacey's just come in with a bottle of cherry brandy – must be kind to Herbert. He shall not sweep out Intelligence office in the morning. Sentries of the 94th Light Aid Detachment kept us supplied with hot tea and rum – good of them and it relieved the monotony somewhat. Showed Sten guns and magazines. Had visions of a court martial today. Couldn't find mosaics of the next op – was really shaking and a tremendous relief when I fluffed where I'd put them.

The Dutch celebrated their Noel on 6th. Nuns sent us apples and biscuits baked in the shape of a cross. Felt jaded today – always do off guard and went with party to the Divisional cinema – pretty good since Jean Arthur was in the show and she's so damned well like Stella that I never miss her pictures if possible to see them. Stacey up with pile of presents. The Dutch kind people and I believe traitors among them in these towns that border Germany a tiny minority.

Some interesting information in Divisional Intelligence summary re new tactical infiltration by small groups of infantry – though this I believe was successfully tried by Ludendorff in his March offensive of 1918. Also an appreciation of merits of British and German infantry – his belief is that his is better than ours. I think that's true as regards this campaign – at least as regards the offensive – but his praise of British troops in defence is generous – and here again he's right I think. He praises Battalion armoured units in general and our artillery.

These summaries make interesting reading, being based upon captured German appreciations and with no propaganda attached – indeed, the only criticism worth considering is that which comes in form of our unbiased intelligence appreciation from the enemy. British infantry is traditionally stubborn in defence but in attack it sometimes seems on this campaign at least, as though when encountering strong opposition they sit tight and leave it to gunners and bombers – and it seemed to me that more could have been done both in infantry attack on the 'Island' to relieve Airborne 1st Division and in clearing out centre line and I could never see why Guards Armoured had to be split into three separate formations: one holding Island bridgehead north of Nijmegen – one 30 miles back to clear centre line along which whole of Second Army was advancing, and one to bolster up American Airborne flank facing Reichswald Forest. Perhaps conservation of troops is a definite policy – certainly a change from 1914–18 when incompetent generals sent thousands of men into impossible terrain and unnecessary death. Our own tank men are inclined to sit back and call for Tiffies when up against Tigers – but here, with the average sacrifice of three or four Shermans to one Tiger there is some justification. Our tanks have the mobility but not the armour or gun-power to engage Tigers, nor for that matter Panthers, in equal combat. A Sherman to a Tiger is as a cruiser to a battleship and such controls are not deliberately sought at sea. Our tank men often bitter about discrepancy in armour. Still – we and Americans under Patton, have exploited full mobility of our armour in a way Germans couldn't do with Tigers, and not even with Panthers. Our Churchills could, perhaps, slug it out with their Panthers, but not a tank on our side can stand up to the Tiger.

Nevertheless our tanks by day should cancel out any success of his infantry infiltration by night. Report on his liquid air shells reads grim. Roll on!

GERMAN "TIGER" (56 TONS)
WITH 88 mm. GUN.

***

On 21 December the 1st Battalion went into billets at Hoegaarden and the surrounding villages and was anticipating a relatively peaceful and comfortable Christmas. However, on 16 December the Germans launched a serious counter-offensive against the Americans in the Ardennes and they succeeded in breaching a 45-mile gap in the Allies' front though nothing decisive was achieved. When the offensive was at its height GAD was moved to Namur and the adjacent high ground overlooking the Meuse as a precautionary measure though the enemy did not reach their positions. The Welsh battalions returned to Hoegaarden for a belated Christmas, which, together with the New Year, was celebrated in some style.

During an increasingly cold January finding billets in Hoegaarden was not a problem:

No need to hunt for billets here – people almost kidnap us off the streets and I hear them asking one another if they have an English soldier yet and those that haven't try to lure away a 'lodger' from those who have two or more.

The Army makes only token payment – they genuinely and sincerely want an English Tommy each. (27 December 1944 – Hoegaarden.)

21 December 1944 – Autgaarden

Moved off 10.00 am – regimental form-up, inspection etc. Still a heavy fog though not as thick as yesterday, but quite thick enough to neutralize our air activity. We ended up here in Autgaarden – a scruffy village with more steaming manure heaps than I've seen yet and place pervaded by the 'healthy' hum that goes with them.

24 December 1944 (Christmas Eve) – Hoegaarden

Fine weather has continued and it has grown colder. Heavy frosts this morning – clear blue skies and hard ground, like iron. If this keeps up all will be well I think. Moon out now in a clear sky. This morning the café below was full of cockerels in little baskets – hearing all the crowing as I dressed I imagined it must be a cock-fight but discovered it was, in fact, a cock-crowing contest – must have been some thirty birds and their owners – latter kept using some fluid administered to birds in fountain-pen fillers – either dope or lubricant – a stimulant maybe. Seemed an odd sport – some crowed long and lustily – some not at all – very strange, but no doubt they'd think a cricket match a peculiar sport too.

Off now for a few drinks – much music from the café. Belgians downstairs often break out into 'The Red Flag'. Seems a very leftish place altogether. The German song *Lili Marlene* popular in cafés in Belgium – people a bit nervous about singing it in our presence at first, but our fellows all for it – a haunting tune that sums up the longings and frustrations of a soldier's life in any country at war. Besides there's no doubt of the Belgians' hatred of the Germans. People below seem particularly fond of Uncle Joe's boys – but we are allies – so what?

Snowy wanted funny drawings for the NCOs' café. I fearfully depressed and in no mood to comply. However, did manage a couple of weak efforts. Very cold today, frost incessant.

25 December 1944 (Christmas Day) – Namur

We are now in the yard of a farm. A glorious but very cold morning.

The CO came into the mess café last night – stood all present a round of drinks and said that it was to be our last as we were moving off before first light in the morning. Caused quite a stir. Plates, tablecloths etc had been hired for the Xmas dinners.

Many were drunk but the news was sobering and we wondered if matters had taken a turn for the worse and it meant battle in the morning. Issued maps – packed kit – the civvies much alarmed. (We are now in Namur – great vapour trails in the sky – but ground haze considerable and must be a nuisance to them up there.) When ready drank more cognac and beer. Roberts didn't turn up with the truck. He went to fetch it as I ordered and suddenly found himself halfway down a lane with headlights full on at 4.30 am – remembered nothing after leaving café – drunk as an owl – we searched for him. Luckily he turned up in time for us to load truck and move off on time.

Indeed, it says much for discipline that a battalion of men, dispersed throughout a small town, disporting themselves in numerous cafés on Xmas Eve, many happily drunk and none expecting a 'call to arms' should, on being warned late at night and at the height of their revelry, be away before light next morning with all equipment and in convoy and moving operationally and not a man missing.

26 December 1944 (Boxing Day) – Namur

Awoke, having slept deeply – colder than ever and the frost makes fascinating patterns on the windows. The map looked different, but, though it has more shape about it there's nothing very encouraging – the *schwerpunkt*[1] seems to be drifting due west – towards here and the enemy still retains the initiative. Brigade seems to think a large-scale counter-offensive brewing. If this weather holds might turn out OK. Jerry is sticking out his neck a long way and is close to the Meuse near Dinant where 29 Brigade of 11th Armoured is in action. It's so easy to look at arrows and plan a counter-offensive on the mauve and green staff maps – but the Ardennes is difficult country and will probably limit the use of our air forces.

Thinking a lot about Stella – should be soon now. Cancellation of England and return rather depressing – roll on!

30 December 1944 – Hoegaarden

We held our Xmas Day yesterday. We (sergeants) waited on the men in the traditional manner. A misty foggy day and only one small gleam of sunshine – Jerry weather in fact. Dinners OK and Battalion did us well – beer, champagne and red wine – then with Doug Marsh to visit 3 Company where we drank gin – then round the cafés and grew drunk as owls – whisky in the sergeants' mess and rum from Peters – that is, we were drinking from 2.00 pm till 1.00 am and I was indeed drunk. Still cold and a very heavy hoar frost.

An American transport unit here. Odd system – instead of being a corps like RASC, they are made up of stragglers and odd men of all units – gunners, infantry, tank men etc – mixed blacks and whites – a few drinks and they fire off guns in the streets – into the air but disconcerting –

---

1. Focal point.

desperadoes. Today cold and foggy and raw. Blokes posted on roadblocks – a whole Brigade of German saboteurs[1] at large, dressed in US uniforms and in captured US vehicles – precautions taken here.

'Red Flag' and *Marseillaise* sung in cafés – not *Marseillaise* as national anthem but as revolutionary song – the Belgian anthem the *Brabaconne*. Am rather drunk again tonight. A bad head this morning. Yanks an odd shower – drink much black-market cognac and some have gone blind – permanently it is said. Belgians prefer British to Yanks. Exaggerated rumours re battle, but not much change.

1 January 1945 (New Year's Day)

Into the mess café where many civilians and Yanks. There had local 'Christmas' beer brewed in M. Vandenbroeck's (my landlord) brewery, and whisky and much gaiety and dancing. Things were going fine and the best night I've had for a long time. A Belgian sang the *Brabaconne* – the British, a little sheepishly at first, 'Land of Hope and Glory' and the Yanks their anthem. American and British soldiers ripping off one another's tapes for souvenirs – Jenks more or less running the show as MC – a slight contretemps between CSM and Drill Sergeant Stevens, but generally all very friendly considering the liquor that abounded. An American played a piano-accordion as accompaniment. At midnight we all sang 'Auld Lang Syne' and taught the Belgians how to join hands in the traditional manner.

Little whisky glasses looking damned attractive on trays and even more so in the hand. Much singing. Yanks, as usual, *pas gentil*, but friendly enough.

I silently toasted my Stella and, perhaps, my son or daughter – wondering how she is facing her lonely ordeal. A man can't visualize what a woman feels in such events.

I watched the Belgian folk – voluble and unrestrainedly happy and the Americans going all out to make their celebrated 'whoopee' on this New Year's Eve, swearing furiously and letting their hair down and the Welsh who grouped together and sang nostalgically their native songs of country or religion and the English who just stood and drank.

Then a Yank, a serious-looking fellow in rimless *pince-nez* glasses, began wanting his tapes back – he was fairly drunk and getting a bit quarrelsome and he started feeling in the pockets of our people and trouble was in the wind. Wondered what the devil line I should take if he tackled me. With misgiving I watched the faces of our people as they pushed away the American's searching hands and noticed the ominous glitter in their eyes as they heard the American threatening to start something that he warned wouldn't be pleasant. He approached Sgt Blackmore who, without

---

1. Skorzeny's commandoes. Lieutenant Colonel Otto Skorzeny – SS officer with a speciality for daring and secret operations.

taking his eyes off the approaching Yank and without changing his position at the bar, slowly closed his fists and the gleam in his eye was a clear danger signal of what was about to happen. The bonhomie was, for most of our people, on the surface so far as the Yanks were concerned. I stepped in – explaining that there were plenty more chevrons to be had. That it was New Year's Eve 1944 and reminding them that at midnight we had all drunk the common toast as allies. Then Jenks took over and approached their senior sergeant who was fairly sober and, as I left I saw the Americans themselves about to eject the bespectacled warrior who had caused the trouble.

As I came down the street shots were fired – but into the air – these Yanks should keep their bullets for the Hun. I fairly sober and entered another café where a gramophone was playing that music so typical of continental cafés and which seems based upon the piano-accordion. In this café were mainly Yanks, black and white – each party with its guns and ammunition 'under the proprietor's counter'. A wise precaution because, from what I see and hear the whites and blacks hate the sight of each other. I learned from one of our fellows that it was the senior sergeant of the blacks who had insisted upon the precaution of 'guns under the table' on this occasion. The whole thing's fantastic – they're gun-crazy like school kids. To us a gun is a necessary evil, and a nuisance that rusts and must be cleaned.

4 January 1945

Was in the mess last night when an orderly came in with a message form for me saying that Charles Nicholas was born and that both were well. Great relief and glad for Stella's sake that it is over for her – the worst part at any rate. And it is a boy – she was certain of it. Well done! So I am a father and, on the strength of it was allowed to buy a bottle of whisky and we drank to the health of Stella and young Nick. I wonder if he'll ever know that his health was drunk in a Belgian café by British soldiers. The people in the café delighted at the news and I became the target for much friendly though pungent leg-pulling and those whose wives had undergone same as Stella told of their circumstances and reactions at the time when their children were born. The RSM came in to see and congratulate me and toasted the birth – adding that it was the quickest job I'd ever done. A load off my mind. Got fairly well-oiled and quite happy. The civvies at the café, and here in billet, very kind in all this.

8 January 1945 – Hoegaarden

Up – a touch of fluey cold and a bit chesty – breakfast. Some 6 inches of snow and all very pretty. The trucks look a bit like iced cakes. Children soon got cracking and Yanks, Tommies and kids soon engaged in terrific snow fights – a good sight indeed – flushed faces – noticed how the veins seem to stand out and red noses appear much redder in the reflected snow light. This is a longish and welcome break but one wonders what future holds in store for us. Roll on – roll on.

Much black market and *Madame* here walks four and a half miles to farm of cousin to get half a pound of black-market butter for which she pays nearly 10/-! Twice a week she sets off on foot on this 9-mile journey – and in this weather she is a heroine – we help out with marge but never see butter.

Cafés here, instead of darts and bowling alleys, have archery galleries attached – haven't tried it yet. Full size long-bows – about 30-yard indoor range.

12 January 1945

Off guard – tired – not too cold and hadn't to start up vehicles [note added later: these, when weather actually below freezing point, had to be started and run for a while by the guard in case of sudden order to move]. However, it snowed throughout most of the night and my moustache kept freezing as my breath condensed. More rumours about going back – they won't take CO's opinion as final. Odd thing is that so many of these 'latrine rumours' prove correct.

25 January 1945

IO told me today of Sergeant Millward's grave – he was killed on patrol – at least was seen to be hit and missing from patrol. CO sent out patrol after patrol to locate and bring in his body but no luck until after we had left Veulen and Second Army advanced – our officers kept in touch and followed up advance and behind the German lines found a very fine cross of SS type – painted on '*Feldwebel* Millward', his regimental number and regiment – all done very decently. Makes us a little ashamed of our rough and ready burial of German dead. Indeed the SS, vandals as they are, seem to conform to a very high military code when dealing with British troops – at least that is the experience within this Division.

There's something reassuring about our officers' interest in retrieving, or at least locating, our own Battalion's dead. They won't rest until the body is found and buried and this task is accomplished at times in the face of considerable hazard. Suppose there are two ways of looking at this. 1) Regiment won't release you from its clutches even after death. 2) Regiment does a 'Priam and Hector' act and mourns its dead. The latter is the just way of looking at it. The humblest rookie 'belongs' and is mourned as a relative in a family – odd thought. SS must behave in much the same way. See what new notebook brings. Roll on!

14

The Rhineland Battle
1 February–10 March 1945

The Welsh Guards moved out of the Hoegaarden area on 31 January. They had made good friends with their host families and there was much sadness at their leaving:

> When I made my adieux *Madame* broke out in tears and then tough old *Maman* started – and the same thing was happening all over the village wherever Welsh guardsmen were saying 'Goodbye'. I didn't know where to look or what to say. I swore that I would return some day and shall do so if humanly possible. They are very kind and very good people and I feel proud that the Belgians think so much of the English. We do so of them.

***

The last fighting of the war in which 1WG was involved was the Reichswald or Rhineland battle. The plan was to clear the enemy from the land between the Maas and the Rhine with the First Canadian Army breaking through from the Nijmegen-Mook line and attacking south-east. Once the Reichswald Forest was won the Guards Armoured Division was to follow up, seize a ridge of high ground north of Sonsbeck and then to push forward a strong mobile column with the object of capturing the Rhine Bridge at Wesel in the unlikely event of it still being intact.

It was also hoped that this attack, known as Operation 'Veritable', would draw off German reserves to enable the First and Ninth US Armies to strike simultaneously north-east from Aachen so that the Germans would be crushed between two converging armies. This was eventually achieved but the American assault was delayed by a fortnight due to the Germans opening some of the Roer dams and flooding the country. The whole battle was characterized by appalling weather conditions as the frozen ground thawed, roads flooded and any movement of either wheeled or tracked vehicles became increasingly difficult and the plan for a quick advance had to be abandoned. In addition the enemy's intense and fanatical opposition was a feature of the battle.

They were then concentrated around Malden. On 13 February, most of the country north of the Reichswald had been won. The Welsh Guards Battalions, or detachments therefrom, took part in actions at Hommersum, Kassel, Hassum (where they remained for a fortnight), Mull and Bonninghardt. Both battalions were extremely fortunate in that, although the Rhineland operation was 'a battle which in intensity and fierceness equalled any which our troops experienced in the war' (Field Marshal Montgomery), the Welsh Guards, though there was heavy fighting, did not experience anything like the resistance they had met in Normandy or at Hechtel and their casualties were light.

THE RHINELAND

13 February 1945

The thaw and atrocious ground conditions are enabling Jerry to bring up strong reinforcements to this front and there's no doubt that his Ardennes counter-offensive, by monopolizing the hard frosty weather, has put a brake on this offensive which had to be postponed to meet his own offensive. In view of ground conditions and particularly of enemy's greatly increased strength I cannot see this Battalion and the 2nd smashing through to Wesel and grabbing the bridge there intact. In fact we, instead of being the star of the show, are little more now than spectators of the work of the infantry divisions.

15 February – 1000 hours

We travelled on in an eerie half-darkness caused by the searchlights on cloud of artificial moonlight – great masses of searchlights reflecting their glow against the clouds – Gennep was deserted except for our truck – in the glow of artificial moonlight it looked horribly sinister and was a contrast to the busy scene of midday. No shells fell until we had cleared the town however, and we moved forward to here.

Houses, trees, everything is shattered here – breaks one's heart to see the looted litter in the houses. A tiny bottle of O-do-ro-us lying on the floor of a room that was full of the Hun smell seemed incongruous – gardens and fields scored with dugouts – dead men lying under a shattered windmill –

poor Holland! The only consolation is to know that 3 miles to the east and across the German border the same thing is happening. Jerry obviously left here in a hurry – bedding and small kit still in cellars and the cellars reek of his smell. I wonder if we have our peculiar odour to Jerry. Seems odd. They're not, as a race, dirty people and the smell isn't entirely one of sour sweat – it is almost as though they ate or smoked something with a pungent smell that is given off from their pores. [Note added later: have read, since then, that it was German soap that caused this peculiar odour.]

Some tea and rum 10.00 pm. Guns sited all around us. Cleared a room of debris – the wind howled and whistled through the smashed windows.

We got down to it but I slept badly – our own guns vibrated everything – the floorboards – loose doors and the pieces of glass still adhering to the broken window frames – this glass amplified the din outside and was unnerving. Some bombs fell near earlier, bringing more plaster and debris down upon our heads and throughout the night the drum-fire of our guns continued. When, for a moment it paused, we could hear the whine and crash of German shells falling outside – too near for my liking and when there was a rare moment of silence from both sides the wind became audible – an icy, howling wind that whistled about our ears and itself dislodged fragments of glass and masonry and loose wood so that, when the guns were tiring we didn't know whether the fragments that fell on us were caused by wind or shell. I scarcely slept at all and would have preferred a slit trench. Indeed I nearly ordered the section to get outside and

BRITISH SELF-PROPELLED
25-POUNDER GUN.

dig trenches as a precaution against shelling – for a shell landing on the battered house and penetrating through roof or window or wall to the room must have killed the lot of us. However, one or two were snoring and I was afraid I might be thought windy if I roused them to dig.

May I never forget all this terror if I live through it. The 'phew-phew' of our own 25-pounders firing – they're off again now.

Was glad to see daylight at last. This produced fog through which could just glimpse stretches of a flat dreary landscape – or seascape of acres of flooded meadows studded with shell-ruined or burnt-out farm buildings. All looked utter chaos and detestable. The casualties in Brigade attack of yesterday were light – may they remain so!

18 February 1945 – Hassum

Still don't know what's happening. Impossible to send soft stuff up any further – tracks impassable to wheeled vehicles.

Still raining and weight of water in ground sheet has just caused it to fall again into the trench and all over my knees. *S'en ne faire rien.* What a life! Fires lit – our legs dreadfully cramped last night. No mail from Dearest – maybe today. Funny to see men stumble out of their trenches first thing – in all orders – their backs hunched. The smokers fishing in pockets for cigarettes – staring abstractedly at a smoky wood fire – all deep in their own thoughts and it's not difficult to guess what those thoughts are about – 'What the hell's going to happen to us today?' Jerry prisoner yesterday – his nose dripping, searching through his rags for his *Soldbuch.*[1]

Some brew being prepared. Civvies passing back through us yesterday with shell wounds – old women among them. They're Huns but we cannot help but feel compassion towards them. What a stupid thing war is and, as one listens to the whining and whooshing steel going overhead it seems crazy. Roll on!

7.00 pm

We now have straw in our trenches – a great improvement – Drill Sergeant Blackmore is using a Jerry bazooka as a chimney for a fire in his trench. Hope he's removed the bomb. Amazing where men scrounge the kit from. The abandoned Jerry trenches nearby have yielded much of it. These trenches part of northern extension of his Siegfried Line – the line at last – but no washing on it.

Supper fifteen minutes late. Rabbit stew and, we hope, rum. Some cattle brought in today and fresh bacon for teas – OK too. A cook has just carried a squealing porker across to cook-house. Pity it isn't Adolf – though not for supper. Roll on!

[End of note book.]

---

1. Pay book – also ID book carried by every German soldier.

<u>19 February 1945 – 5.00 pm</u>

Had to start a new notebook – last one torn and pencil is fading. Have just glanced through my wallet of drawings and diaries – it's growing terribly bulky and am annoyed to find that, in some places the pencil is rubbing out and that in parts diaries are almost indecipherable. Apart from S and N, I am anxious to get these home. To see so much painstaking effort fading away is a dead loss. Kipped OK in trench but bottom very sore through sitting up the whole time. Cannot help smiling to think of fuss mothers and wives make to air a collar – but it's that sort of thing that makes home anyway.

The ennui of all this! Let me presume to address myself at a later date – I say 'presume' as I have no right to believe that any lengthy future lies before me. If ever – if ever I find myself sitting in a chair at home and find myself bored may I remember so many days of the past nine months – may I recall these days – this day – dull and cloudy and dreary – the hillocky ling-covered plain, its black sand tracks – the truck and trailer – the garish yellow sand mounds around the black slots of the slit trenches. The wagons, covered by camouflage nets – the smoke coils and sudden racket of 5.5s behind as they fire – the forlorn drooping little marker flags planted by the Gunners survey sections on various mounds – the bedraggled birch trees and the shell-holes – the nearby German zig-zag continuous trench system – the dragging hours – the cold and the wet – the brackish water with which we make tea (may we not be poisoned) – the occasional crump of landing German shells – the ever-present slight uneasiness that some careless Hun might plaster us for a battery – the hopeless uncertainty of the future – the ever-wet towels – the boredom of everybody – wet feet – sticky hands from jam which is a dead loss once it gets on hands. The depression of it all and the nihilism of it all. The longing for home, and particularly for one's wife. The uncertainty of it. In real danger, oddly enough, one loses this uncertainty. What a life! May I be grateful for fire and bed and peace of mind in Civvy Street – let alone freedom from fear of shells and mortar excursions at ghastly early morning hours. Roll on! Roll on!

<u>10.00 pm</u>

Moved and am on guard here – my first guard on German soil though Battalion Companies were in Germany at Millen and Tuddern for six weeks, so not my first visit. We are dug in beneath a wooden platform at Hassum Station. Place has been typhooned and shelled and is a ghastly mess, and a yellow-painted and shelled house was burning as we arrived – the station shattered and the rails rusty and twisted into odd shapes. A few civvies remain here – they are obsequious and a man doffed his cap to me as I passed.

A hundred yards up the line towards Goch a house blazing merrily – maybe set off by 51 Div or German shells – a nice beacon for a stonking – let's hope not. Disturbing rumours re 2SG – to hell with rumour! Our guns have been firing TFO and German stuff landing round about. Whistling Verey lights and what looked like tracer mortars from Hun. Mauve Verey lights shooting up from burning house opposite – metal of rails twisted and torn by shelling – mud and water everywhere. Hassum Station and its purlieus most depressing.

20 February 1945 – Hassum

Men huddled around fires – rain – rain – rain – but not cold just now. Leather jerkins are a godsend. The rapid scraping of spoons on mess tins. May I never hear this sound after the war – army life puts one off the picnic habit. The rain pattering on the cab tarpaulin and leaking in – windscreen blobbed with rain and the eternal mesh of the scrimp-garnished camouflage net and the wooden banging of the 5.5s and their rolling, clanging echo.

400 mortar bombs fell in front of 4 Company's position last night and not a soul hurt – astonishing. Indeed – it is amazing how much HE is required (on average) to slay a mortal. At least when he's dug in. Shelling on troops caught in the open is another matter. The greyness of everything here and the rain is depressing. Some peculiar white lights in the sky this morning – visibility very limited. Takeover rumour still lingers. How I wish

BREN GUN CARRIER.

it were true. Our companies going forward again today. I sometimes think we're as scared of our own guns as of the enemy's and the gunners seem to enjoy seeing us bob as we pass in front – I am not sure they don't time their salvos to indulge in this pleasure. Not much else in the way of achievement around here. It's an impressive sight as a battery or troop opens fire. Roll on.

Am bored and very wet – what folly war is – the 'Tchk-Tchk-Tchk'– of falling shells and mortars from Hun. The fading red and black feathers in the cab here – now just a faint echo of past glories and the 'swan' to Brussels. And still it rains! Roll on! Roll on!!

22 February 1945 – Hassum – 6.45 pm

Strange how these attacks go. We expected trouble against Hassum – yet Jerry had gone – some attacks are lucky – others deadly.

To mobile baths at Hommersum and Rob and some of company there this afternoon when Huns shelled it – they were all in Adam's order and had a scare – all laughing about it. As I passed through the devastation and extensive flooding that is Hommersum, I saw three or four shells fall, after our road I suppose, but the fountains of water they raised more reminiscent of naval than land warfare. Shells are not so dangerous in this waterlogged soil, being somewhat smothered as they burst.

Hommersum today is a scene of utter desolation and all the way back to Brigade the scene reminded me of the photographs and drawings I have seen of 1914–18 war. Mud, shell-torn buildings, army vehicles and signs everywhere – drooping, multi-coloured signal cables (a miracle how they sort them out) and infantry plodding up to or down from the line.

Through our 25-pounders and medium gun-lines – one blast from four guns nearly blew over the truck as we raced past the barrels. Micks nearly bombed by our own planes – if there's any rudery about the Micks fall for it – they have taken heavy casualties – a fine mob the Micks.

23 February 1945 – Hassum – 12.15 pm

Warned to go with Trevor to search farm in no-man's-land in front of 4 Company. Stacey has gone into dock – with a packet[1] we think. Don't fancy this job at all at 1.00 pm. Roll on! 5 Guards Armoured Brigade passing through station and between railway tracks – seemed endless – a vision of power – sketches – have several of these sketches of Hassum Station (see plate nos. 31 and 32). Meanwhile Jerry dropping muck around environment.

1615 hours

On Bren gun-carrier through devastated and deserted Hassum – littered with dead horses and generally utterly depressing, and on to 4 Company area where a fighting patrol of two sections was waiting.

Set off – Trevor and Hank the Dutchman (as interpreter) with me. We approached the farm cautiously and in single file and hugging hedges. The farm was clear of Jerries and we searched the place. A white flag drooped

---

1. A dose of VD.

from a barn. Four civvies were in farm buildings – an old man and his wife – a woman of about 30 and a boy child. Found nothing of significant interest. As we searched, an OP was being established at a window in the roof. Mr Brinson who accompanied the patrol was going back to 4 Company HQ – said, jokingly, he had no intention of staying there while they directed the fire of our mortars and artillery from the OP.

So, our job done, we left with him and Mr Brinson, but noticed some outhouses we hadn't searched and went back, forced the doors and examined a car in one of them – not much use, and we set off again and were just clear of the farm when our 25-pounders started ranging. Almost immediately a burst of mortars or shells fell on both sides of us – we were crossing a flooded meadow and making for cover of hedges as we heard the whine of the falling explosives. We flung ourselves to the ground and lay in the flood-water with no cover at all to screen us. Most unpleasant. The two officers had gone on some time before.

I decided that the *schwerpunkt* of the stonk was on the farm and could see mortars or shells penetrating the roof. So decided to run for it to the shelter of a hedge and bank about 100 yards away. I watched the shell and mortar bursts and shrapnel falling into the water all around us and it seemed suicide to stay there – could hear some small-arms fire but decided that the splashes around me were shrapnel from HE and not bullets as I could not pick out the distinctive whine of bullets going overhead. It seemed safer, as we were under mortar or shell-fire, to rush for cover together rather than singly. I warned Hank and Trevor and at my shout we all three rose and made what speed we could through flood-water and mud to the bank, but it seemed to take ages. One burst of mortar fire followed us, but we made the bank and threw ourselves behind it. My guess that we were under observation from a Jerry OP and not from a section or platoon must have been correct for, had they had small-arms or a light automatic with them they surely could not have resisted the sporting target we presented.

One is not terribly scared at such time and could be hit, I think, without knowing it. As we reached the hedge and bank, expecting a bump any moment, I felt quite puffed – later we found a deep hole along the bank and there we rested and laughed at our own indignity and lucky escape. We stayed there a while expecting to be shelled or mortared again when OP had had time to redirect weapons but in this case I myself overrated my own importance.

The experience of being shelled and mortared in the open most unpleasant however. I'd left my wallet of diaries and drawings with Brian – just in case I was wounded and captured or killed. Reached the comparative safety of a platoon HQ of 4 Company which was in a house and the carrier turned up which was to take us back and was I glad to see it!

Don't know how many, if any, of the 4 Company fighting patrol were hit. Mr Moss was nearly killed by a shell or mortar that passed his head as he was in the roof establishing the OP.

It is very fortunate for us that the ground was waterlogged and boggy – nevertheless it is unnerving to lie under fire in water as one sees the splash of every piece of shrapnel and it seems that hundreds of such pieces are falling all around one's person. Still, I cannot grumble and I can almost count on one hand the near-lethal misses I've had. I was lucky at Cheux when the shrapnel that got Wilcox missed my head first – the shelling of our OP at Carpiquet when I made a trench only by seconds – the bomb that night at Colombelles when Rose, sleeping beside me, was hit in the head – the blessed dud that fell right alongside me in the ditch at Beeringen and I suppose, this little affair today, though today's was not exactly a near-miss – it was the complete absence of cover that was so disconcerting.

Three battalions of our divisional tanks roared through Hassum station this morning, a most impressive sight. Some of them were extremely well camouflaged and looked more like mobile hedges than tanks. Ah well! I suppose this bizz will go on until one, or some, or all of us are seen off – so unnecessary – nothing gained.

Deg has been out with PoW Company – they also were stonked. I thought Hassum Station and its purlieus a lousy hole, but it seemed like home when I arrived back here. At least I've a hidey-hole here – not much – but something.

24 February 1945 – Hassum – 9.35 pm

Degville detailed for OP job with 4 Company – Brian volunteered but no-go – same sort of job as yesterday's but this time at night and rather more sensible. Unfortunately it's in the wood they were stonking so severely yesterday. Hope all OK with him – feel rather guilty that I didn't volunteer to go – he left his wallet with me – awkwardly – for Deg is a Brummy and undemonstrative and we always stress that it's just in case we lose the wallet or are captured – never if we are killed – to Deg, though he was probably thinking it, it would sound 'sloppy' to say such a thing. Gave him my stick of chocolate – little enough – but he doesn't smoke – he has to stay there for twelve hours tomorrow – it's only the same distance from 4 Company HQ as was our farm and he's going with a fighting patrol – it's not intelligence work at all and I feel rather mad that IO is sending him; he has no specialized work to do and will be simply one of the patrol – they are lying up tomorrow hoping to get a crack at Jerry. It's easy enough to send chaps out from CP and Rob never yet visited us on an OP nor came with us ahead of forward companies. He's a good IO and, of course, being so much with CO he finds himself in enough sticky spots. I feel I should have gone but Deg seemed anxious to get out on a job and yesterday, while I was out with a patrol, put Brian up to suggesting to IO that he went on one – very silly I think.

The lure of these things is loot – a thing I do not worry about. But even if they merely get Luger pistols they can get ten pounds each for them from the Yanks; this is Deg's motive. Shall worry about this until he returns. Let's hope this OP more successful than yesterday's and doesn't get fluffed to and stonked. Cold tonight – the moon is out. About 5.00 pm a crowd of our heavy bombers passed over going westwards. Four Spitfires, we thought they were escorts, were flying around low – suddenly we saw three bombs leave each Spitfire and fall about half a mile along railway and well within our own lines. Very odd indeed – no flak fired at them and they flew off northwards. A mistake – or are they captured planes manned by Huns? Trevor says we stay here now until 27th – so looks as though we'll not go out at all. Roll on!

2 March 1945 – Siebengewald

Typical March day of blustering wind, hail, snow and sleet interposed by momentary periods of quite warm sunshine. Moved from station to here – the old command post. Seemed almost as though drummer should have sounded the Long Reveille and a band played us off with 'Auld Lang Syne'. Billeted here in house but I prefer my straw-lined dugout and privacy. We move tomorrow. An armoured thrust with our 2nd Battalion I think. Unsettled existence. We might even move tonight. Situation is interesting – looks as if Hun right flank will be sandwiched very soon unless he pulls out *tout suite*. We seem to be pivoting on this sector. Depends, I suppose, upon how much Huns can get back across the Rhine. Were we able to bounce the bridges things might happen – if not then Operation 'Veritable' will end along the west bank of the Rhine and a new operation start then. Roll on a more settled life. I'm getting a bit oldish for all this gadding about. Roll on!

3 March 1945 – 6.30 pm

Fairly fine day – cold wind and some sleet and rain. Now at CP with whom, or which, we move off on a 'swan'. This time on the Wesel Bridge 'do' again. Jerry must surely have blown it sky-high by now or be defending it in great strength. Rob returned this afternoon with new engine in our truck. So here we are again – on eve of a mobile battle (or so planned). This battle of the Rhine – or Rhineland rather – going pretty well. Rumours that we are across Rhine – don't know if true. This might be a real advance and exploitation beyond Rhine – but I feel another planned operation will be needed first – don't know.

4 March 1945 – 6.35 pm

Cold, damp, misty morning and has continued thus all day. 5 Armoured Brigade are on their way so guess we shall go tonight, though Jerry's bridgehead this side of Rhine must be contracting and so making less room for more troops to attack him – unless we relieve 11th Armoured or someone. Made some sketches again today of the shell-torn graveyard here at Siebengewald (see plate no. 34) – a tragic sight to see – graves and stones and crosses smashed by high explosives – skeletons disinterred in places and the church itself almost unrecognizable as such. Sketch too of interior of vicarage and of a rather charming shelf group including a particularly pleasantly coloured image of the Virgin. Don't go much on all these ornate religious effigies as a rule, but this one particularly pleasant and very delicately coloured.

Report is that craters are holding up advance of 5 Brigade – through bombing I suppose. RAF a menace to our advances at times. Nightmarish ride with Deg to Battalion HQ to fetch Sten guns in dark last night – crazy to go in dark on a motor-cycle and with so many mines in road verges too. Kipped in Keldar. Boring existence. Wonder if we, or Yanks, will cross the Rhine soon?

Joe should be ready now to advance on the vital sector – towards Berlin – seems worried about his flanks. Shame to see the fine, well-bound books on architecture etc flung into the yard and the rain – their leaves used for toilet paper. This kind of thing depresses me more than the sight of corpses. May all this never happen again! Roll on – roll on when I can see, and be with, Dearest.

6 March 1945

Battalion attacked 10.00 am – the casualties light – six killed and eighteen wounded – Battalion has struck lucky again – we expected a fierce fight – impossible to forecast these battalion battles or to know just where Jerry will make a determined defence – he has a habit of withdrawing from towns and villages and then re-entering and often reinforcing them after the bombardment.

7 March 1945 – Bonninghardt

Moved here – Bonninghardt – but stayed for several hours at a manor-cum-farm-cum-castle. It had been stonked or bombed by RAF having been a Hun HQ of some kind. A fascinating place of moats and flaky grey towers and mellowed red brickwork...the place was full of Russian and Polish slave labour girls – one or two, despite rough clothing, very fascinating and who, when our rifle companies reached here last night, gave themselves to their liberators, and seemed very happy to do so.

Evidently the Count and Countess quite good to them and most of them were carrying on with their jobs pending their departure to DP[1] camps.

As we drove away from the place along a road through fine pine forest I reflected how, pre-war, the Count and his wife had probably returned home through this drive full of pride from Nazi rallies and meetings and, as their car drove in, have gloried in Nazi Germany's might.

Marked out more crosses for our own boys tonight, including one for Sergeant Waters [note added later: Sergeant Waters of Mortar Platoon was, I believe, the last man to be killed in this campaign. Tough luck being the last man to die] – a melancholy business.

The civvies here are servile and still a little panicky from the battle. One elderly man rushed up with a match as I took out a cigarette. I believe, despite my stripes, he took me for an officer. Seemed odd and a little embarrassing – I can't believe that English civvies would have been so servile had Huns taken England in 1940 – but I think these people have had a bellyful and want only peace – so do I – but I wonder if they were as keen on peace in July 1940? Roll on! Roll on!!

On sentry at 5.00 am and must count enemy dead tomorrow. Roll on!

8 March 1945

Dullish sort of day – saw the dawn break on sentry. A lot of German shells and mortars fell around us at breakfast time – and some falling now (midnight). As Deg, Ianto and I were returning from cooker with teas some mortars of 88s fell 20 yards from us as we moved along road – probably 88s as no time to duck, but we weren't hit.

I'd been to Brigade HQ in afternoon where Carey produced a bottle of gin and we drank nearly half each – so that I gained a temporary and ill-gotten reputation for being a 'hard case' to have remained standing on the road while Ianto and Deg were biting its dust. Surprising how a drop of neat gin takes the sting out of enemy 'rudery'. Still feel a little fuzzy from it – had some 100 German prisoners through our hands this evening and tonight – herded them into burnt-out barn when German shelling became too rough and, thanks to the gin, found it no effort at all to present a completely nonchalant front in searching and marshalling them and as one or two were inclined to be cushy and start smoking, we formed them up, drilled them and marched them to the barn.

Amazing how Germans respond to this – there is never any physical bullying of helpless prisoners – but interrogating officers can do little with them once they feel secure and relax, nor can they get much out of men who have been looted of some valuable, or sentimentally valuable trinket, such as a watch, and some bullying is essential in drill form and discipline.

---

1. Displaced persons.

Interrogating officers sometimes deliberately put a man at his ease and for a definite reason, but we are expected to hand them over with a respect for British discipline, and the Germans have high respect for discipline anyway.

Prisoners are always a dead loss though; unlike on stunts in England, they make no desperate attempts to escape. Indeed, all are only too anxious to get back away from their own shelling and it seems cruel to keep them in the line once they've been searched and marshalled, but believe Intelligence officers are coming here to see them and there's no divisional cage handy. Nevertheless, I'd feel pretty sick if shells did fall among them and we gave them spades to dig themselves additional cover to the barn – the Jerries started urinating in a corner of the barn – apparently a Gunner OP dug-in below and they seemed to resent Germans urinating over them. The Jerries very contrite when they learned of their *faux pas*.

9 March 1945

The 'Minnies' are moaning again – a gun – an SP I think – shelled close by here early this morning. One of our fellows down RAP this morning and sobbing like a small child – suffering from battle-strain or, as last war had it, 'shellshock'. CO says there's no such thing, but I wonder that more men don't go haywire – particularly in rifle companies. Battalion has been in constant action, or nearly so, for almost a month now and that's too long – the companies are definitely weary. It is true that the Battalion has been fantastically lucky in its casualties – they are, thank heaven, absurdly small considering the amount of stuff that has been flying around, the attacks made, and the heavy casualties of Micks and other of Division's battalions fighting a few hundred yards away.

Indeed, throughout this operation this Battalion seems to bear a charmed life – I have watched woods and copses and villages smothered in smoke from falling shells and mortars and within a few hundred yards of us – as much stuff, if not more, is coming over from Jerry now as in Cheux and places in Normandy, and back at Brigade I hear of the casualties these stonks are bringing to other Guards' battalions and our men believe, and are saying, that this luck cannot last. Each dreaded attack we've made has proved a piece of cake. We shall bump into trouble one day, we are sure. Were the other units on our flanks getting away with it too we would put it down to Jerry's cracking morale, but he's fighting furiously and we are facing first-class troops – paratroops and the like. Thus our people, despite our luck, feel far from complacent about the lightness of our casualties so far, and no doubt the anticipation of trouble can be increased through man's belief in the odds against such luck continuing and can wear the nerves as much as the acceptance of heavy casualties. Even we feel this strain – the rifle companies have far more reason to do so.

Heber-Percy can do little about it once the MO has certified battle-strain and several, including Sgt R have been given base jobs as a result of it, but I think H-P will have little time for any of them later, and while he is still CO of the Battalion.

Coldies out again tonight. Apparently no German can cross a Rhine bridge without a pass signed by a general – and it's death to try otherwise. Don't know what we'd do without Hitler – he's put the German Army into some hopeless situations during past two years.

Patton has gained a bridgehead – quite a boy. Germans say America will grab the British Empire and Russia will take what's left – they firmly believe this and some show high standards of intelligence. Our prisoners are not all true parachutists, i.e. they haven't all actually at some time or other made an assault from the air, but some of them are, and one can tell them at a glance. Nevertheless, they are all imbued with the fanaticism of the German paratrooper.

$$\overline{15}$$

Return to England
12 March–26 March 1945

With the end of the Rhineland Battle the war was over for Charles Murrell and the 1st Battalion Welsh Guards. On 11 March they withdrew to the Nijmegen area for rest. GAD and the 2WG stayed in Europe to the end of the war. X Company Scots Guards who had fought with them for so long ('and a wonderful Company of fighters they are – admired by us all and their original Commander "Feathers"[1] with his big whiskers and sallow countenance was a great hero and beloved by them all and admired by us') joined the 2SG. After a 'Farewell to X Company and RASC' dance and a farewell parade in Nijmegen stadium, the Battalion sailed from Ostend to England on 23 March.

On the same day Field Marshal Montgomery began operations to secure crossings of the Rhine and everywhere in Europe Allied forces were preparing for the final battles of the war.

11 March 1945 – Malden, Holland

The Battle of the Rhine – or Rhineland rather, has ended – for us at any rate and we are back here at Malden in Holland and in same billets as before and I am actually in the same corner! How odd.

The German women seemed sorry to see us go from Bonninghardt – the men, once they lost their fear, became less obsequious and watched us go with impassive faces, though at first it was the men who cringed and not the women. So like men, and particularly German men, once assured that the invading armies do not massacre or ill-treat civilians, they forget their fears and begin to recall the past 'glories' of the military Reich – for the men were elderly and probably knew service under the Kaiser. But the women, fearful of their children's safety and their own and their men's, and realizing that the invaders are human enough, seem only too thankful and turn from fear to friendliness and gratitude for a bar of chocolate gruffly given to *Der Kleine* and whatever we gave we always stressed it was for the kids as a sort of alibi against fraternizing with adults. Alibi seemed a little

---

1. Major Steuart-Fotheringham.

far-fetched when we gave some cigarettes however. The men scared, obsequious and then, their fear alleviated a touch – only a trace – of arrogance returned. The women scared, grateful, friendly, as though Nazi pride meant little or nothing to them – at least that's how it struck me. Doesn't do to get sentimental over any of them, but the women's attitude by far the less contemptible.

But how nice to be back here in Holland where we can cheerfully greet the civvies and where they are all glad to see us! We can still hear distant guns firing, but it seems peaceful here. We came back through Geldern, Kevelar, Weeze and Goch and Gennep today. A trail of ruin and desolation and all in Germany. Our fellows worried now about slaughter of livestock and smashing of German houses etc as we realize British money will have to help keep Germans going if disease and famine are not to overwhelm Europe. As we came through the shattered battlefields they seemed prosaic enough to us who have grown used to them, but I thought again of the Horsemen – how fine their work in that zone we passed through today.

Must get to kip and must write Dearest tomorrow. England now looks certain unless H-P has his way. Don't care so much either way now. There's the Rhine to cross, but end of the war seems near now and I'd have liked to cross the Rhine at last. Still, to see Stella and the kid is everything. So ends yet another battle, or operation I've survived. May I come out of them all as well as this. What amazing luck the Battalion's had this time.

12 March 1945

We were officially told today that the Battalion is to return to England – seems a cert and I for one, very pleased. But no longer as desperately excited as at Schinveld. Then, things were in the doldrums. Today it is spring – the bushes and trees are budding – even flowering – spring and dry campaigning weather are on the way and I feel that soon the armies will be going ahead across the Rhine – this Division and others, swarming ahead and the war over. At least all organized resistance is at an end. I think it is quite possible Nazis may try a 'Thermopylae'[1] at Berchtesgaden or a last-ditch stand at the Alps.

Germans will know they've been licked in the field, but a death-or-glory stand might give future generations something – a legend – upon which to build new myths.

Oddly enough, many of the men are depressed – anti-climax I suppose – that and bobbing on Burma. Italy would be OK and a change. But I am glad we shall see England again and if we go away on another campaign, I shall see to it that we leave 50 per cent of present kit off the Intelligence truck. Cannot believe that I may never again have to set up maps of battle

---

1. The Battle of Thermopylae, 480 BC. The Spartans, under Leonidas, wiped out the Persians.

area and pack the truck for war. Realization will come to us gradually I think. Showed battle-dress, caps, belts and greatcoats today – many drill parades in offing. I can stand these, I think.

18 March 1945

Coldish day – sunny intervals. Some gunners outside in SP 25-pounders – they say the Canadians turned them out of their billets – some Canadians apparently convinced that their Army liberated Nijmegen and area. Admittedly it is now a Canadian zone but they were many miles away when GAD entered Nijmegen – in fact Canadian attitude has caused some resentment among us – everywhere here and at Nijmegen are maple-leaf signs and there's some bull with all this – we see their signs reading, 'Verges cleared of mines' where our trucks stood last September and where there never were any mines at all. And now some of them actually believe their Army liberated this zone – it's incredible, and sometimes almost alarming, how facts can be so easily distorted. Not that this matter is important, but other things more serious, politics, atrocities etc could as easily be 'put over' and believed.

24 March 1945 – Channel – 1120 hours

Coast of Belgium still in sight – indeed, we're travelling due west at present and it looks as though we're heading towards Dover – though we actually land at Tilbury.

Over on the port side we must be passing very near the beaches and town of Dunkirk – still held by the Huns, and I cannot help thinking of my last departure from the Continent – how very different this is! Then I sat stark naked aboard the ship and so dog-tired I didn't much care what happened. In defeat I felt humiliated – the future, if I thought of it, was grim to contemplate.

It seems rather like the ending of a nightmare and soon, I believe, even the great universal nightmare will end for all of us. Patton's across the Rhine and German reports say that Monty's going all out north and south of Wesel. The Battle of Germany has, I believe, already been fought, west of the Rhine and in our last operation, even as Eisenhower said. We shall see.

1645 hours

Have just passed the sea-forts on our port side. We have a meal at 1700 hours. We shouldn't be long docking now. How wonderful to know that this is English land we can see now!

Some Thames barges – that's home and no mistake. And we see all the odd little coastal craft, and pass the wrecks we saw coming the opposite way – in June of last year. How different now! Then we didn't know what lay in store for us but guessed it was something pretty grim – and it was.

I want to taste and savour and appreciate every second of this voyage home. We're obviously close to England – the weather that has been so sunny and warm hitherto has become dull and chilly. But who cares? This is England, and this the voyage home, our fighting done, that I used to anticipate in my slit trenches.

Now, with a wallet bulging with diaries and sketches that record nine months of campaigning and victory. I never believed really and implicitly that I should make this return journey. Now, whatever happens, I have seen English soil again, and soon we shall be standing upon it – and, somewhere beyond this muddy estuary is Stella! How tremendous that is! And how childish of me to gloat so. Men here are playing cards with English money – government-bevelled half-dollars and florins and banknotes that look and feel and smell sound to us – like real money. What a great moment this is! Today, on this ship and on her consort sail only 6 per cent or so of the original Battalion that sailed from here and Newhaven last June. Even now I am in the waters we sailed down then. Must go up for another quiz at the land now.

<u>2310 hours – Chelsea Barracks</u>

This seems all a dream – England – London – Chelsea Barracks! So many pleasant and some unhappy memories of '35 and '39. And here I am again. The same old iron bedsteads, the red and white walls and the tin lockers and the inevitable black line about four feet up the walls dividing the red paint from the white colour wash – dear old Chelsea – the great windows looking out upon trees, and the Chelsea Hospital on one side and upon the vast barrack square on the other. The barracks are the same, but the men are changed. Thunder Thomas is here somewhere with a rifle company, but I seem alone of those men I lived with in 1935 – many are dead or wounded – some, Tex Richards, Swain, the elder Chugg and others, are, presumably, still with Police or Fire Brigade; Barlow and Tony Hibbott wounded – Happy Jenkins, Griffin, Corporal Holder God knows where – Angus an officer in a line regiment – I feel a bit like the last of the ten little nigger boys and there's sadness as well as joy in Chelsea revisited.

We docked at Tilbury about 7.00 pm and boarded at last an English train – how pleasant! Though the flat Essex landscape was not the treat and change from Dutch scenery that Kent would have been. However, it soon grew dark. Folks cheered us from the rail-side houses just as they did after Dunkirk. Guess they thought us a train-load of wounded, and they may well be forgiven for mistaking us for a train-load of shellshock cases. We were a little slap-happy to be in England and the Dutch and German and French phrases must have sounded gibberish to them.

26 March 1945 – Charing X Station – 2050 hours

Now here – in the train actually at Charing Cross Station and still I cannot believe it! Have, so far, spoken to only one civilian, a boot-black in the kerb outside Victoria Station – at least to hold a conversation. Had some English beer and am feeling almost shy to meet my wife. How odd all this is. Full lights are blazing in this carriage.

I still cannot believe it. Charing X – it's Charing X, you fool! You're at Charing X! It might as well be desolated and battered Hassum station in Germany.

In the buffet were two Canadians bumming their loads about battle and gory details of dead Germans to listening civvies who were lapping it up. It pays to advertise indeed.

It's very wonderful that, within two hours, I shall be with my wife and child – how odd the dear old Cockney voice sounds announcing train arrivals and departures through the loudspeakers. And only a fortnight ago we came out of the line at Bonninghardt!

The Lieutenant Colonel gave us a talk today. In it were broadish hints of our being sent to Burma or China. Wrap up! Roll on!

Bibliography

Ellis, Major L.F., *Welsh Guards at War*, Gale and Polden Ltd., 1946

North, John, *North-West Europe 1944–45*, Her Majesty's Stationery Office, 1953

Retellack, John, *The Welsh Guards*, Frederick Warne Ltd., 1981

Rosse, Captain the Earl of, and Colonel E.R. Hill, *The Story of the Guards Armoured Division*, Geoffrey Bles, London, 1956

Index